Country Walks Near Baltimore

Third Edition

by Alan Fisher

RAMBLER BOOKS

Baltimore

COUNTRY WALKS NEAR BALTIMORE

By Alan Fisher
Maps and photographs by the author

Rambler Books
1430 Park Avenue
Baltimore, MD 21217

If you notice errors in the text or maps, please point them out in a letter to the publisher. Conversely, we also welcome letters that let us know we are doing a good job and that contain "quotable quotes" for promotional use.

Printed in the United States of America

THIRD EDITION   1 2 3 4 5

ISBN 0-9614963-3-9

CONTENTS

MAP 1 — Orientation

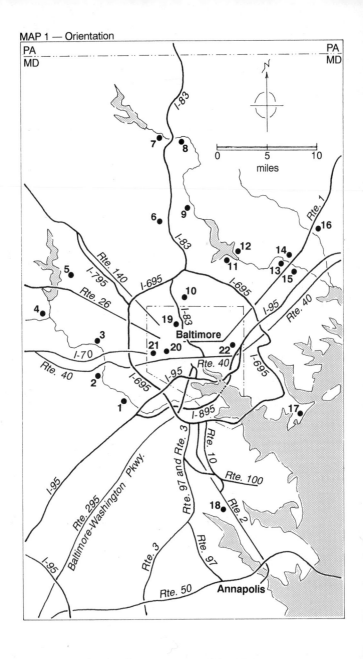

PREFACE

THIS BOOK IS FOR PEOPLE who want an outing in the country without wasting half the day getting there and back. If you live in the Greater Baltimore area, the excursions described here are close at hand. The walks show the best parts of our area's large parks and extensive trail networks. Some of the trails are suitable also for ski touring and bicycling, and of course all are open to the public. The excursions cover the gamut of Maryland's Piedmont and Coastal Plain landscapes, and successive visits during different seasons provide added variety and enjoyment.

Each chapter of this book includes a brief introduction, a discussion of the area's natural or social history or other pertinent issues, detailed directions, and one or more maps. Most of the commentary is general in character and is intended to be read ahead of time. The discussions, directions, and maps have all been updated for this third edition, and several new walks have been added.

For this edition I have omitted the bibliography, which threatened to add to the cost of the book, and which I never knew anyone to look at. For the most part it was merely a long list of old newspaper articles that are on file at local libraries. Instead, I have informally noted pertinent publications at the ends of some of the chapters. However, I must acknowledge here my debt to John W. McGrain for his books and many articles—some of which he has been kind enough to send to me—on Maryland mills and Baltimore-area ironworks. For this third edition Fraser Bishop, Cal Buikema, Edward S. Corbett, Brent Hartley, Lisa Hite, Jacques Kelly, Jody Landers, Joseph L. Mullen, and Malcolm Wilkerson have also been helpful. Many, many thanks.

Alan Fisher
Baltimore

COMFORT AND SAFETY

PLEASE READ THIS. It is customary, in guidebooks such as this, to include a catalog of cautions about possible nuisances and hazards. Such matters do not make for scintillating reading, but really, I think that you will be glad to have read here about a few potential problems—so that you can avoid them—rather than learn about them through uncomfortable (or even dangerous) experience.

Wear sturdy shoes that you do not mind getting muddy or wet. In winter wear hiking boots that will keep your feet dry and that will provide traction in snow. I usually carry a small knapsack containing a snack, a water bottle or juice carton, insect repellent, and an extra layer of clothing, such as a sweater or rain parka.

Some of the excursions described here are suitable for bicycling. Cyclists should wear helmets, yield to other trail users, pass with care, and keep their speed to a moderate, safe pace.

Several of this book's more rugged hikes are in the Patapsco and Gunpowder valleys, where there are steep, rocky slopes and even cliffs. Don't, like some people I have encountered, undertake impromptu rock climbing, only to find yourself perched on a ledge and unable to extricate yourself. Stay back from the edges of cliffs, and keep in mind that terrain presenting only moderate difficulty when dry can be treacherous when wet or icy.

Ticks can be a problem from early spring through autumn; some may even carry Lyme disease. So check your clothing occasionally while walking through woods or tall grass, and also when you return to your car. And check your body for ticks when you get home.

Every year the newspapers carry stories about people who pick up a squirrel, a raccoon, or some other animal and get bitten. They then have to undergo a series of painful anti-rabies shots. Don't be one of these people; don't handle *any* animals. In somewhat the same vein, remember that the Baltimore region is inhabited by poisonous copperhead snakes. Be careful where you place your hands and feet, particularly in rocky areas.

During winter, all too often drownings occur when people fall through the ice after venturing out onto frozen ponds, rivers, or even the shelf of ice that sometimes extends from shore into Chesapeake Bay. I am sure that you have heard this before; everyone has. And yet each winter a few more people die in this manner. So stay off the ice. And tell your kids.

Other sound advice that is ignored with puzzling regularity concerns lightning. If you are in an exposed or elevated area and a storm approaches, return to your car immediately. That is the safest place to be—safer even than a small shelter. And if a storm arrives before you get back to your car, hunker down in a low spot. Don't worry about getting wet or feeling stupid as you lie there with the rain pouring down. Clearly it is better to get wet and yet be safe than to try to stay dry by huddling under an isolated tree or pavilion or some other target for lightning.

Where the trails described here follow roads briefly, walk well off the road on the shoulder to minimize the risk of being hit by a car, and use caution, especially at dusk or after dark, where the routes cross roads. Studies show that in poor light conditions, motorists typically cannot even see pedestrians in time to stop, so your safety depends entirely on you.

Finally, one of the pitfalls of writing guidebooks is that conditions change. Just because I say to do something does not mean that you should forge ahead in the face of obvious difficulties, hazards, or prohibitions.

In sum, use good judgment and common sense to evaluate the particular circumstances that you find. Heed local regulations and signs, and do not undertake any unusual risks.

1

PATAPSCO VALLEY STATE PARK

Avalon, Orange Grove, and Ilchester

Walking and bicycling—4.0 miles (6.4 kilometers) or more, depending on whether you turn back at Orange Grove or go on from there to explore other trails. The route shown by the bold line on Map 2 on page 23 starts at the Avalon area and follows River Road upstream along the southwest bank of the Patapsco River. Cross the swinging bridge at Orange Grove, then return downstream on a paved path along the northeast bank. River Road is closed to cars on Saturday, Sunday, and major holidays. However, in order to cross back over the river at Avalon, the last 0.3 mile of the circuit follows park roads that remain open to automobile traffic, so in this area, extra caution is necessary. As is also shown on Map 2, several footpaths follow the side of the valley above River Road. These trails, which are popular with mountain bikers as well as hikers, provide a strenuous alternative to the riverside road. And as shown on Map 3 on page 26, spur trails lead from Orange Grove to nearby attractions. Finally, as outlined on Map 4 on page 29, a circuit from Orange Grove leads still farther upstream to Ilchester.

   If you are looking for a country setting in which to push your child in a stroller, the paved path along the river's northeast bank makes an excellent promenade, as does River Road during the period that it is closed to cars.

These paved ways also provide a good opportunity for children to bicycle.

The park opens daily at 8 A.M. during the warmer months and at 10 A.M. during the colder months. Year-round, the park closes at sunset. It is also closed on Thanksgiving and Christmas. An admission fee is charged on weekends during March and every day April through October. All pets are prohibited. The park is managed by the Department of Natural Resources, Maryland Forest, Park and Wildlife Service; telephone 461-5005.

BETWEEN WOODSTOCK (west of Baltimore) and tidewater at Elkridge, the Patapsco River falls more than 200 feet in a distance of 17 miles, much of it through a steep-sided valley. The potential of this stretch of river for water power was not lost on the ironmongers, millers, textile manufacturers, and other early industrialists of the eighteenth and nineteenth centuries, and during that period many dams and factories were built in the narrow valley, notably at Elysville (now Daniels), Ellicotts Upper and Lower Mills, Oella, Ilchester, Orange Grove, and Avalon. The excursions described here and in the next two chapters pass these sites. At some places the old mill buildings still stand, and at a few sites factories that are descended from early industries still operate. Other areas, however, are just stretches of wooded valley where, except for a few ruins or faint remnants, whole factory villages have been torn down or obliterated by fire and flood. In some places the names of these company towns survive only in local roads or as designations for different sections of the Patapsco Valley State Park.

≈   ≈   ≈   ≈

Avalon is one of these lost towns. It got its start in the 1760s when Caleb Dorsey, ironmaster and owner of Elkridge Furnace (established in 1755), built a forge upstream from his furnace for fashioning implements from the approximately 1,000 tons of pig iron that he produced annually. According to the nineteenth-century memoirs of Martha Ellicott Tyson (a descendant of the Ellicotts of Ellicott City), the only iron tools made in Baltimore County prior to the American Revolution were crowbars produced at Dorsey's Forge. Most other tools were imported, as was intended under the British mercantile system by which the colonies were to provide raw materials—including pig iron—to England and to purchase finished goods in return.

During the Revolution, the Avalon forge was leased by William Whetcroft of Annapolis, who had received a government loan voted by Maryland's revolutionary legislature. Whetcroft made cast-iron parts for muskets that were assembled in Annapolis. Whetcroft also built a rolling and slitting mill, and by 1777 his Patapsco Slitting Mill was producing nails. This was the first nail factory in Maryland; apparently it was quite primitive, since the nails had to be headed one at a time by hand. Whetcroft's lease with Caleb Dorsey's son Edward (known as Iron Head Ned) stipulated that Dorsey would raise his forge dam at Avalon an additional foot and dig a race to Whetcroft's mill for water power to run the bellows and other machinery; in exchange, Whetcroft would not only pay rent for use of the site but would also buy all of his raw iron from Edward Dorsey, who later purchased the Whetcroft mill for himself.

In 1815 the forge and slitting mill were purchased at auction by two members of the enterprising Ellicott family. By 1820 the Ellicott ironworks—one at Avalon (the name was first used by the Ellicotts) and another a few miles upstream at

Ellicott City—were listed together in the census as having between them four rolling mills, six pairs of rollers with the necessary furnaces, and twenty-four nail machines, each capable of cutting 1,200 nails per minute. The works employed fifty men and thirteen boys and used 800 tons of iron annually to make not only nails but also iron bars, sheets, and plates.

During the next half-century, the Avalon ironworks were sold and expanded a number of times. In 1845 the nail factory burned. Three years later a mill was constructed for rolling rails for the Baltimore & Ohio Railroad. After being pulled down and rebuilt on a larger scale in the early 1850s, the factory reached its peak in about 1856, producing 44,000 kegs of nails from forty-four steam-driven machines. In a panoramic depiction of Avalon in 1857, the ironworks are shown as two long buildings resembling train sheds side by side, standing parallel with the river on the east bank near the present-day park automobile bridge at Avalon. The roofs were supported on brick piers. Four tall smoke stacks rose between the mill sheds, one of which bore a sign saying "Rolling Mill 1855" and the other a sign saying "Puddling Mill Built 1853." ("Puddling" means simply to work molten metal.) Around the factory was a small village, including a church, a school, stores, and about thirty mill houses.

The ironworks at Avalon continued in operation until July 24, 1886, when a monstrous flood swept down the Patapsco Valley. There appear to be no eyewitness accounts of what happened at Avalon that morning, but the events at nearby Ellicott City, as recalled by Charles F. Kreh, who was there at the time, give some idea:

> At about 9:15 o'clock the mail train from Baltimore arrived, and at that hour there was little evidence or intimation of impending disaster in the Patapsco. Only a lowering of the clouds and an unusual darkness, together with some fierce bolts of lightning, appeared to cast their shadows before them and to

indicate the coming of a storm. But, as yet, few if any had
thought of what was in store for them. Soon, however, came
reports of terrible cloudbursts in various places east of the
Ellicotts. The Baltimore train left the station and had only
reached Union Mills about a mile distant, when it was met by an
avalanche of water. The bounds of the river were already broken
and only the weight of the train held it to the tracks. Fortu-
nately for the passengers, it stood close by the mountain side,
and they were thus enabled to clamber up and return to the city.

Hardly had a few minutes elapsed before the mad waters (in all
their intensity and fury and without any warning) burst upon the
good people of Ellicotts living along the river course on the
Baltimore County side, and almost in a twinkling their homes
were surrounded and all avenues of escape cut off. Then began
scenes that almost beggar description, many of them pitiful and
heartrending. The waters, filled with logs and trees and debris of
all kinds, arose as if by magic and seemed to gloat in their
power of fierce destruction. Opposite the railroad station across
the Patapsco stood a row of houses, some brick, some frame and
others stone, extending over a space of about 1,000 feet from
the bridge to the mill structure . . . and in a remarkably short
time these were seen to begin to crumble from the beating of the
waves against them. Now could be seen the dwellers breaking
through the roofs from house to house and barely escaping the
collapse of their homes. The last house in the row was a brick
building owned by William Partridge and in this, thirty-odd
persons sought refuge. Many were the prayers that went up to
the Most High from those looking on from the opposite shore
that this house might be spared, but it was not to be, and soon
all were engulfed and swallowed up in the angry waters. School
children, who had come across the river in the early morning,
stood on the banks and saw their parents go to their watery
graves.

The flood crest reached 40 feet above normal. At Ellicott
City thirty-two buildings were destroyed. Workers fled the
factories as the riverside industries were inundated. The
massive Granite Cotton Mill just upstream from Ellicott City

collapsed into the torrent, taking with it one man who had been too slow to leave. Bodies from Ellicott City were recovered near Baltimore, 15 miles downstream. Those of one man and his wife and child were found caught in the top of a tree. In all, about fifty people drowned that morning in the Patapsco Valley.

At the Avalon ironworks, the chimneys collapsed and very nearly all the machinery was smashed by flood-borne debris. The *American and Commercial Advertiser* for July 25, 1868, reported that "the Patapsco washed entirely through the lower portion of the large nail factory at Avalon . . . and the machinery at the works was damaged to a very great extent, and the stock on hand carried away. The houses of the workmen, surrounding the factory and like it situated on low ground, were inundated, the water reaching the second story of some of them. It is not known that any lives were lost at this place, but many families lost all their household property."

After the flood, some Avalon residents returned to their company-owned houses, but the ironworks never operated again. The machines were sold for scrap, and what was left of the factory was torn down. By the turn of the century, even most of the tenant dwellings had vanished. Today only two stone houses survive, of which the more conspicuous is the former mill superintendent's residence located on Gun Road above the railroad crossing.

Since 1868 the Patapsco Valley has experienced lesser floods (as it always had) on a more or less regular basis. Tropical Storm Agnes in 1972, however, was of a different order of magnitude; it was comparable to the flood a century earlier. Beginning June 21, the storm lumbered across Maryland in three days of almost constant rain. At Ellicott City, one of the early stone Ellicott houses that had survived the prior flood was toppled. Over $1,800,000 in damage occurred in the Patapsco Valley State Park alone. At Avalon, the high water washed out the northeast end of the old ironworks dam over

which the river used to flow. (Damaged by the 1968 flood, this dam had been rebuilt in 1901 by the Baltimore County Water and Electric Company, which until 1928 operated a filtration plant at Avalon.) Now the dam, bypassed by the river, is barely visible in a thicket of trees that have grown up since the 1972 flood. At the same time, the automobile bridge at Avalon was destroyed, as were most other small bridges. Shelters were swept away and the swinging footbridge at Orange Grove was pulled down. Between Ilchester and Avalon the current ate away long stretches of River Road and the B&O railbed, and the large sanitary sewer that runs down the valley was ruptured in four places.

Since 1972 much of the damage has been repaired. The swinging bridge has been replaced and River Road has been reconstructed between Avalon and Orange Grove. New rest rooms and picnic shelters have been constructed. For information about the use and reservation of these shelters, call the park office.

≈   ≈   ≈   ≈

Orange Grove, like Avalon, is the site of another lost company village. Formerly located in the vicinity of the present-day swinging bridge, the mill and hamlet survived the flood of 1868, but they have vanished since just the same. Only a few traces remain, among them the massive stone wall shown on page 17. The wall was once part of the C. A. Gambrill Manufacturing Company's Mill C, which in the second half of the nineteenth century was said by the management to be the largest flour mill east of Minneapolis. Two of the mill's better known brands of flour were Orange Grove and Patapsco Superlative Patent. Gambrill flour products were marketed throughout the mid-Atlantic region and eventually as far away as Europe, South America, and the West Indies.

A flour mill was first constructed at Orange Grove in 1856,

when George Worthington and George Bayly brought land there on both sides of the river. According to the deed, the property included parts of tracts know as "Talbot's Last Shift," "Small Bit," "Joseph and Jacob's Invention," and all of "Vortex." It is thought that the new mill and its company village became known as Orange Grove because of the Osage-orange trees that were common in the area. In 1860 Worthington and Bayly sold the entire property to the C. A. Gambrill Manufacturing Company, which had also taken over the Ellicott family's flour mill farther upstream. In 1882 the Gambrill company, trading under the name of Patapsco Flouring Mills, opened a third mill in Baltimore and gave letter designations to the three plants. The one at Ellicott City was Mill A, the Baltimore plant was Mill B, and Orange Grove was Mill C.

In 1873 the Gambrill company added a Corliss steam engine and boilers to supplement water power at Orange Grove. In 1880 output was 171,381 barrels of flour. Three years later the millstones were replaced by modern steel rollers, and output increased further. By 1900 the mill building, which measured 150 by 175 feet, had six stories, four of brick topped by two more of frame and metal siding. A massive rectangular grain elevator 100 by 150 feet and eight stories high flanked the mill on its upstream side, and on the downstream side there was a tall, tapering, square smokestack and a three-story structure housing the Corliss engine, coal bins, and a dynamo that generated electricity to light the mill and the nearby superintendent's house.

The entire mill complex was crowded onto a shelf of land between the railroad and a high retaining wall along the river. There was so little room to spare that the former Gun Road (now the riverside path) used to pass through the building in an arched passageway. Because the mill and elevator were set into the hillside, trains picked up flour at the fourth story, which was even with the floor of a box car on the siding.

Coal was dumped from trains into a chute that is still discernible as a stone lintel and boxlike foundation opposite the end of the swinging bridge. A wooden dam about 10 feet high and slightly curved against the pressure of the impounded water created a millpond stretching upstream as far as Ilchester.

According to the memoirs of a former Orange Grove resident—Thomas LeRoy Phillips, whose father was superintendent of the mill from 1891 to 1904—"the subdued rumble of the mill was heard from early Monday morning to late Saturday evening; the muffled roar of water pouring over the high wooden dam was unbroken; and long freight trains rolled by day and night." William A. Clayton, the day engineer in the early 1900s, was so impressed by the mill's steam engine that he named one of his sons Corliss.

On the southwest bank of the river, across from the mill, a small company-owned village of seven houses was strung out along the Patapsco where a parking lot and rest rooms are now located. There was also a combination one-room school and church. Then, as now, the river was spanned by a swinging bridge, which was snagged and pulled down by an ice jam in January 1904, and again washed out by Tropical Storm Agnes in 1972. A hand pump provided water for the community. Itinerant grocers and butchers with horse-drawn carts supplied some food; other shopping entailed a short train ride to Ellicott City, Elkridge, or Baltimore on one of the twelve passenger trains that stopped daily at Orange Grove. On every third Sunday church services were conducted by a traveling reverend who also preached at Elkridge and at Locust Chapel near Ilchester.

The mill at Orange Grove operated until May 1, 1905, when it was gutted by fire. Rebuilding was not worthwhile. Baltimore's flour trade was in decline, and anyway, the advent of steam engines made access to water power of minor importance, especially when balanced against the risk of flooding. At Orange Grove the mill's walls were torn down. From the middle of the swinging bridge, however, the stone abutment of the old wooden dam is still visible (during the leafless season) about 100 yards upstream on the southwest bank of the river. On the northeast side of the river, the stone foundations of the former mill stretch upstream 75 yards along the railroad embankment. The walls are obscured by trees and are best examined close up.

AUTOMOBILE: The section of the Patapsco Valley State Park explored by this walk is located southwest of Baltimore. The entrance is off South Street near its intersection with Route 1 (Washington Boulevard) 0.2 mile northeast of the Patapsco River.

From Baltimore, take Interstate 95 south toward Washington. Interstate 95 southbound can also be reached from Exit 11B off Interstate 695 (the Beltway). Follow Interstate 95 about 1.7 miles southwest from the Beltway, then take Exit 47A for Interstate 195 east toward BWI Airport. Follow Interstate 195 for 0.8 mile, then take Exit 3 for Route 1 (Washington Boulevard) south toward Elkridge. Bear right onto Route 1, then immediately turn right again onto South Street. Go only 100 yards, then turn left into the entrance for Patapsco Valley State Park—Avalon Area.

Follow the entrance road 1.2 miles, passing a pay station and going under the B&O's stone Thomas Viaduct and the high Interstate 95 bridge. At a T-intersection, turn left. Cross the Patapsco River and turn right into the large Avalon parking lot.

WALKING and BICYCLING: (See Map 2 opposite.) With the Patapsco River in the distance on your right, follow the road that starts at the end of the parking lot and that leads 1.6 miles to the swinging bridge

MAP 2 — Avalon to Orange Grove

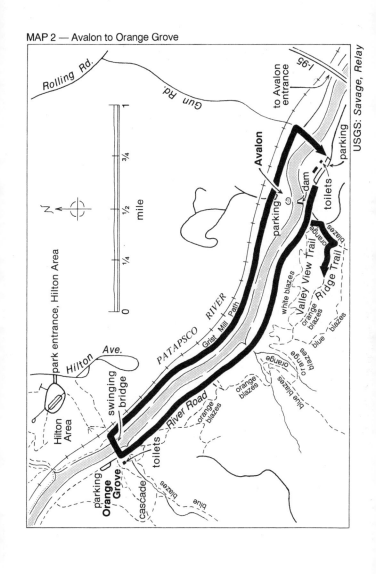

at Orange Grove. The road is closed to motor vehicles on Saturday, Sunday, and major holidays, but the wisest policy is always to be alert for cars. (Incidentally, from the top of the first rise along the road, look down at the old Avalon dam, now nearly lost from view in a thicket of woods growing from what used to be the riverbed.)

With the river on your right, follow the road to the swinging bridge. Or, if you prefer, take one of the more strenuous paths that follow the side and rim of the valley. These trails are shown as dashed lines on Map 2. The main alternative to the riverside road is the Ridge Trail, blazed with red-orange paint and starting from the riverside road 90 yards beyond the point where a gravel road veers off to the left.

Once you reach the swinging bridge at Orange Grove, there are several opportunities for exploration beyond what is shown on Map 2. The maps and directions on pages 25 through 31 outline four alternatives.

To return from Orange Grove to Avalon along the northeast bank of the river (as shown by the bold line on Map 2), cross the Patapsco on the swinging bridge, then turn right. With the river on your right, follow the paved path downstream. After 1.5 miles, you will reach a parking lot next to a pond. Continue straight along the road, but be alert for cars. With caution, follow the road 0.3 mile, then turn right at an intersection near a railroad crossing, where the factory village of Avalon stood. Cross the Patapsco River and return to your starting point at the large parking lot.

SIDE TRIPS FROM ORANGE GROVE: In case you want a longer walk or ride than the 4-mile route shown by the bold line on Map 2, other excursions that start at Orange Grove are outlined on Map 3 and Map 4 and are described below.

Bloede Dam: (See Map 3 on page 26.) The most obvious and easiest side trip from the swinging bridge at Orange Grove doesn't lead aside at all. Rather, with the river on your right, simply continue straight along the riverside road for 0.7 mile to the Bloede Dam. The road deteriorates toward the end but nonetheless is easily passable even by bicyclists.

The **Bloede Dam** was built in 1906 by the Patapsco Electric and Manufacturing Company, which generated power here until 1924. Named for the company's president, Victor Bloede, the dam was among the first reinforced concrete dams in the United States, and the first to house generators within its hollow interior. (Under no circumstances should you enter the dam.)

River Road used to continue upstream from the dam, but the floodwaters of Tropical Storm Agnes in 1972 carved deeply into the bank, eradicating some stretches of the road.

Cascade: (Walking only; see Map 3 on page 26). A few dozen yards upstream from the swinging bridge at Orange Grove, a trail marked with blue paint blazes starts at some stone steps and leads 100 yards straight uphill, then continues (more or less level) for 160 yards along the side of a ravine to an attractive cascade. Be careful here; the rocks may be slippery when wet or icy. By crossing the stream below the main fall of water, you can follow the trail farther upstream, switching from one bank to the next as necessary.

Buzzard Rock and Saw Mill Branch: (Walking only, see Map 3 on page 26). This 2.5-mile side trip from Orange Grove is rugged and involves some scrambling. It follows trails that in some places barely exist, but the reward is an impressive view of the Patapsco Valley from the top of the cliff at Buzzard

MAP 3 — Side trips from Orange Grove

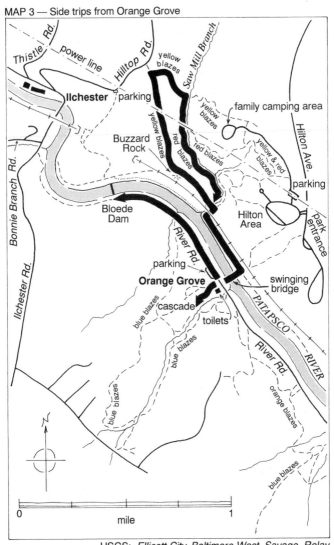

USGS: *Ellicott City, Baltimore West, Savage, Relay*

Rock and also the chance to follow Saw Mill Branch as it cascades and twists through a relatively secluded valley. The rocks here can be slippery if they are wet or icy, so be cautious.

At Orange Grove cross the swinging bridge toward the railroad, then turn left and follow a footpath upstream past the stone foundation of the old flour mill below the railroad. Continue as the path follows the top of a large pipe (the Patapsco interceptor sewer), then turn right and pass through a tunnel that carries Saw Mill Branch under the railroad. (Watch your footing; do not enter the tunnel unless there is ample room to walk next to the stream.) After emerging from the tunnel, go upstream about 25 yards, then turn left across the stream and scramble steeply up the slope until you are on a level with the railroad. Continue climbing straight over rocks and roots on a rough trail marked with yellow paint blazes. Follow the yellow-blazed trail steeply uphill, with the Patapsco Valley on your left and the deep ravine of Saw Mill Branch on your right. About 175 yards after the path levels off, a rock outcrop (Buzzard Rock) provides a particularly good view of the Patapsco Valley and Bloede Dam.

Continue on the yellow-blazed path to Hilltop Road. As you approach Hilltop Road, turn sharply right onto a narrow footpath marked by yellow blazes. (If you reach a steel gate at Hilltop Road, retrace your steps 80 yards to locate the place where you should have turned.) Follow the narrow, yellow-blazed footpath through the woods and down into the valley of Saw Mill Branch.

When you reach the stream, do not cross. Instead, turn right onto a trail marked with red paint blazes. With Saw Mill Branch on your left, follow the red-blazed trail downstream. At some places, the streambank and trail are obviously in the process of being undermined by erosion; in these areas, stay back at least 10 feet from the edge, even though the trail appears to follow the brink. Use common sense to avoid an accident here.

Continue downstream with Saw Mill Branch on your left. At times the red-blazed trail follows the streambed, but for the most part the trail is along the side of the bluff. Eventually, within sight of the railroad, descend steeply to the left and return through the tunnel and downstream along the river to the swinging bridge at Orange Grove.

Circuit to Ilchester: (Walking only; see Map 4 opposite). This 3-mile circuit upstream from Orange Grove to Ilchester is rugged and involves some scrambling. In a few places the trail is very muddy and scarcely exists. Also, part of the route follows local roads for about a mile, so extra caution is needed because of the presence of cars. And why, you ask, would I recommend such a route? Because at Ilchester, where the old paper mill still operates, this excursion provides a fascinating and unprettified look at a factory hamlet typical of the mill villages that used to be nestled at intervals in the Patapsco Valley. The route also passes Buzzard Rock and the Bloede Dam and for about half a mile follows the remains of River Road, where the destructive power of the 1972 Agnes flood is still plain to see.

At Orange Grove cross the swinging bridge toward the railroad, then turn left and follow a footpath upstream past the stone foundation of the old flour mill below the railroad. Continue as the path follows the top of a large pipe (the Patapsco interceptor sewer), then turn right and pass through a tunnel that carries Saw Mill Branch under the railroad. (Watch your footing; do not enter the tunnel unless there is ample room to walk next to the stream.) After emerging from the tunnel, go upstream about 25 yards, then turn left

MAP 4 — Circuit from Orange Grove past Ilchester

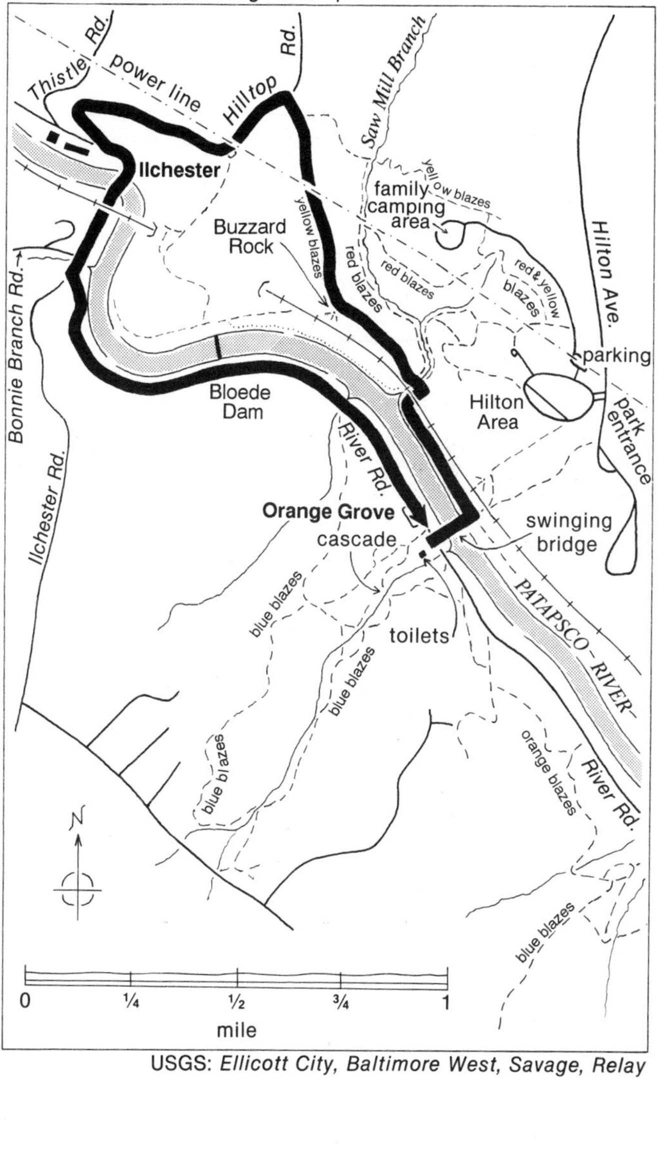

Thistle Rd.
power line
Hilltop Rd.
Saw Mill Branch
Ilchester
family camping area
yellow blazes
Buzzard Rock
yellow blazes
red blazes
red blazes
red & yellow blazes
Hilton Ave.
parking
Bloede Dam
Hilton Area
park entrance
River Rd.
Orange Grove
cascade
swinging bridge
Bonnie Branch Rd.
Ilchester Rd.
blue blazes
toilets
blue blazes
PATAPSCO RIVER
blue blazes
River Rd.
orange blazes
blue blazes
N
blue blazes

0   ¼   ½   ¾   1
mile

USGS: *Ellicott City, Baltimore West, Savage, Relay*

across the stream and scramble steeply up the slope until you are on a level with the railroad. Continue climbing straight over rocks and roots on a rough trail marked with yellow paint blazes. Follow the yellow-blazed trail steeply uphill, with the Patapsco Valley on your left and the deep ravine of Saw Mill Branch on your right. About 175 yards after the path levels off, a rock outcrop (Buzzard Rock) provides a particularly good view of the Patapsco Valley, the Bloede Dam, and the road along the opposite bank by which you will return.

Continue on the yellow-blazed path to Hilltop Road, and there turn left and follow the road, walking on the far left in order to minimize the risk of being hit by a car approaching from behind. Follow Hilltop Road past houses, then steeply downhill. Turn sharply left downhill past stone houses overlooking the mill complex. (Many of these houses have been torn down, and all may be gone by the time you get there.)

This is **Ilchester**: a dam, a paper mill, and a few stone and frame mill houses up the hill. In the 1820s, George and William Morris, two Scottish brothers from Philadelphia, established their Thistle Mills here for making cotton print. (A flour mill owned by the Ellicotts already existed on the opposite bank, wedged between the railroad and the river.) The name *Thistle* still survives in Thistle Road, which links Frederick Road with the river just beyond the upstream end of the mill complex. In 1850 the mill employed 71 male and 106 female workers. Its water-powered looms produced 1.3 million yards of sheeting and drill annually. By 1900 the mill had been converted to spinning silk. About 300 hands were employed, and the *Baltimore Sun* said that Thistle made "goods that rival the silk works of France." In 1920, however, new owners operating as the Thistle Cotton Mills, Inc. retooled the plant to manufacture automobile tire fabric. Then in 1928 the Bartgis brothers of Baltimore moved their paper carton business into the old Thistle factory, which has since passed through other hands. The Agnes flood and a fire in 1972 inflicted $1 million in damage, but the works were rebuilt within the old stone walls. The factory now recycles wastepaper to produce paper board, the kind of cardboard used in cereal boxes. Most of the old mill houses—at one time there were thirty-five dwellings crammed along River Road and up Hilltop Road—have been torn down.

At the bottom of the valley, bear left onto River Road and follow it across the river and under the railroad. Again, be alert for cars. Continue 200 yards past the railroad, then—a few yards beyond the intersection with Bonnie Branch Road—turn left across the guardrail onto an old, decayed road.

This old road remnant is part of River Road, which downstream from here was washed away by the flood during Tropical Storm Agnes in 1972. The stone arch and abutment at the river's edge are the remains of the B&O Patterson Viaduct, destroyed by the flood of 1868.

With the river on your left, head downstream on the remains of the road. When it disappears (as it does in some places), follow the rough footpath over jumbled rocks next to the river. Continue to the Bloede Dam, built in 1906 and discussed on page 25. With the river on your left, follow the remains of River Road downstream to the swinging bridge at Orange Grove.

Further reading: John W. McGrain's profusely illustrated *From Pig Iron to Cotton Duck* (published by the Baltimore County Public Library) and Paul J. Travers' *Patapsco: Baltimore's River of History* (Tidewater) contain enjoyable accounts of industries and mill villages in the Patapsco Valley.

2

ELLICOTT CITY and OELLA

Walking—1.5 miles (2.4 kilometers). Stroll along Ellicott City's steep, narrow streets, passing old granite and clapboard structures that now house a host of interesting specialty shops. The route (which is shown on Map 5 on page 41) passes the B&O Railroad Station Museum, which is open Friday, Saturday, Sunday, and Monday from 11 to 4; telephone 461-1944. Also interesting is the small Firehouse Museum, open Saturday and Sunday from 12 to 4.

Near Ellicott City is Oella, a self-contained mill community that is well worth touring by car.

_____

AS A NAME AND ANACHRONISM, **Ellicott City** is on a par with Baltimore Town (as colonial Baltimore was known when it was founded in 1729). The Ellicott City charter was revoked, in fact, by the General Assembly in 1935 after a half-century of economic decline in the Patapsco Valley caused by the advent of steam engines as an alternative to water power. Subject to periodic flooding, the valley lost its luster as a site for industrial plants. Over a period of decades many old mills were allowed to slip into obsolescence until they were eventually abandoned following some disaster or other.

Today, despite a glossy new varnish of antique chic, Ellicott City retains much of the flavor of the mill town, quarries, and early railroad terminus of its origin. Its stone and frame buildings are jammed along a narrow valley where Frederick Road crosses the river. A mile upstream on the opposite bank is the industrial village of Oella, which offers to the sightseer a remarkable concentration of nineteenth-century mill housing.

In 1772 Joseph, John, and Andrew Ellicott, Quaker brothers who milled flour in Bucks County, Pennsylvania, bought land on both sides of the Patapsco River above and below the future site of Ellicott City. Their newly-acquired stretch of valley was uninhabited, uncultivated, and inaccessible except by footpath, although most of the surrounding upland had long been farmed by tobacco planters. The attraction of the valley site lay in the steep gradient of the river, for the Ellicotts' purchase included exclusive water and power rights for 2 miles above and below the dam and mill that they proposed to build. Most of their 700-acre purchase was bought cheaply from an Englishman who may have feared the approaching Revolution, but another 20 acres were obtained under a 1669 law that allowed entrepreneurs to gain control over riverside land for fifty years if they built and operated a gristmill. In 1774 the Ellicott brothers also purchased an existing dam and mill for grinding corn 4 miles upstream, where the then-Frederick Road (now *Old* Frederick Road) crossed the river.

Prior to their purchases in the Patapsco Valley, Andrew and John Ellicott had traveled on horseback over the middle counties of Maryland between the Patapsco and the Blue Ridge. They had concluded from their tour of inspection that the region was suited for growing wheat and had ample water power for grinding grain. Tobacco was then the main cash crop near Baltimore, but the European demand for American tobacco had slumped, payment from European dealers was slow, and yields were declining as the soil became depleted. Wheat was the rising crop, demanded by the growing cities of the Eastern seaboard and exportable also to southern Europe and the Caribbean. Maryland's upper Eastern Shore was prospering as a region that grew wheat shipped out through the port of Chestertown. Baltimore, which had access to a vast western and northern hinterland, offered still greater possibilities, and the Ellicotts were determined to be part of the region's burgeoning grain market. Already, as a matter of agricultural heritage, the new German settlers in central Maryland (where Frederick had been named for the kings of Prussia) preferred to grow wheat. Between 1749 and 1774 the export of wheat and flour from Annapolis had increased by nearly 600 percent, and the growth of wheat exports from Baltimore had been even more dramatic.

From the outset Joseph Ellicott concentrated his attention on the improvement of the upstream site where Frederick Road crossed the Patapsco; this became known as the Upper Mills. John, Andrew, and Andrew's sons undertook development of the lower stretch of river. Their household goods, tools, and farm implements were brought by boat from Philadelphia to Elkridge Landing. At that time Elkridge Landing (located on the turnpike to Washington) was the head of navigation on the Patapsco River and was an important regional tobacco port from which ships sailed directly to England. From Elkridge, the Ellicotts' possessions—and those of their workmen whom they had persuaded to come with them—were carried by wagon along a riverside road that the party had to hack and build as they went. For the final mile, everything was carried by hand on a footpath along the river to the new settlement. Even the wagons themselves had to be disassembled and carried in.

By 1774 the Ellicotts had supervised the clearing of land and the construction of a low dam, a sawmill, a gristmill, a log boarding house, and a number of wooden houses. At first the brothers grew and milled their own wheat in order to demonstrate to the nearby tobacco planters that wheat could be cultivated and sold profitably. Charles Carroll of Carrollton, one of the largest and most forward-looking planters in Maryland, became a financial backer of the Ellicotts. After the brothers built a road extending 5 miles west from their mill to

Carroll's vast plantation at Doughoregan Manor, Carroll converted much of his land from tobacco to wheat.

By the end of the American Revolution, the flow of wheat from nearby plantations to Ellicotts Lower Mills had increased to the point where the Ellicotts decided to enter the export trade as soon as peaceful conditions returned. In 1783 the Ellicotts built a wharf at the corner of Light and Pratt streets in Baltimore, where they used a dredge of their own invention to deepen the channel. They not only exported flour but also imported ironware, tea, mirrors, dinner sets, glassware, linen, silks, satins, brocades, liquors, wines, and other goods, which they sold to the planters through their new store (erected in 1790) of Ellicott & Company at the Lower Mills. Planters from throughout the region congregated at the store and post office, bringing their wheat in exchange for credit at the store. The Ellicotts also built and operated a school at the Lower Mills.

In 1791 Ferdinand M. Bayard, a member of the French Academy of Arts and Sciences, recorded his impression of a visit to the Lower Mills:

> The river, upon the borders of which Mr. Ellicott has built his mill, is enclosed by two chains of uncultivated hills. . . . The bottom of the river, whose channel can hardly be decried, is full of broken rocks which the waters have not yet worked smooth. Some masses are raised above the surface of the river, whose waters, dashing against them, keep up continually a dull noise, truly sepulchral. The advantages to be derived from a mill in this place render the proprietor insensible to the horrors which surround him. It can only be a regard for pecuniary interest which enables him to live undisturbed by the noise of the waters which dash over the rocks. The leanness of the sheep and cattle attest to the poverty of the soil. The miserable garden, from which the productions seem forced; fields where the scantiness of the grain leaves the soil exposed; plains incapable of producing a middling sized oak; such is the melancholy aspect presented by the country from Baltimore to Ellicott's Mills.

In time, the Ellicotts erected iron-smelting furnaces, forges, rolling mills, and nail factories in their stretch of the Patapsco Valley. Another mill was added later for the production of copper sheathing. The Ellicotts sold or leased land to other entrepreneurs who established a paper mill, an oil mill, and a carding mill. After reading an article in a horticultural journal and conducting their own experiments with plaster, the Ellicotts instructed the surrounding planters in the use of lime as a fertilizer to restore the exhausted soil. They imported blocks of gypsum from Nova Scotia and ground it for fertilizer. They constructed bridges and a road east to Baltimore at their own expense and, with the assistance of Charles Carroll and other planters, they built a road west to Frederick, opening the new wheat country of the interior to Ellicotts Lower Mills. In 1804 the Baltimore and Frederick Turnpike was established though the Lower Mills, supplanting the old Frederick Road through the Upper Mills. The turnpike was soon linked with the Ohio Valley by the National Road through Cumberland and Wheeling, so that by 1818, when the Ellicotts' settlement on the Patapsco had a population of about three thousand people, Maryland's most important land thoroughfare to the West passed through the Lower Mills.

During the same period, granite quarrying became a significant industry in the vicinity of the Lower Mills. Between 1806 and 1821 granite for Baltimore Cathedral—at the time one of the nation's most significant structures because of its large size and distinguished neoclassic design—was hauled from Ellicotts Lower Mills along the Frederick Turnpike in huge wagons drawn by nine yoke of oxen.

Ellicotts Lower Mills received another boost in 1827, when the Baltimore & Ohio Railroad was incorporated by several leading Baltimore merchants and bankers. They feared that the Erie Canal, which in 1825 linked Lake Erie at Buffalo with the Hudson River at Albany, and the newly planned Chesapeake & Ohio Canal, with its eastern terminus in Washington, D.C., would each divert commerce away from Baltimore. The first leg of the experimental railroad was laid up the Patapsco Valley, and Ellicotts Lower Mills was selected as its inland terminus until the line could be extended farther west.

During the next forty years Ellicotts Lower Mills continued to grow and prosper, although in the aftermath of the financial panic of 1837, the Ellicotts at the Lower Mills, "trading under the name of Jonathan Ellicott & Sons, being embarrassed in their circumstances and largely indebted to many individuals" (as recited in the deed of trust), were forced to convey the flour mill to trustees for the benefit of their creditors. Colonel Charles Carroll III acquired the mill in partnership with Charles A. Gambrill, who eventually became the firm's principal. The mill continued to be owned by the C. A. Gambrill Manufacturing Company until 1923, and during that period it was rebuilt at least twice after being destroyed by flood or damaged by fire. Most of the currently existing structure, still in use as a flouring mill, dates from 1917. It stands on the east side of the river opposite the town and is flanked by huge grain silos.

In 1840 Ellicotts Lower Mills was selected as the site of the courthouse for the new Howard District of what was then Anne Arundel County. In 1851 it was made the county seat when Howard County was organized. The Lower Mills became Ellicott City with the granting of a municipal charter in 1867. The next year, however, much of the city's industry was destroyed in a devastating flash flood, as described in Chapter 1. Although some of the mills were rebuilt, many were not, and the community never fully recovered its former economic importance.

AUTOMOBILE: Ellicott City is located west of Baltimore where Route 144 (Frederick Road) crosses the Patapsco River.

From Interstate 695 (the Beltway) west of Baltimore, take Exit 15B for Route 40 west toward Ellicott City. Follow Route 40 about 4.4 miles to an intersection with Rogers Avenue at a traffic light. Turn left and go as straight as possible for 1.1 miles, passing the intersections where Rogers Avenue and Ellicott Mills Drive turn right downhill. Continue straight on Courthouse Drive to the large parking lots serving the Howard County courthouse.

WALKING: (See Map 5 on page 41.) From the courthouse parking lots, head toward the granite courthouse complex. Pass to the right of the courthouse buildings (the front—or downhill—section was built in 1840-43), then turn downhill to the right on Court Avenue. At the bottom of Court Avenue, turn left onto Main Street and follow it down past the intersection with Old Columbia Pike. Continue downhill on Main Street to the depot square, located at the intersection with Maryland Avenue next to the old railroad station. The discussion below mentions some of the buildings that you will pass along the way.

On the left (north) side of Main Street at the intersection with Old Columbia Pike, there is a large granite building with an ironwork porch. This is the Howard House, built as a hotel about 1850. Because it was caved into the hillside with its back door at ground level on the third floor, the hotel's central stairs became a thoroughfare between Main Street and Church Road on the way to and from the courthouse. The first floor, as later expanded, had a bar, a lunchroom, and an ice cream parlor. The second floor included a dining room for hotel guests and a separate banqueting hall. Following the construction of the railroad, tourists flocked to the town in order to combine the novelty of a train ride with a country excursion. Also, the granting of a municipal charter gave Ellicott City the right to license the sale of liquor. The city became the only "wet spot" in Howard County and the site of lavish parties held in the function rooms of the town's various hotels and victualing houses.

About 25 yards downhill from the Howard House (just before a large boulder), is the stone Walker-Chandler house, built about 1790. It has served successively as a private residence, a bootmaker's shop, offices, funeral home, tavern and dive, then offices again, before becoming Ellicotts Country Store.

The five-story building at the intersection with Maryland Avenue is the former Colonial Inn and Opera House, purportedly where John Wilkes Booth made his debut as an actor. Another prominent inn was the Patapsco Hotel, built in 1830 with one end butting up against the railroad. Rather than depositing the hotel's guests at the station across the street, the train pulled forward a few dozen yards and made another stop at a platform along the side of the hotel's second floor, so that guests could enter the hotel directly from the railroad carriages.

From the intersection with Maryland Avenue, continue east on Main Street under the railroad to the middle of the bridge over the Patapsco River.

The site of the original Ellicotts Lower Mills is now occupied by the Wilkins-Rogers flour mill and silos at the bend in the river downstream from the Frederick Road bridge. Most of the early settlement was on the east bank of the river but was destroyed by the flood of 1868. The row of houses where thirty-six people died (as discussed in Chapter 1) stood between the mill and higher ground. Opposite the mill near Frederick Road is the stone house of George Ellicott, a son of Andrew Ellicott. Built in 1789, the house originally stood on the

MAP 5 — Ellicott City and Oella

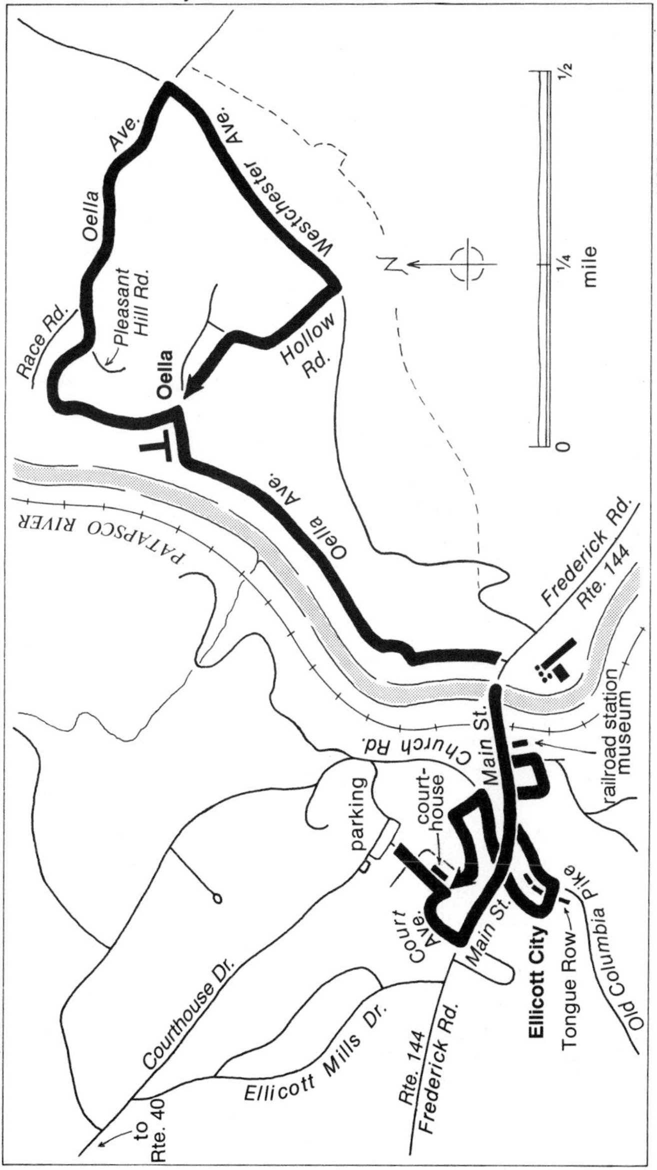

USGS: Ellicott City

Oella Ave.

Westchester Ave.

Race Rd.

Pleasant Hill Rd.

Oella

Hollow Rd.

PATAPSCO RIVER

Oella Ave.

Frederick Rd.
Rte. 144

railroad station
museum

Main St.

Church Rd.

parking

court-
house

Court Ave.

Main St.

Ellicott City

Tongue Row

Old Columbia Pike

Courthouse Dr.

Ellicott Mills Dr.

Rte. 144
Frederick Rd.

to
Rte. 40

N

½   ¼   0
mile

other side of Frederick Road at a somewhat lower elevation, where it was partially destroyed by the 1972 Agnes flood. Under the auspices of Historic Ellicott City, Inc., it was moved to its present site in 1987 and restored for use as offices.

The mill village of Oella, mentioned at the outset of this chapter, is located on Oella Avenue about 0.7 mile upstream from the eastern end of the bridge over the Patapsco River. Oella is well worth touring by car after your walk in Ellicott City, and directions are provided at the end of this chapter.

Back on the west bank of the Patapsco River (which no longer has much flow because nearly all water from the river's North Branch is impounded at Liberty Reservoir) is another old stone building, located between the river and the railroad. This structure is believed to have been built as a house for mill hands. For a period during the nineteenth century, it served as a general store called Radcliffe's Emporium. Neighboring houses upstream were swept away by the flood of 1868.

Return back under the railroad bridge and turn left to the railroad station, located on Maryland Avenue at the depot square.

The B&O station dates from 1831, when the railroad first reached Ellicotts Lower Mills. The building has been restored to its early nineteenth-century appearance and now houses the B&O Railroad Station Museum.

From the curved stone wall next to the railroad station museum, cross the street and enter Tiber Alley opposite. Turn right over Tiber Run, then left onto Main Street. At the next intersection, turn left up Old Columbia Pike and continue to Tongue Row, a group of stone houses (now shops) built by a Mr. Tongue in the early 1800s.

At Tongue Row descend on narrow stairs between the buildings. Bear right in front of a parking lot in order to cross over Tiber Run and return to Main Street. Cross Main Street and climb half-right up Church Road past the former firehouse, which is now a museum where an excellent collection of old firefighting equipment is displayed. Turn left onto Emory Street opposite the Emory United Methodist Church, then turn left again onto Court Avenue. (If Court Avenue is closed—as it was early in 1993 because the retaining wall had collapsed—retrace your steps back down around the corner onto Church Road and follow stairs that climb to Court Avenue.) Follow Court Avenue up past small law offices and the former First Presbyterian Church, now the headquarters of the Howard County Historical Society. Pass the courthouse, then turn right to return to the parking lot.

≈   ≈   ≈   ≈

As noted earlier, the village of **Oella**, which in physical terms remains an enclave of mill housing surrounding the former textile plant, is located on the east bank of the Patapsco River about 0.7 mile upstream from Frederick Road. Oella got its start in 1808 when the founders of the Union Manufacturing Company of Maryland purchased land from the Ellicotts and started selling stock. By October 1809, the first textile mill had been completed. In 1811 the company employed over 300 workers and had its property resurveyed under the name of "Oella," which the patent said was "in commemoration of the first woman who applied herself to the spinning of cotton on the continent of America." However, the identity of this mysterious (or fabled) Oella has yet to be discovered.

The Union Dam (now breached at its western end) is located below the Route 40 bridge about 1.5 miles upstream from the mill. From the dam a millrace, said to have been constructed with slave labor and one of the country's longest races feeding a single mill, runs along the eastern bank of the river to Oella, creating a vertical drop at the mill of nearly 50 feet. The mill generated its own power until the construction of Liberty Dam in the early 1950s diminished the flow of water.

For a time the Union mill at Oella was among the nation's largest makers of cotton goods, but in 1889 financial difficulties forced its sale to William J. Dickey of the Dickeyville mills, who proceeded to manufacture a variety of woolen and cotton fabrics at his Oella plant. In 1918 the three main mill buildings and a warehouse burned down, but these structures were replaced by a new mill that was later expanded several times and still stands. The plant prospered during World War II, employing (as of January 1945) 382 people working in three shifts. Production for 1945 was 445,471 yards of woolen cloth of which 60 percent was for military coats. Operations at Oella reached their peak in the 1950s, when the plant employed 500 workers producing fancy woolen fabrics for men's sports coats and suits. In the 1960s, however, the upsurge in imported textiles and synthetics engulfed domestic woolen manufacturers. The decline at Oella became even more precipitous with the advent of double-knit fabrics that could not be produced on the machinery used there. The plant closed in 1972.

For the decade following the mill's closing, the future of Oella even as a residential community was in doubt because there was no public water or sewer system. Raw sewage from the mill housing was pumped into leaky septic tanks, and for a period Baltimore County considered condemning much of the mill housing. During the mid-1980s however, the county installed water and sewer lines through the rocky terrain at a cost of more than $5 million. Now the community, where mill employees lived for generations, is becoming gentrified as the old housing is restored, new luxury residences are built, and a variety of retail enterprises and artisans occupy the mill.

AUTOMOBILE: (See Map 5 on page 41.) To reach Oella from the Howard County Courthouse parking lots, follow Courthouse Drive back toward Route 40. After 0.5 mile turn left off Courthouse Drive onto Ellicott Mills Drive. Descend steeply 0.5 mile, then turn left onto Frederick Road (Main Street) at a T-intersection. Go 0.4 mile downhill through Ellicott City and across the bridge over the Patapsco River. Immediately after crossing the bridge, turn left onto Oella Avenue.

Follow Oella Avenue past the low shelf of land that was the site of the Ellicott ironworks at the beginning of the nineteenth century and later the site of the Granite Cotton Mill, which was destroyed by the flood of 1868. Continue on Oella Avenue along the side of the valley above the river and past mill housing. Bear right past the large mill, then turn sharply left so as to continue around the mill. Follow the road past more mill housing. Curve right and continue past intersections with Pleasant Hill Road on the right and Race Road on the left. Eventually, turn right near the rim of the valley onto Westchester Avenue. Go 0.4 mile, then turn right downhill onto Hollow Road, which is very steep, curved, and two-way, so go slowly. At the bottom of the hill, fork left past the mill to return to Frederick Road by the way you came.

Further reading: A book-length treatment of Ellicott City is Celia M. Holland's *Ellicott City, Maryland: Mill Town U.S.A.* (Adams Press). John W. McGrain has written *Oella— Its Thread of History* (published by the Oella Community Improvement Association).

3

PATAPSCO VALLEY STATE PARK

Daniels

Walking—3.0 to 6.5 miles (4.8 to 10.5 kilometers)
depending on how far you continue past Daniels.
Although this section of the Patapsco Valley State Park
has no official activity centers or even parking lots for visitors, it nonetheless has many foot trails and horse paths
that provide outstanding opportunities for walking. The
route shown by the bold line on Map 6 on page 57
follows the remains of Alberton Road (now closed to
cars) west along the winding Patapsco Valley to the dam
and partially-ruined mill complex at Daniels. From there
the broad trail continues upstream and eventually turns
into a narrow and somewhat rugged footpath through a
particularly isolated section of the valley. Return by the
way you came.

This section of Patapsco Valley State Park is open daily
from sunrise to sunset. Dogs must be leashed. The park
is managed by the Department of Natural Resources,
Maryland Forest, Park and Wildlife Service; telephone
461-5005.

FIVE HUNDRED FIFTY ACRES fronting on the Patapsco
River. A factory complex consisting of a three-story stone
mill, 48 by 230 feet, and various brick and cement-block struc-

tures for the manufacture of heavy canvas, denim, industrial belting, and hose. A concrete dam furnishing 400 horsepower and generating surplus electricity that was sold to the Baltimore Gas and Electric Company. A post office, a community hall, and a general store. And 118 single-family, two-family, and rowhouse dwellings, most of them brick, averaging five rooms each, many without interior plumbing. In 1940, this was Alberton. Before that, the town was called Elysville. It has since been renamed Daniels. For three generations it had been a company town owned by James S. Gary & Sons. But on November 23, 1940, the entire town—houses, factory, and machinery—was sold for $65,000 to the C. R. Daniels Company of Newark, New Jersey, at a auction held in front of the general store to foreclose Gary & Sons default under its mortgage. The company simply had been unable to survive the Depression.

A few years later, however, stimulated by the immense demand for canvas and cotton duck during World War II, the factory was again humming. Operations continued until the rain-generated floodwaters of Tropical Storm Agnes churned through the mill in 1972, but not before the Daniels Company itself, in a remarkable exercise of milltown proprietorship, had razed all the houses in 1968, destroying a town since named to the Register of Historic Places, evicting about a quarter of the mill's employees and many of its pensioners, but perhaps saving their lives and certainly their property from the subsequent devastation of Agnes.

Elysville got its start in the 1840s when the Elysville Manufacturing Company, consisting of Thomas Ely, his three brothers, and Hugh Balderson, started building the original stone mill, now largely ruined but with walls still standing. The Baltimore & Ohio Railroad already passed through the stretch of curving valley bottom. Constructing, equipping, and operating the mill were more costly than anticipated, and in 1845 the Ely brothers decided to convey it to a new corporation funded with more capital from additional shareholders. Accordingly, in 1846 the Elysville Company sold the mill to the newly-incorporated Okisko Company in exchange for $25,000 of Okisko stock. Six Baltimore merchants, who would soon wish they had never heard of Thomas Ely and his slippery brothers, paid another $25,000 for their shares in Okisko.

Further improvements were made, the fresh capital was spent, but still the enterprise floundered. In 1849 a suit was brought by unpaid contractors and other creditors demanding that the mill be sold to satisfy their claims. At this point the Elysville Company brought its own suit asserting that the sale of the mill to Okisko was a nullity and urging that the mill, complete with its recent improvements, be returned to the Elys or sold for their benefit on the grounds that the contract with Okisko had required the Elysville Company to be paid in cash and not stock, that Thomas Ely (as president of the Elys' corporation) had lacked power to sell the mill, and that the Elysville Company had been without charter authority to hold stock in another company such as Okisko. When the court attempted to sell the property, Hugh Ely, a state senator who was one of the brothers, bought the mill at the auction but then repudiated his purchase on the grounds that the advertisement describing the property, which was based on an inventory that the Elys themselves had prepared when selling the mill to Okisko, was inaccurate and misleading. The intertwined litigation dragged on until 1853, reaching the state's highest court three times. The property was finally sold for the benefit of creditors.

During the 1850s, the mill was bought and sold by a succession of corporations, some of them simply reorganizations of prior owners. For a time, the property was owned by the Alberton Manufacturing Company, one of whose principals was Jacob Albert, an Okisko creditor whose name stuck to the community. In 1861 the mill and town came under the firm control of James S. Gary, a self-made man whose fortune propelled his son, James A. Gary of Baltimore, to the position of Postmaster General for President McKinley and to leadership of the Maryland Republican party until his death in 1920.

Under Gary ownership, the mill at Alberton became a solid financial success for the first time, helped by large contracts for canvas tents during the Civil War. In 1860 the mill employed 50 men and 120 women running 120 looms. An oakum factory was also in operation making caulking from cotton waste. By 1895 the mill had grown to 340 looms, presumably run by an equal number of women and children. (During the 1890s, the Maryland cotton manufacturing industry employed more children under age sixteen than any other type of manufacturing enterprise, with an average starting age of twelve.) By 1915 more than 400 hands were employed at Alberton.

During most of the period between the Civil War and World War I, the mill and the surrounding town were managed by Samuel F. Cobb, remembered by his former workers and subordinates as an Old Testament-like figure with a long white beard who was not only boss but *de facto* mayor as well, summoning outside authority only as need arose. Cobb's diaries describe the practice of sending recruiters to Virginia and West Virginia to attract employees—especially families with many girls, since inexpensive female labor was preferred. One recruiter supposedly enticed a family to move to Alberton to work in the mill by telling them that bananas, free for the picking, grew in the surrounding woods. When the new employees complained to Mr. Cobb that there were no bananas, he is said to have replied that the monkeys had eaten them all. Although almost certainly apocryphal, the story may nonetheless accurately reflect the tenor of Mr. Cobb's regime.

The company policy for management of the mill was a combination of long hours and low wages matched by equally low rents for comfortable houses, according to the standards of the times. Even as late as 1968, the C. R. Daniels Company was charging a top rent of $4.50 per week for a seven-room house, provided that the head of the family worked in the mill. The company also provided free firewood, Christmas gifts for children, a school, support for a growing variety of community activities, and charity for those of its "family" who suffered misfortunes. This paternalistic system was in fact the norm at company towns like Daniels, nor was it resented by most employees. At Oella, for example, unemployed workers were allowed to remain in their company-owned homes free of rent during the Depression, and in return the workers repeatedly voted not to unionize.

Aside from the mill, the center of town life at Alberton was the churches. James A. Gary built the Gary United Methodist Church on the hill south of the mill in 1879 as a memorial to his father. It is the only building in the community undamaged by flood or fire. Other churches were encouraged, including the Catholic chapel of St. Stanislaus Kostka, whose priest in winter sometimes skated down the frozen river from Woodstock College of the Sacred Heart to conduct Sunday service. In the 1920s the chapel was struck by lightning and burned. Its ruins are located on the hillside across the river and slightly downstream from the mill. An Episcopal congregation existed until World War I. Subsequently, its stone church with a squat, square tower and cupola was incorporated into the mill complex. In 1940 a small Pentecostal church was built near the railroad bridge across the river from the mill. At one point during the 1972 flood, only the roof and tower of the church were visible. (Although the church still stands, it is not safe to enter.) Dozens of company houses used to front the road above and below the church. The residents crossed to the mill on a pedestrian suspension bridge like the one at Orange Grove, discussed in Chapter 1.

Following World War I, the company's business began to

decline as the owners failed to modernize the mill. During the Depression, operations nearly stopped altogether. Many employees worked only one or two days a week in order to spread wages among as many people as possible. Gary & Sons obtained a loan from the federal government's Reconstruction Finance Corporation, but when the firm was unable to keep up with the payments, the entire enterprise was sold to the C. R. Daniels Company. Daniels renovated the mill and much of the housing but eventually announced that it was going to demolish the dwellings because it could not afford the cost of still further repairs and improvements—estimated at $750,000—in order to bring the residences up to housing code standards. Despite an outcry from local housing-assistance agencies and historic preservation groups, the town ceased to exist in 1968, although the mill continued in business.

In 1972 Agnes struck. The water rose so fast that five people were caught in the mill building and had to be evacuated from the roof by helicopter. The town store was pushed off its foundation and swept away. When the flood receded, cars, trucks, flotsam, and wreckage were left heaped against the buildings, which were coated inside and out with mud. Snarls of nylon yarn trailed from windows and the tops of telephone poles. The C. R. Daniels Company suffered a very large uninsured loss—as high as $2.7 million, according to some newspaper accounts—and pulled out of the valley. (The company now has a plant near Ellicott City.) Then in 1978, the mill, while being used as a warehouse, was gutted by fire. Its roofless walls remain. Other structures are used by a variety of marginal businesses. Across the river, where much of Elysville-Alberton-Daniels used to stand, the land has been incorporated into the Patapsco Valley State Park.

AUTOMOBILE: The section of the Patapsco Valley State Park explored by this walk is located west of

Baltimore, not far upstream from where Interstate 70 and Old Frederick Road cross the river. The trailhead is on Alberton Road, which intersects with Dogwood Road at the point where Dogwood Road most closely approaches the Patapsco River. Two avenues of approach are described below: the first from the Beltway and the other from Interstate 70 at Route 29.

From Interstate 695 (the Beltway) west of Baltimore, take Exit 17 for Security Boulevard, then fork west toward Rolling Road. Follow Security Boulevard west past Security Square Mall and the intersection with Rolling Road. Continue straight west on Security Boulevard, then turn left onto Greengage Road. Follow Greengage Road 0.3 mile, then turn right onto Fairbrook Road. Follow Fairbrook Road 0.4 mile, then turn left onto Johnnycake Road. Follow Johnnycake Road 1.4 miles as the road eventually winds downhill into the Patapsco Valley. At a T-intersection with Hollofield Road in front of the river, turn right. Go 0.3 miles to a T-intersection with Dogwood Road. Turn left over a bridge, then turn left immediately onto Alberton Road. With caution, follow Alberton Road about 150 yards to an oval drive in front of a house. Turn left to park as far from the house as possible. As a courtesy to the owners of this house, do not park in their oval drive, nor anywhere near the green park gate. Finally, if "no parking" signs are posted, park elsewhere—such as the shoulder of Alberton Road near the intersection with Dogwood Road.

The starting point at Alberton Road can also be reached from Interstate 70 by taking Exit 87B for Route 29 toward Route 99. Route 29 also provides a good approach from the vicinity of Columbia. Follow Route 29 north to its end at a T-intersection with Route 99, and there turn right (east). Go 0.6 miles on Route 99, then turn left onto Old Frederick Road. Follow Old Frederick Road 1.7 miles as the road eventually descends into the Patapsco Valley and crosses the river. About 100 yards beyond the bridge, continue straight on Hollofield Road where Johnnycake Road intersects from the right. Continue 0.3 mile to a T-intersection with Dogwood Road. Turn left over a bridge, then turn left immediately onto Alberton Road. With caution, follow Alberton Road about 150 yards to an oval drive in front of a house. Turn left to park as far from the house as possible. As a courtesy to the owners of this house, do not park in their oval drive, nor anywhere near the green park gate. Finally, if "no parking" signs are posted, park elsewhere—such as the shoulder of Alberton Road near the intersection with Dogwood Road.

WALKING: (See Map 6 on page 57.) With the Patapsco River toward your left, follow the remains of Alberton Road past a gate. Continue along the road upstream for about 1.0 mile to Daniels.

Where you first come within sight of the ruins of Daniels, a grassy road intersects from the rear-right. This road leads uphill and around the shoulder of a ravine to the left. The ruins of the old Catholic chapel of St. Stanislaus Kostka are located in the woods on the far side of the ravine shortly after the roads bends left away from the river.

From the riverside road opposite Daniels, continue around the big bend in the river. After passing under the railroad, do not follow the rutted road where it curves abruptly right uphill next to the railroad; instead, continue straight on a less worn trail. Follow this trail (which is quite narrow and muddy in places) as it gradually curves right past several obscure side trails that lead left toward the Daniels dam. The path eventually rejoins the river on the left, then joins the railroad. Be alert for trains, and do not walk on the tracks; if a train passes, stand well back.

With the river on your left and the railroad tracks on your right, go about 100 yards to a bridge over a stream. Immediately after crossing the bridge, cross the railroad tracks, then follow a rough, eroded path that climbs along the side of the valley. With the river on your left, continue along the side of the valley for about 0.7 mile. After descending to the level of the railroad, turn sharply right to follow the main path steeply uphill away from the tracks. (This sharp, uphill turn occurs about 100 yards before the railroad enters a tunnel.) When the path levels off, turn left at a four-way trail junction. Follow the path across the top of the hill through which the railroad tunnel passes. Continue as the path narrows and zigzags downhill, eventually descending steeply to the bottom of the valley.

With the river on your right, follow a faint trail downstream through the bottom of the curving valley. There really is no set path here, or perhaps it would be more accurate to say that nearly every year the path changes as the area floods or as trees fall. However, you should have little difficulty threading your way through the bottomland woods next to the river. Eventually, as the shelf of bottomland narrows, the trail hugs the foot of the slope on the left, then rises along the side of the hill to join the railroad near the mouth of the tunnel. With caution, cross the tracks and rejoin the trail that you followed earlier in the opposite direction. With the river on your right, follow the trail along the valley passed Daniels and back to your starting point at Alberton Road.

MAP 6 — Daniels

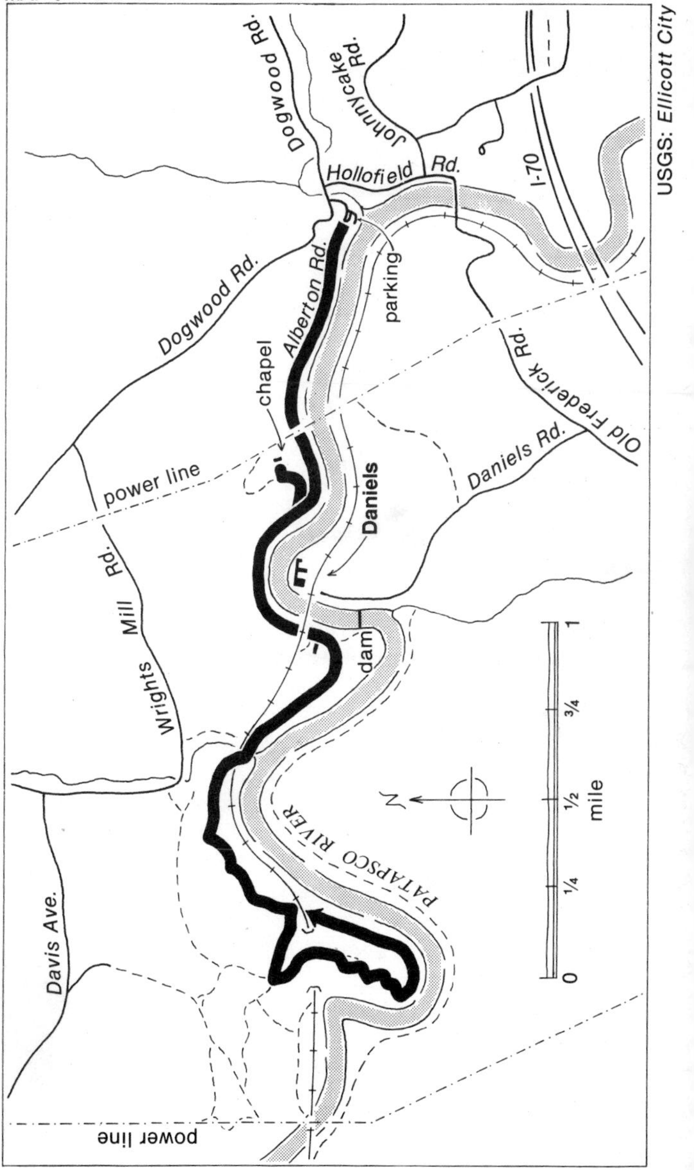

USGS: Ellicott City

Dogwood Rd.

Johnnycake Rd.

Hollofield Rd.

I-70

Dogwood Rd.

Alberton Rd.

parking

chapel

power line

Old Frederick Rd.

Daniels Rd.

Daniels

Wrights Mill Rd.

dam

PATAPSCO RIVER

Davis Ave.

N

1/4   1/2   3/4   1
mile
0

power line

Ellicotts Upper Mills

While you are in the vicinity of the Daniels walk, you may be interested to know that the point where Old Frederick Road crosses the Patapsco River was formerly Ellicotts Upper Mills. As noted briefly in Chapter 2, the Upper Mills were purchased by the Ellicott family in 1774 from James Hood, who in 1768 had built a dam and mill for grinding corn. Four years earlier the Ellicotts had bought undeveloped land farther downstream at what became the Lower Mills and later Ellicott City. At that time the Upper Mills was more valuable than the Lower Mills because it was located where the main road linking Baltimore and Frederick forded the river. When the Ellicott property was divided, the Upper Mills was assigned to Joseph Ellicott, the oldest of the three Ellicott brothers. Ironically, nothing now remains at the Upper Mills.

When Joseph Ellicott moved his family from Pennsylvania to Maryland in 1775, he tore down the mill built by James Hood and constructed another for milling wheat using the latest inventions and improvements, many of his own design. On the shelf of land at the west end of the present bridge, he also built a large house and (on land later taken by the railroad) an ornamental garden with a fish pond and fountain spouting water 10 feet high. When the Upper Mills tract was resurveyed in 1797, it was called "Fountainville."

Like his brothers at the Lower Mills, Joseph also built a general store that sold dry goods, silks, satins, and brocades, as well as the usual groceries. Although the store reportedly did a good business, society must have been limited. Four of Joseph's nine children married the orphaned brothers and sisters of the Evans family, whom the Ellicotts had brought with them from Pennsylvania.

When Joseph Ellicott settled at the Upper Mills, he was already wealthy, having traveled to England ten years before to claim and liquidate his great-grandfather's estate to which he was heir. In Pennsylvania he had been high sheriff of Bucks County and a member of the provincial assembly. His preoccupation with mathematics, clockmaking, mill works, and mechanics had also earned him prominence in scientific circles, and it is said that as he got older, these interests almost completely precluded social intercourse even with his own family. One of his projects was a four-faced musical grandfather clock that played twenty-four tunes and marked seconds, minutes, hours, days, months, years, phases of the moon, and motions of the planets.

Joseph died in 1780 but his widow, Judith, maintained her household at the Upper Mills until her death in 1809. By then the mill and store had greatly declined in value. The Frederick Turnpike had been relocated through the Lower Mills, which in time utterly eclipsed the small settlement farther upstream.

Further reading: When it is published by the Baltimore County Public Library in 1994, Volume II of John W. McGrain's *From Pig Iron to Cotton Duck* will include a comprehensive discussion of Daniels.

4

PATAPSCO VALLEY STATE PARK

McKeldin Recreation Area

Walking—4.0 miles (6.4 kilometers). The McKeldin
Recreation Area provides some of the best walking in the
Baltimore region. The route shown by the bold line on
Map 7 on page 68 follows well-marked footpaths through
the deep valleys and woods at the confluence of the
South and North branches of the Patapsco River. A spur
trail leads to McKeldin Falls, among the largest of our
local cascades.

The park is open Thursday through Sunday, 10 A.M. to
sunset. It is closed Thanksgiving and Christmas. An
admission fee is charged on weekends and holidays
during March through October. Pets are prohibited. The
park is managed by the Department of Natural
Resources, Maryland Forest, Park and Wildlife Service;
telephone 461-5005.

"FRANKLY, I LIKE THE SOUND of the Governor Theodore
R. McKeldin Recreation Area," said Governor Theodore R.
McKeldin at the dedication ceremony for this section of the
Patapsco Valley State Park in 1957. For more than a decade
McKeldin had been one of the leading advocates for the expan-
sion of the park to include the entire Patapsco Valley down-
stream from Sykesville as well as the North Branch below

Liberty Reservoir. As governor, McKeldin was in the enviable position of being able to implement what he described as a "brilliant plan" for park expansion that he had come across after taking office—a plan developed earlier at his recommendation while mayor of Baltimore but shelved by the previous governor. The plan called for the extension into the greater Baltimore area of the system of stream-valley parks first proposed in the Olmsted Brothers report fifty years earlier (as discussed in Chapter 20).

Prior to the 1950s, the Patapsco Valley State Park included less than 1,500 acres in a patchwork between Route 40 (Hollofield) and Route 1 (Avalon). The park—or Patapsco River Forest Reserve, as it was at first called—had started with a gift to the state of 434 acres in 1907, at a time when President Theodore Roosevelt (for whom McKeldin was named) and his chief forester, Gifford Pinchot, were popularizing the philosophy of conservation and were adding millions of acres of land to federal ownership, withdrawing immense public tracts from sale to the private sector, and setting apart federal forest reserves. In 1912, the state legislature for the first time appropriated funds for the purchase of forest lands to be managed by the Maryland State Board of Forestry. By the time of the Depression during the 1930s, the Patapsco River Forest Reserve included about 1,300 acres; during this period the area was improved with trails, picnic grounds, shelters, and campsites constructed by workers of the federally sponsored Civilian Conservation Corps, which had a camp at the Avalon area (Chapter 1). As the primary use of the area shifted from forest preservation to recreation, the name was changed to the Patapsco Valley State Park under the newly consolidated Department of State Forests and Parks (now the Department of Natural Resources).

In 1946, the Patapsco River Valley Commission, appointed by then-Mayor McKeldin, drew up a plan for enlarging the state park to 15,000 acres connected by a riverside parkway for cars. The road was never built but other aspects of the plan reappeared in a study prepared by private consultants for the Maryland State Planning Commission in 1950. The new plan called for a linear park of 8,500 acres averaging half a mile in width and extending 37 miles along the river from the Hanover Street Bridge in Baltimore to Sykesville. Improvements were to include not only the usual hiking and riding trails and picnicking and camping facilities, but also golf courses (even miniature golf), swimming pools, a miniature railroad, a carousel, dance pavilions, restaurants, cabins, and lodges. The total cost was estimated at $6 million and a period of twelve years was thought sufficient to complete the project.

During the next twenty-five years the park grew in fits and starts. For a period, land acquisition stalled at about 4,500 acres as funds were exhausted and state and local officials and a citizen advisory committee debated which land should be given priority for purchase. A major area of contention was the marsh along the lower Patapsco, where gravel mining had left a series of small lakes in the flats beside the river. (This area has since been acquired at the urging of officials of Anne Arundel County and—although not yet developed for recreation—promises to be a very unusual and interesting section of the park.) By 1972, when much of the Patapsco Valley was devastated by flooding from Tropical Storm Agnes, the park included about 7,000 acres in Carroll, Howard, Baltimore, and Anne Arundel counties and was visited yearly by an estimated 4.5 million people.

Yet at the same time that millions of dollars were being spent to expand the park, industrial pollution and suburban growth were turning the Patapsco River into a regional sewer. At first the problem was not without drollery. Children who swam at Ellicott City in the early 1900s had to post a lookout on the rocks upstream to warn the others to get out of the water when the Dickey Mill at Oella released dye into the river. But by mid-century swimming was unthinkable. Sykesville, Ellicott City, and other communities and institutional facilities dumped their untreated waste into the river.

Industries added oil, solvents, and other chemicals, and cannaries and distilleries poured in slurries of food scraps, pulp, and grain. The river stank. Newspaper accounts during the 1960s reported floating islands of bubbling sludge and a river bottom coated with decomposing matter. Detergents produced a frothy surface that gave the appearance of snow and ice year-round. Massive fish kills occurred annually during periods of particularly toxic discharges. By 1967 a study by the Maryland Department of Water Resources classified the Patapsco River below Ilchester, where effluent from the paperboard mill used to be discharged into the river, as "grossly polluted."

Since then, however, water quality in the Patapsco has improved significantly. Industries and communities along the river have been required to connect into the large Patapsco interceptor sewer line that during the late 1960s was run up the valley from the Patapsco Wastewater Treatment Plant at Wagners Point. Also, the torrent caused by Tropical Storm Agnes flushed the accumulated filth from the riverbed (and dumped it in the tidal portion of the Patapsco at Baltimore City). Still, however, incidents of industrial pollution and sewage overflows occur regularly, and sediments from erosion and stormwater runoff give the water its characteristic murky appearance.

After the 1972 Agnes flood, the Maryland Department of Natural Resources undertook to re-evaluate previous park plans for the Patapsco. The job was assigned to the Department's own staff of professional land planners. Working with members of the Maryland Park Service and a newly appointed citizen advisory committee, the state's design team developed a revised master plan that was adopted in 1979 and on the basis of which the General Assembly authorized a park totaling 15,200 acres. This figure has since been increased to 16,082 acres, of which 13,447 had been acquired as of the beginning of 1993. Previously, the state had concentrated on buying only the valley bottom and slopes because they were visually and environmentally sensitive (and in most cases cheap as

 What is this? Answer on page 66.

well), but much of the acreage bought since 1979 is outside—though still adjacent to—the immediate valley. In these areas, the plan called for development of extensive campgrounds and picnic areas set back from the valley rim, where the pavilions, toilets, and offices would be beyond the reach of flood, easily accessible from nearby roads, and yet visually isolated in the woods. The valley slopes and bottomland were reserved for low-cost improvements and low-key uses, such as riding and walking trails.

Aside from calling for a larger park, the 1979 Patapsco master plan was generally more austere than earlier plans. The Department of Natural Resources adopted the policy that the chief purpose of state parks is to promote the enjoyment and protection of natural, historic, and scenic features rather than to provide tennis and basketball courts, skating rinks, swimming pools, golf courses, and other recreation facilities that are more appropriately the responsibility of local governments. This policy will probably become even more pronounced when the 1979 Patapsco master plan—by now rather dated—is next revised. For example, many of the big picnic areas and campgrounds contemplated for Patapsco Valley State Park have never been built and probably will be postponed indefinitely—or at least be scaled down—in recognition of the fact that Patapsco visitors no longer use these types of facilities as much as they once did, preferring instead to walk or bicycle for the day in a natural setting.

AUTOMOBILE: The McKeldin Recreation Area of the Patapsco Valley State Park is located west of Baltimore below Liberty Reservoir. The entrance is on Marriottsville Road north of Marriottsville.

From Interstate 695 (the Beltway) west of Baltimore, take Exit 16 for Interstate 70 west toward Frederick. Follow Interstate 70 west about 8.0 miles to Exit 83 for Marriottsville Road. Bear right and follow Marriottsville

Page 65: Tree trunk stripped of its bark by beavers.

Road north 4.0 miles to the park entrance on the right. Park your car in the lot just beyond the small ranger station at the top of the entrance road.

The park entrance can also be reached from the intersection of Liberty Road and Marriottsville Road west of Randallstown. In this case, follow Marriottsville Road southwest 4.7 miles.

WALKING: (See Map 7 on page 68.) From the parking lot and tiny ranger station at the top of the entrance road, follow the entrance road back downhill toward Marriottsville Road for 70 yards. At the first bend, head straight off the road onto a wide path entering the woods. This is the Switchback Trail, and it is marked with white paint blazes. Except for a few stretches noted below, the route described here follows this trail.

Follow the path through the woods, then down and around to the left by Marriottsville Road. Continue along the bottom of the slope. At a trail junction where the white-blazed path curves left uphill, continue straight downhill to the river's edge. You will rejoin the white-blazed trail later.

Turn left along the valley bottom and continue with the river on your right. Eventually, turn right at an intersection and rejoin the white-blazed trail. Follow the path along the river bank, then up and straight across an asphalt road. Descend through the woods, at one point forking right downhill where the white-blazed trail veers left. At the river's edge, a spur trail along the bank leads upstream several hundred yards to McKeldin Falls.

From McKeldin Falls, head downstream. With the river on your right, follow the riverside path over jumbled rocks and across a large, bare rock surface sloping into the river; **but** if you prefer not to cross the rock slope (which can be slippery when it is wet or icy),

67

MAP 7 — McKeldin Recreation Area

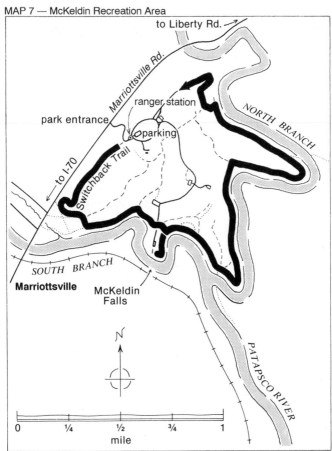

USGS: *Sykesville, Ellicott City*

retrace your steps 50 yards and detour up and around the rocky area and back down to the path by the river. As you continue downstream, be alert for places where the path is in danger of caving into the river because of erosion.

Follow the riverside path downstream to the confluence of the South and North branches of the Patapsco River. (Because of the dam at Liberty Reservoir, the North Branch usually has little water.) With the river on your right, follow the North Branch upstream. After about 0.7 mile, fork right and continue on the white-blazed trail, still with the river on your right, although it is often out of sight. Follow the path along the valley bottom, around to the left, and along the river. Eventually, the trail crosses a jumble of rocks shortly before the river bends slightly to the right. After about 220 yards, turn left to climb very steeply away from the river. (If you run into a cliff blocking further progress along the river's edge, you will know that you have gone too far and should retrace your steps 70 yards.)

Follow the white-blazed footpath as it climbs steeply away from the river and turns right. Continue obliquely uphill along the side of the valley, with the river downhill to your right. At a trail junction near the crest of the slope, turn right. Follow the white-blazed path along the top of the slope, then gradually downhill and to the right along the side of the valley. Continue as the trail gradually climbs, then curves sharply left. Follow the path to a picnic area and then along an asphalt road that at one point provides a view of Liberty Dam to the north. Continue straight to the parking lot by the ranger station. Be alert for cars.

5

SOLDIERS DELIGHT NATURAL ENVIRONMENT AREA

Walking—3.0 or 4.0 miles (4.8 or 6.4 kilometers) depending on whether you continue east of Deer Park Road. The two routes shown by the bold lines on Map 8 on page 79 explore an unusual landscape of rocky meadows and stunted, piney woods.

The park is open daily from sunrise to sunset. Dogs must be leashed. Mountain bicycling is prohibited. The visitor center is open Monday, Wednesday, and Friday from 9 to 4 and Sunday from 12 to 4, but these hours are subject to change. The area is managed by the Department of Natural Resources, Maryland Forest, Park and Wildlife Service; telephone 922-3044 or 922-9651. If there is no answer at either number, call the Patapsco Valley State Park at 461-5005.

THERE'S CHROME IN THEM THAR HILLS at Soldiers Delight northwest of Baltimore.

Perhaps this news lacks the galvanic impact of a gold strike, but the fact remains that during the second quarter of the nineteenth century, ownership of chromite mines in the Soldiers Delight district and at other outcroppings of serpentine rock in Maryland and southeastern Pennsylvania enabled Isaac Tyson, Jr., founder of the Baltimore Chrome Works, to control the world chromium market and to become a very wealthy man.

The serpentine formations that break the surface in a few locations north and west of Baltimore are like nothing else in the region. They are commonly called serpentine *barrens,* and appropriately so. Blackjack oak, post oak, and Virginia pine (all small, drought-tolerant species) grow from the meager soil. The shallow, stony earth here not only lacks organic matter but also contains heavy concentrations of magnesium, which inhibits the ability of plants to absorb nutrients. Scattered throughout the stunted woods are meadows of yellow and red-tinted grass. The faded colors and stunted pine forest offer hikers a refreshing change from the deep-soiled farmland, river gorges, and tall deciduous woods so typical of Maryland's Piedmont region. Even if you have no interest in botany, you can enjoy the look of the Indian grass, little bluestem, purplish three-awn, beardgrass, turkeyfoot, broomsedge and other grasses typical of mid-western prairies. Depending on the season, visitors can also find birdsfoot violets, fameflowers, blazing stars, gerardias, sundrops, asters, knotweed, goldenrod, fringed gentians, and other wildflowers. At least 34 rare or endangered plants are found here, many of them showing special adaptations (such as hairy surfaces or leaves that curl up at midday) in order to cope with the drought and heat of summer. The best way to learn more about these plants is to join a walk led by a qualified naturalist. Call or stop by the visitor center for information on flower walks and other programs at Soldiers Delight.

Serpentine is a greenish metamorphic rock found near Baltimore not only in the Soldiers Delight region but also in the Bare Hills west of Lake Roland. At Cardiff in Harford County, serpentine is quarried and sold under the trade name of Maryland Green Marble, although it is not a limestone, as are true marbles. The rock is used primarily for interior trim in banks, hotels, and office buildings (including the lobby of the Empire State Building). Serpentine has also been tried as a structural building stone, despite the tendency of the rock surface to flake off due to weathering. The exterior of Baltimore's Mount Vernon Place Methodist Church, which has a distinctly greenish hue, is built of local serpentine. Perhaps, too, you are familiar with the old greenish stone school on Falls Road in the Bare Hills just uphill from Princeton Sports.

More significantly, the occurrence of serpentine in Maryland is associated with the presence of chromium. In 1808 or 1810 chromium ore was discovered in the serpentine outcroppings at the Bare Hills estate of Jesse Tyson, a wealthy flour and grain merchant. The Tysons' gardener showed some black rocks to Tyson's son, Isaac, who was a student of geology, mineralogy, and chemistry. He identified the rocks as chromite, and analysis established that the ore was of a salable grade.

With financial assistance from his father, the young Tyson started mining the ore on a small scale. Ore was extracted at the Bare Hills as early as 1811, and by 1817 Tyson was also mining chromite from stream deposits (called placers) in the serpentine barrens at Soldiers Delight. As with gold mining, the stream sands were washed in a sluice (called a buddle) to concentrate the heavy chromite. The ore was then shipped to paint and ceramic factories in England, for at that time chromium was used chiefly to make brilliant pigments, dyes, and glazes (hence chrome-yellow, chrome-orange, chrome-green, and other chrome hues).

Chromite mining was only a small part of Isaac Tyson's business as a manufacturer of chemicals, but in 1827 he hit pay dirt. He noticed that a cider barrel that had been brought in a wagon to Belair Market in Baltimore was steadied by rocks that he recognized as chromite. He traced the stone to the Reed farm near Jarrettsville in Harford County, obtained mineral rights to the property, and there, at what came to be called Chrome Hill, found a massive deposit of ore only 8 feet below the surface. The Reed Mine was developed quickly and became so profitable that Tyson temporarily suspended his mining operations at other sites.

Tyson continued, however, to search out serpentine formations in Maryland and Pennsylvania, and he bought or leased property wherever there were indications of chromium. Not long after the Reed discovery, Tyson opened the Wood Mine in the State Line district of Lancaster County, Pennsylvania. This operation was another bonanza, eventually proving to be the richest chromium mine in the United States. Isaac Tyson's mines were far more productive and economical than other sources, with the result that between 1828 and 1850 virtually all of the chromium used in the world came from his mines.

Tyson's search for chromite also led to his involvement in the mining and smelting of iron and copper. He had a copper works at the Bare Hills, faintly recalled nowadays by Copper Hill Road and Coppermine Terrace off Falls Road. In league with his partners, he eventually owned most of the copper deposits in Maryland. He visited pits, smelting plants, and ironworks up and down the East Coast. He was a leader in the use of new and more efficient methods of refining ore, such as smelting with hard coal, and pre-heating air to create a hot blast. Engrossed with mining and minerals and intent on holding down competition, he or his agents sedulously investigated deposits and mining claims from Maine to Virginia, west to Arkansas and Missouri, and even in Cuba and Spain. "I am now going to Stafford in Vermont and for what purpose?" he wrote in his journal on December 1, 1833:

All for the sake of gain and how great the sacrifice. My beloved wife not yet out of her bed and requiring the sympathy and solace of her husband. My little children requiring the care and attention of their father & and my business neglected. . . . I am able to talk philosophically on these subjects and show the unreasonableness of avarice and the folly of accumulating wealth for children and yet I find myself pursuing the beaten track.

In 1845 Tyson and his associates established the Baltimore Chrome Works for the manufacture of chromium compounds

from raw ore. The plant was located on Block Street at the entrance to the Inner Harbor, south of what is now Little Italy. Tyson's timing in this venture was fortunate because the export market for unprocessed ore began to decline after the discovery of high-grade chromite in Turkey in 1848 by a geologist who had gained some of his experience working for Tyson. Although the export of chrome ore from the United States had practically ceased by 1860, the manufacture of chromium compounds at Baltimore continued and was carried on by Tyson's sons after his death in 1861. Local mines were eventually closed as the Baltimore Chrome Works obtained ore more cheaply from company-owned mines in California and later in New Caledonia. Until a rival plant was established in Philadelphia in 1882, the Baltimore Chrome Works supplied virtually all the chromium chemicals used by American industry.

Tyson's principal operation at Soldiers Delight was the Choate Mine. It was opened before 1839 and was worked intermittently until about 1886. It consisted of an inclined shaft sloping to the southwest for as much as 200 feet and fanning out to a mine face 160 feet wide. During World War I, when chromium was needed to make high-grade steel for armaments, the Choate Mine was reopened for a brief period. The ore was washed and concentrated in a local buddle operated by the Triplett family, who in 1893 had bought mineral rights to 6 acres from the Tysons. The entrance to the Choate Mine is still visible, but the sloping shaft should not be entered. Visitors should also be cautious around other old shafts in the area, where a variety of minerals were mined at one time or another. For example, talc was mined at Soldiers Delight and ground at local mills to make talcum powder.

Soldiers Delight is now a state "natural environment area," meaning that aside from the visitor center and trails, no recreational development is planned. The state first began to purchase land here in 1970 after ten years of lobbying and fund-raising by local conservation groups, including the Citizens Committee for Soldiers Delight and Soldiers Delight Conservation, Inc. Money has been supplied by private donations and by the county, state, and federal governments. About 2,000 acres has been purchased as of 1993.

Rather different is the present-day status of the old Baltimore Chrome Works, which in 1908 combined with two rival firms to form the Mutual Chemical Company of America. During the next half-century, Mutual greatly expanded its Inner Harbor plant for processing chromium compounds, and in the early 1950s the facility was the world's largest chromium chemical plant. In 1954 Mutual was acquired by the Allied Chemical Corporation (now Allied-Signal, Inc.), which in 1984 ceased operations at the Inner Harbor. As of 1993 the site was undergoing decontamination after the production there of toxic chromium compounds for more than 140 years. Soil under the site is impregnated with cancer-causing chromium chemicals that leak into the Patapsco River at a rate of about 60 pounds per day. The cleanup effort includes sealing the chromium in the soil under a 7-foot cap of clay, gravel, and heavy plastic sheeting. An impermeable barrier will be installed around the shoreline. Scheduled for completion in 1995, the cleanup will cost Allied-Signal up to $100 million, which the company hopes to recoup by using the site for a $200-million complex of offices and housing.

AUTOMOBILE: Soldiers Delight Natural Environment Area is located northwest of Baltimore near Liberty Reservoir. For walkers the best place to park is the overlook on Deer Park Road, where the area's five loop trails all start and end. Even if you intend to stop by the visitor center, I suggest that you walk there from the overlook.

From Interstate 695 (the Beltway) northwest of Balti-

more, take Exit 18B for Route 26 west toward Randallstown. Follow Route 26 (Liberty Road) about 5.0 miles
to an intersection with Deer Park Road on the right
near a large water tower. Bear right onto Deer Park
Road and go 2.3 miles to the Soldiers Delight overlook
on the left (or west) side of the road, about 0.3 mile
past the entrance to the Soldiers Delight visitor center.
The overlook, incidentally, occupies a site called Berry
Hill, where in 1853 John Berry was gibbeted for the
murder of his mother and the attempted murder of his
father.

WALKING: (See Map 8 opposite.) The trails at
Soldiers Delight are marked by red, orange, yellow,
green, and white blazes that indicate five routes of
different lengths. The red route is about 1 mile long,
the green and orange routes are each 2 miles long,
and the yellow and white routes are each 3 miles long.
In my opinion, the best excursion is the white route,
followed by the red route, and these two are described
below. Even though the routes are blazed, you
should pay close attention to the map and to your
progress, since the wooden posts on which the blazes
are marked have a way of falling down or even being
vandalized.

  White Route: Start at the overlook on Deer Park
Road. With the road on your left, follow the path south
next to the road for 50 yards, then veer half-right into
the woods. Follow the footpath for several hundred
yards as it runs parallel to Deer Park Road before turning right onto a gravel road. Follow the gravel road to
the visitor center, where there are interesting exhibits.
  From the visitor center, continue on the gravel road
past the side of the building. Stay on the gravel road

MAP 8 — Soldiers Delight

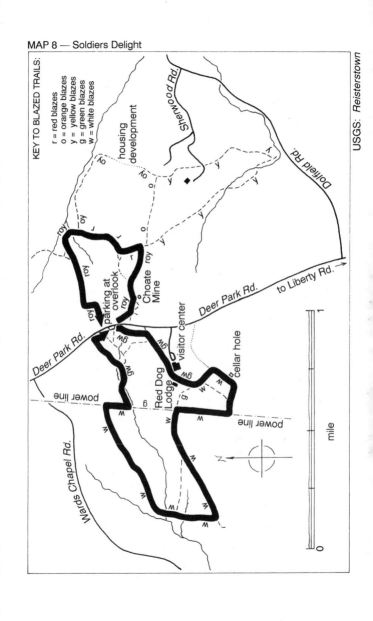

KEY TO BLAZED TRAILS:

r = red blazes
o = orange blazes
y = yellow blazes
g = green blazes
w = white blazes

USGS: *Reisterstown*

as it curves left past Red Dog Lodge, then past a rutted road intersecting from the rear-right. When you reach a large field with power lines visible in the distance, turn left. Skirt briefly through the edge of the woods, then continue on the worn track clockwise around the field and toward the power lines.

Turn right under the power lines and follow the track downhill, then up to the crest of another hill, where there is a four-way trail intersection. Turn left here. Follow the trail downhill away from the power lines, passing through clearings and piney woods. At a fork in the rutted road, bear left. Eventually, after passing a large field on the left, turn sharply right. If you reach a field behind some houses, you have gone too far and should retrace your steps about 80 yards.

Continue gradually downhill through woods and past small clearings, across a very small stream, and uphill. Go more or less straight past a trail intersecting from the right. Descend across another stream. Climb through a clearing and a short stretch of woods, then bear right along the edge of another clearing. Continue uphill on the rough track through a series of clearings. When you reach the power lines, turn right downhill under the wires.

At the bottom of the hill, turn left and follow a brook upstream. For the most part, the brook is to the right of the path, but eventually the trail crosses the stream. After about 70 yards, bear left back across the stream. Follow the path uphill to Deer Park Road, and there turn right onto a trail that leads to the overlook.

Red Route: From the overlook, cross Deer Park Road. With the road on your right, follow the shoulder south 60 yards to where the trail veers left into the woods. Go 125 yards, then bear left at an intersection of several trails. Bear left again in 40 yards near the entrance to Isaac Tyson's Choate Mine.

Continue along the path through the woods. After about a quarter of a mile, turn left at a T-intersection.

Continue through the woods, then fork right at a trail junction. Follow the path gradually downhill. Pass a trail intersecting from the right at the center of a small clearing. Re-enter the woods and cross a small stream, then turn left and continue straight uphill through more clearings. Eventually, turn left, then right to follow the main track uphill to Deer Park Road, with the overlook to the left as you emerge from the woods.

Further reading: An account of Isaac Tyson's career is contained in Abbot Collamer's "Isaac Tyson, Jr.—Pioneer Mining Engineer and Metallurgist," which appeared in *Maryland Historical Magazine* for March 1965.

6

OREGON RIDGE PARK

Walking—4.0 miles (6.4 kilometers) round-trip. From Oregon Ridge Nature Center, hike to Ivy Hill Pond and Baisman Run. The figure-8 route shown by the bold line on Map 9 on page 95 crosses and recrosses a wooded ridge on well-marked trails.

The nature center building is open from 9 to 5 daily, except Monday and major holidays. The park is open daily from sunrise to sunset. Dogs must be leashed. Mountain bicycling is prohibited. Oregon Ridge is managed by the Baltimore County Department of Recreation and Parks; telephone the nature center at 887-1815 or the Towson office at 887-3817.

THE VIEW FROM OREGON RIDGE looks over the agricultural valleys of Oregon Branch and Western Run. To the north is Hayfields, long the estate of the Bosley and Merryman families, where in 1824 the Marquis de Lafayette visited Colonel Nicholas Merryman Bosley and presented him with a silver trophy from the Maryland Agricultural Society for the best-cultivated Maryland farm. Immediately to the east is the Hunt Valley business community, since 1962 a major center of nonagricultural employment. Farther north is Loveton Center, another new industrial complex (visible as a white smudge in the right-center of the photograph). Just beyond the fields in the center of the picture is Interstate 83, putting this attractive agricultural landscape within a half hour's drive of downtown

Baltimore. Not surprisingly, in many places during recent years farm fields have been replaced by new subdivisions and townhouse developments.

Hayfields itself, in fact, has been the subject of a series of development proposals. In the early 1980s, efforts to change the zoning to permit 1,600 residential units at Hayfields were unsuccessful. In 1986 the 470-acre farm was sold to another developer who planned a golf course bordered by 69 expensive residences on one-acre lots. The proposal called for altering the zoning on some of the land at Hayfields—a change which Baltimore County refused to approve in 1992. No one, however, expects the issue to go away, and the owner has announced his intention to pursue development of Hayfields for as long as it takes to get his project approved.

The patchwork quilt of farms, subdivisions, and commercial development in the vicinity of Oregon Ridge and all along Interstate 83 into northernmost Baltimore County epitomizes areas that are the subject of growing national concern about the loss of farmland. The concern is both aesthetic and economic. The conversion of farmland to scattered, low-density subdivisions (by far the most voracious use of land) not only chews up the countryside but also imposes on local governments the obligation to develop public services and capital improvements that typically cost much more than similar improvements for high-density housing—and more, too, than is generated in new tax revenues. Also, land that is easily developed for residential use because of level, deep, well-drained soil is for the same reasons excellent for crops, but will never again be used for producing food.

The rapid growth of suburban Baltimore, Washington, and other cities and towns has made Maryland a national leader in farmland loss, although not all of the decline is attributable to land development. When the suburban explosion began after World War II, Maryland farms accounted for 4.2 million acres, or 67 percent of the state's total land. By 1980 farm acreage had dwindled to about 2.4 million acres, or 38 percent of the state's land area. By the year 2000 Maryland is expected to lose an additional 1 million acres of farmland.

Faced with the steady transformation of farms into suburbia, Maryland has developed a variety of programs intended to encourage the continued use of land for farming. In 1965 Maryland was the first state to enact a law (now Section 8-209 of the Tax-Property volume of the Annotated Code of Maryland) requiring that farmland be assessed for property taxes not on the basis of its full development value but rather on the basis of its use for farming, as though that were all the land was good for. This preferential assessment was intended to provide staying power to farmers on the urban fringe, where high taxes based on the land's enormous development potential were supposedly forcing farmers out of business (that is, causing them to sell their land for huge profits).

The remarkable thing about the preferential tax program, which with a few modifications has weathered a series of stormy attacks, is that landowners are required to give almost nothing in return. At most, an owner who sells or subdivides his farm property is simply required to pay an agricultural transfer tax equal to 5 percent of the sale price. As the result of various exceptions, the tax is usually less than that. Also, if the new owner signs a letter to the Department of Assessments and Taxation saying that he intends to farm the land for at least five more years, the sale does not trigger the agricultural transfer tax at all, and the land retains its preferential assessment until farming ceases or the land is sold again.

To get some idea of the magnitude of the agricultural tax preference, consider a hypothetical 100-acre farm in northern Baltimore County, where in 1993 most cropland commanded prices ranging between $7,000 and $10,000 per acre—not, of course, because of the land's suitability for farming but because of its potential for residential development. If the farm were assessed on the basis of its market value (and for this purpose I selected the lower figure of $7,000 per acre and—to keep things simple—assumed that there are no structures), the annual property tax would be $8,610. But because of the artificially low assessment that is assigned to agricultural land, the tax is only $461. The difference—or annual subsidy to promote farming—is $8,149, so you can see why farm owners love this law. Were the farm sold for $700,000 and immediately developed, the 5 percent transfer tax would amount to $35,000, which is less than five times the annual subsidy. For anyone who holds this hypothetical farm for more than five years, preferential assessment provides ever-increasing tax savings that are never recouped by the state and county governments.

Equally remarkable is that despite the revenue loss of tens of millions of dollars annually suffered by the state and county treasuries, no evidence exists that the preferential assessment helps to preserve farmland. In some instances, the law is simply silly, giving a tax break to "farms" that are as small as 2 or 3 acres. More significantly, studies suggest that preferential assessment of agricultural land results merely in a temporary postponement of the development of farmland. Over a period of several decades, the tax benefits are simply not strong enough to deter farmers near Baltimore and Washington from eventually selling out at prices which in 1993 ranged up to twenty or even thirty times the farm-use value of their land. If common sense does not lead to this conclusion, a passing glance at the landscape does.

Some land use experts argue that preferential farm assessment even encourages suburban sprawl of the kind that is spreading throughout northern Baltimore County and neighboring areas of Harford and Carroll counties. The artificially low taxes on farmland near cities enable owners, at minimal cost, to hold land off the market while prices climb higher still, with the result that development leapfrogs farther out. Even if preferential assessment does not encourage inefficient patterns of land development, there is little doubt that the tax break heavily subsidizes speculators by reducing their holding costs, since any land that is farmed, regardless of ownership, qualifies for lower taxes. Land that has been sold to real-estate syndicates at prices reflecting full development value continues to be assessed as though it were fit only for farming. For example, Hayfields, which was bought by a large developer in 1986 for $4.5 million, was assessed for tax purposes in 1990/91 at $330,290. Were it not for the fact that the property includes a large, handsome house, the assessment would have been even less. Nor was an agricultural transfer tax collected; instead, Hayfield's new owner merely signed a letter stating that he intended to farm the land for at least five years, during which development plans for Hayfields were formulated and discussed with local community groups and government officials.

Farm owners, of course, argue that preferential assessment is essential to their economic survival and that they cannot continue to farm the land without it. There are, however, other approaches to the problem, some of which are discussed below. As for preferential assessment, if the law is not repealed (which would be extremely difficult), it should at least be reformed so that the public gets more in exchange for the property tax revenue that is not being collected. For one thing, the 5 percent agricultural transfer tax should be increased substantially.

Recognizing the ineffectiveness of preferential assessments to prevent the loss of farmland over the long term, Maryland has yet another program to obtain a more binding preservation commitment from farm owners. Of course, the usual way to gain permanent control over land is to buy it, but purchasing the full interest—the so-called fee interest—is not necessary. Instead, the state buys easements restricting development of the land. The term "easement" is slightly misleading because these development right easements are *negative*, entailing nothing more than the extinguishment of the owner's right to develop his farmland to a more intensive use. The public is not granted the right of access, as with an *affirmative* easement. Nor does purchase of the development rights enable the state to develop the land; it merely gives the state the enforceable right to prevent the landowner from doing so. And because the owner retains the right to farm his land just as he always has, acquisition of the development rights does not cost as much as purchase of the fee interest.

The preservation of farmland through the purchase of development right easements is one of the chief purposes of the Maryland Agricultural Land Preservation Foundation, which was established in 1977 as an agency of the Maryland Department of Agriculture. As spelled out in Sections 2-501 through 2-515 of the Agriculture volume of the Annotated Code of Maryland, the acquisition process begins with the filing of a petition by landowners to establish an agricultural preservation district. If the petition is approved by the local government and the Agricultural Land Preservation Foundation, landowners within the district must agree to maintain their land in agricultural use for at least five years. In return the local government must adopt an ordinance permitting and promoting agricultural activities within the district in order to protect farmers from nuisance suits and restrictive legislation filed by suburbanites who, for all their talk of the joys of country life, frequently are annoyed by the normal smells, sounds, and dust of farm operations. This protection for normal agricultural use is an important consideration in developing areas, where what some studies call an "impermanence syndrome" can arise among farmers who see land use patterns changing and who fear that their political clout in local government will be overwhelmed by new suburban residents.

Once farmland is located within a preservation district, its owners may sell easements disposing of their development rights to the Agricultural Land Preservation Foundation. If the sale is approved, the purchase price is set by law as the difference between the value of the land with and without the bar on development (unless the owner's asking price is lower). A deed containing covenants that restrict the farmland to agricultural use is recorded among the county land records. The covenants are perpetual, although an owner can apply to buy the development rights back after twenty-five years if profitable farming is no longer feasible. If the resale is approved, the landowner must pay the then-market value of the development rights.

As of January 1993, about 251,000 acres of farmland had been placed in 1,877 agricultural preservation districts, and easements restricting development had been acquired on 677 properties totaling about 99,000 acres, mostly (in descending order) in Carroll, Caroline, Baltimore, Queen Anne's, Frederick, Harford, and Howard counties. The cost of the easements varies greatly depending on the location and development value of the land. Since inception of the program, the easements have cost (on average) $1,105 per acre, which is about 45 percent of the land's full market value. Revenue to support this program comes from the state's transfer tax on the sale of agricultural land (discussed earlier), from county matching funds, and from Program Open Space, which in turn is funded by yet another state transfer tax—this one applicable to the sale of *all* real estate and set at one half of one percent of the purchase price. Because of the dependence on revenues from real-estate transactions, funding for the Maryland Agricultural Preservation Foundation fluctuates widely from year to year depending on the strength or feebleness of the real-estate market.

A glaring anomaly affecting the program of the Agricultural Land Preservation Foundation is that a major incentive for farmers to participate would exist were it not for the law granting preferential farm assessments. Because the sale of development rights to the state reduces the value of land, the owners of such land are entitled to have their property taxes reduced accordingly—yet preferential farm assessment *already* grants all farmers this favored treatment even though they do not participate in the preservation program and instead retain development rights. Obviously, if farm assessments reflected market value, a great many more owners would be eager to do business with the Agricultural Land Preservation Foundation.

Moreover, the average price of easements sold to the state would be lower, because farmers would not be subsidized by artificially low taxes to hold onto their development rights while the price soars.

And one of the reason the price soars is the preferential tax itself. Like any commodity that receives a subsidy, farmland is more valuable as an investment vehicle because of it. Not surprisingly, many investors—some even from Europe—have taken advantage of this tax shelter by buying Maryland farmland, which simply drives up the price, including, of course, the price that must be paid by the state's Agricultural Land Preservation Foundation to buy development rights. And to buy these rights the state uses tax revenues that are all the scarcer because of the failure to collect full taxes on farmland.

Another state agency that is active in the preservation of farmland (as well as other undeveloped areas) is the Maryland Environmental Trust within the Department of Natural Resources. The Trust does not buy restrictive easements but merely acts as the recipient of donations by owners who share the Trust's goal of preserving scenic countryside and who welcome the large income tax deductions and estate tax savings that their donations produce. If the land has a substantial development potential, the charitable deduction resulting from a gift of the development rights to a government body can be very great. Also, of course, once the owner conveys the development rights, the fair market value of the property for estate and property tax purposes drops correspondingly. As of the beginning of 1993, the Maryland Environmental Trust held easements on 240 properties totaling about 40,000 acres.

Because of the expense entailed in the purchase of development right easements and the understandable reluctance of most owners to give them away, some of the county governments are experimenting with a related approach designed to attract *private* money to the purchase of *transferable* development rights. For example, in Montgomery County a farm owner in

certain areas can sell his development rights to a developer who holds land in designated development zones. Purchase of added development rights enables the developer to build residential units on his own land—not the farmer's land—at a higher density than he would otherwise be permitted. This approach helps to restrict farmland to farm use while at the same time promoting the more compact and efficient use of land in designated development zones, all at no cost to state or local governments. As of July 1992, $24 million worth of development rights for 4,880 residential units had been transferred in Montgomery County in order to steer development away from an agricultural reserve that extends along the Potomac River and around the county's western and northern boundary. Of the 90,000 acres within Montgomery County's agricultural reserve, 34,000 acres have been protected (as of 1992) by the transfer out of development rights. The county's goal is to protect the remaining 56,000 acres within the agricultural reserve by the turn of the century. To help achieve this goal, Montgomery County has since 1987 had its own program, similar to the state's Agricultural Land Preservation Foundation, for buying development rights. As of 1992, the county had spent $9 million to buy and extinguish development rights on 3,000 acres of farmland. Some other Maryland counties have also established—or are considering establishing—programs for transferring or buying development rights.

Many counties, however, are reluctant to rely on programs entailing compensation to landowners in order to restrict the development of farmland. Instead, some local zoning ordinances attempt to discourage development in such areas by requiring very large residential lots, such as 3 acres or more. However, large-lot zoning has proved to be ineffective in preventing conversion of farmland to residential use. Instead, it simply squanders farmland by forcing developers to use more land for fewer houses, which are then touted as "estates," "farmettes", and "executive homesites" on the subdivision signs. In Howard County, where 3-acre zoning has not slowed the residential development of farmland, the zoning law was changed in 1992 to permit, and in some cases to require, clustering of houses on smaller lots. For example, in Howard County's rural conservation zone, tracts of 20 acres or more can only be developed on a cluster basis by which one lot remains a large estate or farm subject to conservation easements and occupying about two-thirds of the acreage, and the rest of the houses are clustered on lots not exceeding 1.4 acres in size.

Some counties have gone a step further by establishing agricultural preservation zones where farming is promoted and other land uses are severely restricted. For example, in Baltimore County's agricultural preservation zone, properties of at least 2 acres but less than 150 acres can only be split into two lots, each of at least 1 acre. A 150-acre parcel can at most be split into three lots, and from there each additional 50 acres entitles the subdivider to another lot. None of the resulting lots can be resubdivided.

In addition to state and local governments, various private conservation groups are active in the preservation of agricultural land and other scenic areas. Many of these groups, including The Nature Conservancy, the Chesapeake Bay Foundation, and the Conservation Trust of the Greenspring and Worthington Valleys, themselves acquire restrictive easements and even fee interest in land. The Valleys Planning Council is a local group active in the preservation of land in north-central Baltimore County. Also, there are many *ad hoc* groups working to preserve specific sites. Of these, an outstanding example is Save the Ridge, Inc., which in 1989 led a campaign to buy—for $3.1 million of government and privately-donated money—199 acres for addition to Oregon Ridge Park. Finally, the Oregon Ridge Nature Center Council (telephone 771-0034) is an ongoing-group that focuses on land-use issues affecting properties in the vicinity of Oregon Ridge.

AUTOMOBILE: Oregon Ridge Park is located north of Baltimore near the Hunt Valley business community. The entrance is off Shawan Road 1.0 mile west of Interstate 83.

From Interstate 695 (the Beltway) north of Baltimore, take Exit 24 for Interstate 83 north. Go about 5.7 miles, then take Exit 20B for Shawan Road west toward Oregon Ridge Park. Follow Shawan Road west about 1.0 mile, then turn left at a traffic light onto Beaver Dam Road. Go only 20 yards, then fork right toward the lake and nature center. Follow the park road 0.4 mile to the nature center parking lot.

WALKING: (See Map 9 opposite.) From the end of the parking lot, follow the asphalt road to the Oregon Ridge Nature Center, which has exhibits on the history, wildlife, and vegetation of Oregon Ridge.

After visiting the nature center, locate a pedestrian bridge leading from the end of the building across a ravine and into the woods. Cross the bridge and turn left downhill at a T-intersection with the red-blazed Loggers Trail. Go 150 yards, then turn very sharply right uphill onto the Laurel Trail, which is marked with blue paint blazes. Follow the blue blazes uphill. Cross the wide swath of a gas pipeline right-of-way and continue uphill on the blue-blazed trail. The blue trail ends at a skewed four-way intersection.

From the end of the blue trail, cross the red-blazed Loggers Trail and follow the yellow-blazed Ivy Hill Trail through the woods, across another gas pipeline right-of-way, and downhill to the spillway from Ivy Hill Pond on the left (next to Baisman Run on the right).

You can return from the pond the way you came, or you can continue on the figure-eight circuit shown by the bold line on Map 9. For the figure-eight circuit,

MAP 9 — Oregon Ridge Park

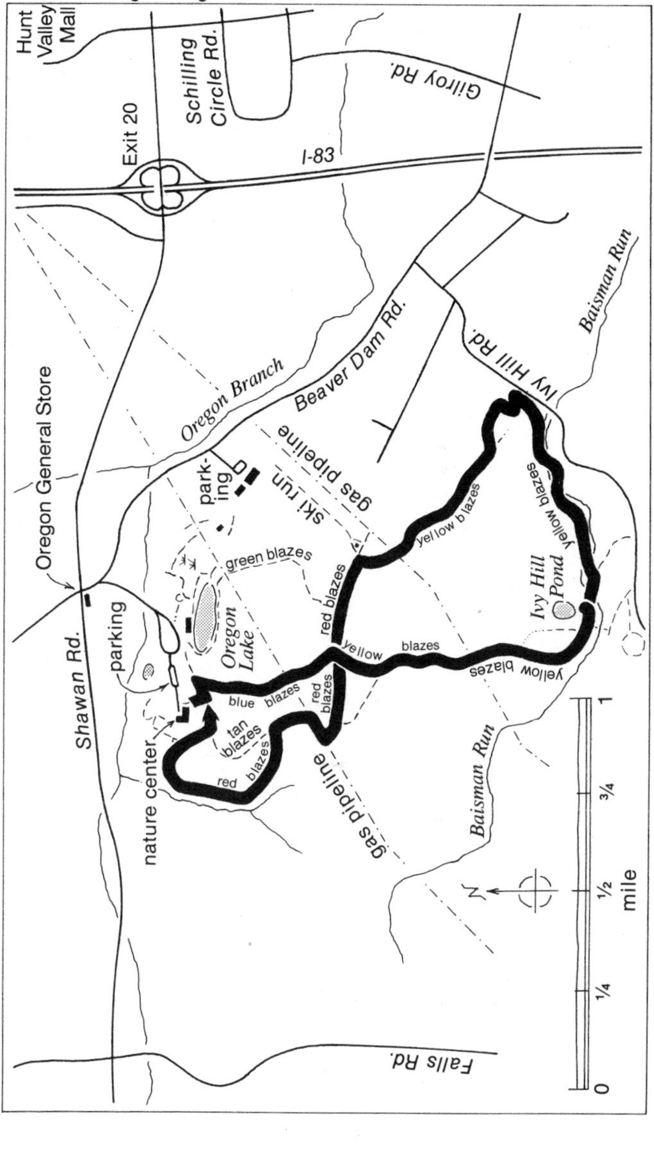

USGS: *Cockeysville*

Hunt Valley Mall

Schilling Circle Rd.

Gilroy Rd.

Exit 20

I-83

Oregon Branch

Beaver Dam Rd.

Ivy Hill Rd.

Baisman Run

Oregon General Store

parking

ski run

gas pipeline

green blazes

yellow blazes

red blazes

Shawan Rd.

parking

Oregon Lake

yellow blazes

Ivy Hill Pond

yellow blazes

yellow blazes

nature center

blue blazes

tan blazes

red blazes

red blazes

gas pipeline

Baisman Run

N

mile

0   1/4   1/2   3/4   1

Falls Rd.

descend from the dam at Ivy Hill Pond and turn left onto the yellow-blazed trail. With Baisman Run toward your right, follow the yellow blazes 170 yards to where the path fords the stream. (Usually Baisman Run is easily crossed, but you will have to assess conditions for yourself when you are there; the rocks, of course, may be slippery.)

After crossing the stream, go 75 yards, then turn left to continue on the yellow-blazed trail, now called the Campbell Trail, for S. James Campbell, who played a leading roll in raising money from local corporations and foundations to buy this part of the park. After only 25 yards, ford back across Baisman Run, then continue on the yellow-blazed trail along the foot of the slope, with the stream toward your right. Before long, ford Baisman Run again and yet again. Eventually, as the yellow-blazed trail approaches Ivy Hill Road, the path curves left and climbs away from Baisman Run. Continue as the trail curves still father left and climbs away from the road, then zigzags to reach the top of the slope.

Follow the yellow-blazed trail along the broad crest of a ridge, rising very gradually as you go. Eventually, the trail cuts diagonally across a pipeline right-of-way, then continues for 140 yards through the woods to a junction with the red-blazed trail. Here you should turn left, but first you may want to take in the view from the head of the ski slope, which can be reached by passing to the left of a large concrete foundation.

As noted above, turn sharply left from the yellow-blazed Campbell Trail onto the red-blazed Loggers Trail. Follow the red blazes along the broad crest of Oregon Ridge and past intersections with the green-blazed Virginia Pine Trail, the blue-blazed Laurel Trail, the yellow-blazed Ivy Hill Trail, and yet another trail on the left. Follow the red blazes all the way to a gas pipeline right-of-way, and there turn right to follow the right-of-way 150 yards before veering half-left at the top of the hill. Re-enter the woods on the red-blazed trail and go 190 yards, then turn left (where the tan-blazed Ridge Trail continues straight). Follow the red-blazed path downhill and along the side of a ravine, then eventually to the right. Continue straight past a memorial to Ann Franklin Ridgely. Go more or less straight on the wide, red-blazed trail where the tan-blazed path intersects from the rear-right. Continue to the bridge leading left across a ravine to the starting point at the nature center.

The "ravine" crossed by the bridge is actually one of the open pits or banks from which iron ore was dug for Oregon Furnace during the middle of the nineteenth century. Oregon Lake swimming pond is another ore bank, now flooded by ground water. Several dilapidated structures from the Oregon Company's hamlet still stand downhill from the park road, and at the intersection of Shawan and Beaver Dam roads is the handsome and well-preserved Oregon General Store, formerly the iron village's company store. Many of the counters and other accouterments in the store are original. There is a display on Oregon Furnace in the nature center.

Oregon furnace was built about 1850 and operated until 1857. In 1852 the unincorporated enterprise was merged with the Ashland Company, whose furnace was located at what is now the southern end of the Northern Central Railroad Trail (Chapter 9). Mining at Oregon continued until Ashland Furnace closed in 1884. Thomas Kurtz, the last foreman at the Oregon pits, bought the 457-acre tract and carried on the general store. His family held the property until 1969, when Baltimore County bought it for inclusion in the park.

7

GUNPOWDER FALLS STATE PARK

West Hereford

Walking—5.5 miles (8.8 kilometers) round-trip. Well-marked footpaths wind along the valley slopes, ridge tops, and river bank bordering Big Gunpowder Falls. The route shown by the bold line on Map 10 on page 109 starts at the Bunker Hill park entrance and explores the rocky gorge upstream. The trails are sometimes rugged and the circuit is rather strenuous.

For a still longer walk in the Hereford section of Gunpowder Falls State Park, see the Hereford Hike, outlined at the end of this chapter on pages 112 through 115.

The park is open daily from sunrise to sunset. Dogs must be leashed. The park is managed by the Department of Natural Resources, Maryland Forest, Park and Wildlife Service; telephone 592-2897.

LONG STRETCHES of Big and Little Gunpowder Falls have been developed into a linear valley park. Most of the park follows Big Gunpowder Falls diagonally across Baltimore County from northwest to southeast—from just below Pretty-boy Reservoir to the river's mouth at Chesapeake Bay.

Another arm follows the roughly parallel course of Little Gunpowder Falls, which forms the boundary between Baltimore and Harford counties. Some sections of the park, notably at Hereford, provide an outstanding opportunity for walking in a rocky and wild setting.

Compared to Baltimore City's basic park system, which was created about the turn of the century, Gunpowder Falls State Park is relatively new, having been planned and acquired in response to the rapid suburbanization of Baltimore County after World War II. Since 1958, when the Maryland State Planning Commission first recommended a system of unconnected parks along both branches of Gunpowder Falls, the Maryland General Assembly has authorized acquisition of 15,787 acres, of which more than 90 percent has now been purchased. These figures do not include several thousand more acres at North Point State Park (Chapter 17), Hart and Miller Island, and the Northern Central Railroad Trail (Chapter 9), all of which are administered through Gunpowder Falls State Park.

With the exception of the Hammerman area, which has swimming and picnicking facilities for thousands of people, most of Gunpowder Falls State Park is undeveloped for uses other than hiking, horseback riding, and fishing. Visitors to the Hereford section in particular (which I think is a model of what a wilderness-style, stream-valley park should be) would never guess at the many years of controversy, of planning and reconsideration, and of patient negotiation and compromise that have gone into creating the simple and beautiful park seen today.

Although highly popular with the general public, state park projects are often the subject of vociferous local opposition. For example, when the immensely successful Northern Central Railroad Trail was being planned in the mid-1980s, several hundred people residing near the old railroad right-of-way signed a petition to quash the project on the grounds that it would increase traffic, noise, litter, and crime in their vicinity. At hearings in the early 1990s on the plan for North Point State Park, many residents expressed disgust and outrage that the state would spend money to attract *outsiders* from the city to their remote bayside corner of Baltimore County. As one speaker at a similar hearing on the development of the Hereford section of Gunpowder Falls State Park once asked, "Why can't they go to places that are *closer*?

By holding a series of public hearings—sometimes occurring over a period of years—and enlisting the suggestions and cooperation of a local citizens advisory committee, the state's park planners try to diffuse prejudice and to address legitimate concerns and requests. If nearby residents feel that they are not being adequately consulted, however, the reaction can be sharp. In 1977, when the Maryland Park Service tried to develop an equestrian center and a large complex of picnic pavilions and toilets for three thousand visitors at Bunker Hill Road in the heart of the Gunpowder's Hereford section, residents of the area formed a group called the Northern Baltimore County Citizens Committee and, with the help of their state senator, succeeded in having funds for the project deleted from the state's budget. They pointed out, accurately, that smaller crowds were already problematic at Bunker Hill, where gatherings sometimes continued into the night and where the covered bridge that once spanned the river had been burned down. When the state put forward a new park plan in 1978, the Northern Baltimore County group attacked it too, and then, at the invitation of the Secretary of the Department of Natural Resources, prepared its *own* park plan for the Hereford section.

In the fall of 1979 the Northern Baltimore County Citizens Committee released its counter-plan, and during the following year a series of meetings were held to resolve, point by point, the differences between it and the state's plan. No proposed structure or improvement was too small for scrutiny. Among the issues debated was whether a toilet should be built at each of the two parking lots upstream from Bunker Hill (suggested by the park planners but opposed by the community), whether parking lots should be provided near bridges downstream from Bunker Hill (opposed by the community), and whether camping should be allowed at Bunker Hill (again opposed by residents of the area). A local bow-and-arrow club wanted an archery range, and joggers suggested that an exercise course be built. Owners on Bunker Hill Road wanted a new access road to bypass their houses that occupy small inholdings within the park. An entire meeting was devoted to canoeists and "tubers"—kids of all ages who float down the river in inner tubes. Local fishing groups, which by this time had joined the fray, wanted part of the river closed to boats. Even owners of streamside property below the park took the occasion to complain of canoeists and tubers trespassing on what they viewed as their river and wanted to know what the Department of Natural Resources was going to do about it. Finally, there was much ado about picnicking. The Department of Natural Resources favored building group picnic pavilions at Bunker Hill, but the citizens committee adamantly opposed them or any other feature that might attract partying crowds, produce litter, challenge vandals, or detract from the natural appearance of the park.

Although trying for all concerned, this lengthy process of negotiation has resulted in a substantially better park at Hereford than either the state or the Northern Baltimore County Citizens Committee would have arrived at on its own. (See Map 11 on page 113.) All the essential ingredients for public use of the area are present. And absent—happily—are overdesigned and inappropriate features that were contemplated at one time or another. In addition to the main parking lots on both sides of the river at Bunker Hill Road (where there is no longer an automobile bridge), smaller lots have been developed at the four roads that cross the river. Contributing to the park's low-keyed tone and natural appearance is the fact that all the parking lots are paved with gravel rather than asphalt. Bunker Hill Road has been maintained as a narrow country lane rather than upgraded to the exalted and sometimes ridiculous standards seen at other state parks. Camping by supervised youth groups is permitted at Bunker Hill, and areas of grass accommodate any number of picnickers without marring the scene with playground equipment and cookie-cutter pavilions. Stocked with trout, the river attracts fishermen from throughout the region, and canoeists and tubers float down the stream without troubling anyone. An archery range has been tucked away in a corner. Finally, at the Hereford section a network of hiking trails traverses more than 3,300 acres of twisting gorge, tributary ravines, and adjacent highlands.

Acquiring all this land for public use is another facet of the protracted process of park creation. The work begins as soon as the proposed boundary is approved by the Secretary of the Department of Natural Resources and may continue for decades as funds become available, as negotiations mature, as unanticipated opportunities present themselves, and as the boundary (or "take line") is changed to include more land—or at any rate different land—than was originally planned. It is a painstaking and sometimes painful process. So far Gunpowder Falls State Park has been pieced together from about four hundred different parcels. Most owners, particularly owners of vacant, unproductive valley slopes, have been amenable to selling, but some unhappiness is inevitable when the states sets out to purchase nearly 25 square miles and as many as three dozen houses—although the state tries to avoid buying houses unless absolutely necessary for a viable park.

Price, of course, is the principal issue. To protect the interests of both the property owner and the state, the Department of General Services, the agency that handles land acquisition for Maryland's parks, is required to hire two independent appraisers to make separate determinations of fair market value of each property. The appraisals are reviewed by the Department's staff and if one or the other is approved, an offer in that amount is made to the owner. Sometimes a third appraisal is necessary if the first two figures are far apart, for the evaluation of real estate is not a precise technique. Occasionally an owner will obtain yet another appraisal which may convince the state's reviewers and the Board of Public Works (which must approve all acquisitions) that a higher price is justified.

If a price cannot be agreed upon, the Department of General Services in consultation with the Department of Natural Resources may simply wait in order to try again later with a new appraisal and offer. Or, in a very few cases (about 30 so far at Gunpowder Falls State Park), the matter may be turned over to the Attorney General's Office for condemnation, so that eventually the value of the property is decided by a jury unless the case is first settled by agreement. If the state declines to pay the amount set by the jury and instead abandons the acquisition, the owner's legal costs are paid by the state. Sometimes where title to the land is clouded, the state will condemn the property simply to obtain a clear title.

The procedural safeguards of appraisal and condemnation are intended, of course, to provide a neutral determination of fair market value. For some properties, however, a price may be *fair* but nonetheless *inadequate*. For example, if forced to sell for fair market value, the owner of an unusually small house or a dilapidated or substandard house may not be able to buy another home in his community for what his own is worth. The result is a dilemma that, for a period, was an impasse in the acquisition of some such properties for Gunpowder Falls State Park. In 1979, however, when the Gunpowder project began to receive federal funds. the payment of relocation assistance became mandatory under federal law. As of 1993, payments of up to $15,000 (in addition to the agreed acquisition price) were authorized to help displaced homeowners buy comparable houses nearby that are also "decent, safe and sanitary." Also, state aid has long been available to cover actual moving costs.

For some owners, however, the problem has not been price but preference: a simple desire to stay where they are. These cases have dragged on for years until only the most difficult are left, often involving holdings entirely surrounded by park property or wedges of private ownership penetrating deep into the park. In some cases the state has not pressed the issue, partly because requiring people to sell their houses generates bad public relations, and also because condemnation typically results in above-average prices. In a few cases the Department of General Services has tried to reach a variety of arrangements with people who do not want to move from their homes or established businesses. Elderly owners have been offered a life license under which the state acquires the property outright for its full value while the former owners retain the privilege to occupy the house for the rest of their lives. They maintain and insure the property but pay no taxes or rent. Another option is a life estate, which requires that the purchase price be reduced by the value of the sellers' right of continued occupancy, as estimated by their life expectancy. If they live longer, they in effect get a windfall; if they die early, the state gets a windfall. Owners of the life estate continue to pay property taxes. Finally, in some cases the state has bought houses or farms and then leased them back to the former owners. This is an arrangement that has been attractive to owners who are approaching retirement but want to continue to farm their land for a few more years. The state, too, finds purchase-and-lease-back to be attractive because the arrangement enables park authorities to have a large measure of control over how the property is used.

Around the perimeter of the park, the state has had trouble buying parts of individual holdings needed to form a readily identifiable boundary that bears an intelligent relationship to the topography of the area and to local roads. Owners have sometimes complained that their "back yards" are being taken—that is, tracts stretching hundreds of feet into the woods behind their houses. With these owners, the Department of

General Services is experimenting with a variety of affirmative and negative easements. The former allows certain public uses of the land and the latter prohibits development or logging. All of these techniques not only ease the acquisition process but also reduce the state's purchase expenses and maintenance costs. Also, as time passes, landowners discover that having a state park for a neighbor is not the nuisance they initially feared but rather increases their property values substantially.

Finally, a word about where the money for the acquisition and development of Maryland's state parks comes from. The principal source is Program Open Space, enacted in 1969 and funded by the state tax of 0.5 percent on the transfer of title to real estate. (For example, the sale of property for $100,000 entails payment of a transfer tax of $500.) At first all transfer-tax revenues went to Program Open Space, and Maryland made great strides in implementing its various park plans. However, since 1984 much—and in some years most—of the transfer-tax revenues have been diverted from Program Open Space to the state's general fund, despite the fact that the responsibilities of Program Open Space have been greatly expanded to include not only park acquisition and improvement, but also the preservation of agricultural land (as discussed in Chapter 6) and other environmental programs. As of 1993, about 70 percent of transfer tax revenues had been diverted away from Program Open Space during the preceding eight years.

The result of this annual raid on Program Open Space is that all too often tracts of land slated for inclusion in state parks have been lost permanently to residential or commercial development because the public money to buy them was not available. When this sort of thing happens, it is a double misfortune. Not only is the land in question lost to the park, but its development for other purposes often renders the remaining park—on which the state has already spent tens of millions of dollars—less coherent, less usable, less manageable, and less attractive. In short, balancing the state budget by switching funds away from Program Open Space to other uses is in the long run a false economy. Revenue from Maryland's real-estate transfer tax should again be allocated exclusively to Program Open Space so that the state can reach its goals for acquiring parkland and preserving farmland as quickly and economically as possible. As some have suggested, it probably even makes sense to issue revenue bonds—backed by transfer-tax revenue—to purchase open space immediately.

AUTOMOBILE: The section of Gunpowder Falls State Park explored by this walk is located north of Baltimore near Prettyboy Reservoir. Park at the end of Bunker Hill Road, which is reached from York Road in Hereford.

From Interstate 695 (the Beltway) north of Baltimore, take Exit 24 for Interstate 83 north toward Timonium and York, PA. Follow Interstate 83 north 12.4 miles, then take Exit 27 for Route 137 (Mt. Carmel Road) and Hereford. At the top of the exit ramp, turn right (east) onto Route 137 and go 0.4 mile to a T-intersection with Route 45 (York Road). Turn left (north) onto Route 45 and go 0.9 mile to an intersection with Bunker Hill Road on the left. Turn left onto Bunker Hill Road and follow it 1.1 miles to the large parking lot next to Big Gunpowder Falls. (There are no falls as such; for a discussion of the word "falls," see Chapter 8.)

WALKING: (See Map 10 opposite.) Start at the parking lot where Bunker Hill Road meets the river. A pedestrian bridge over the river is planned for this location. If it has been built, you may—near the end of your walk—want to return along the north bank of the river, as noted below at the appropriate point in the directions; but look now to see if the bridge is there.

Locate the Gunpowder South Trail, which is blazed

MAP 10 — West Hereford

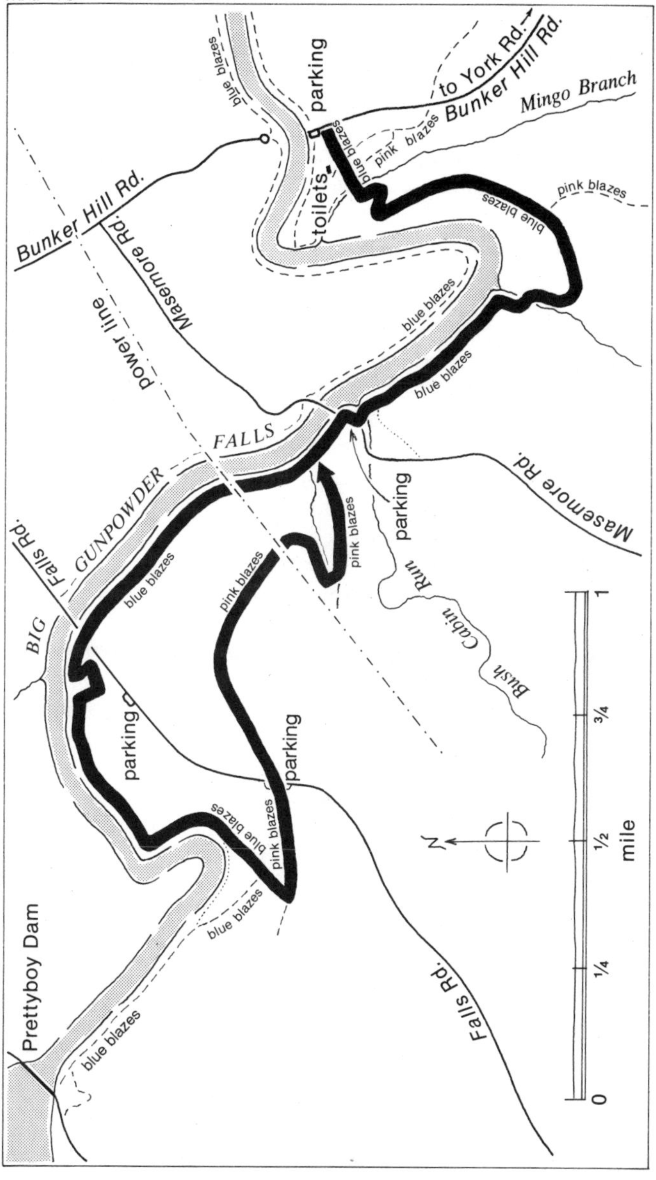

USGS: *Hereford*

with blue dots and crosses the road a few yards uphill from the parking lot. The route described here follows the blue-blazed trail upstream past Falls Road, then eventually turns back on the pink-blazed Highland Trail.

With your back to the river and the parking lot, turn right off Bunker Hill Road and follow the blue-blazed Gunpowder South Trail obliquely uphill and straight through a stand of pines at the top of the slope. Cross the Bunker Hill Trail (pink dots) and continue straight downhill on the blue-blazed trail. Cross a stream (Mingo Branch) and turn left. Zigzag uphill, then continue along the top of a broad ridge between the valley of Mingo Branch on the left and the valley of Big Gunpowder Falls on the right. Pass a trail junction where Mingo Forks Trail (pink dots) intersects from the left. Continue downhill on the blue-blazed trail and along a ravine. Cross a stream and continue on the blue-blazed trail to the edge of Big Gunpowder Falls. With the river on your right, follow the blue-blazed path upstream. Be alert for places where the path is being undermined by erosion. Just before reaching Mase-more Road, bear right to cross Bush Cabin Run on stepping stones (but do not cross if the water is flowing over the stones).

From the south (or near) end of the Masemore Road bridge, continue upstream with the river on your right. At a junction with the pink-blazed Highland Trail, fork right to continue along the river on the blue-blazed trail and across a small stream. Follow the riverside path upstream to Falls Road.

Cross Falls Road and continue upstream with the river on your right. After only 90 yards, turn left uphill to bypass a large rock formation; climb steeply to the left for 20 yards, then bear slightly left and climb some more on the blue-dot trail. (Give wide berth to any snakes sunning themselves on the rocks; some people claim to have seen copperheads in this area.)

After climbing far above the rock formation, descend steeply to the river's edge. With the river on your right, continue upstream. Pass through a long area of jumbled rocks where the path is very obscure; simply continue upstream. Eventually, as the valley bends sharply left, the riverside path becomes smoother. Then, as the valley begins to turn right, fork left uphill on the blue-blazed trail. Follow the blue dots obliquely uphill to the intersection with the Highland Trail (pink dots).

Leave the blue-dot Gunpowder South Trail and follow the pink-dot Highland Trail uphill. (Or, if you want, you can follow the blue-dot trail half a mile each way to the base of Prettyboy Dam and back. However, the trail is rough and rather tiresome.)

Follow the pink-blazed Highland Trail uphill, at one point turning left where another trail intersects from the right. Cross Falls Road and continue past a steel gate and into the woods on the pink-dot path. (A parking lot may be built here, and also a new trail leading downhill to the river.) Follow the pink-dot trail straight through the woods. Cross a right-of-way under high electric transmission lines and re-enter the woods on the foot-path blazed with pink dots. Descend to a stream and follow it upstream. Cross the stream just short of the power line right-of-way. Turn left and climb to an inter-section with another path. Bear left and follow the path gradually downhill to the Gunpowder South Trail (blue dots) next to the river. With the river on your left, bear right downstream and continue to Masemore Road.

If the pedestrian bridge at Bunker Hill has been built, cross the Masemore Road bridge and turn right down stream on the riverside path that leads to Bunker Hill Road. Otherwise, follow Masemore Road right for 60 yards to pick up the blue-dot trail where it crosses Bush Cabin Run on stepping stones a few yards from the end of the guardrail at the parking area. This is the trail that you took earlier from Bunker Hill. Follow it back to your starting point.

HEREFORD HIKE: (See Map 11 opposite.) This strenuous 10.5-mile circuit follows the valley of Big Gunpowder Falls through nearly the entire length of the park's Hereford section. Of course, you can shorten the trip by crossing the river at Masemore Road or York Road, but why would you want to do that? With its wooded bluffs, rock outcrops, and dramatic twists and turns, the gorge provides constant variety, to which the trail adds by sometimes following the Big Gunpowder's bank and at other times climbing high above the river.

The walk starts at the Bunker Hill Road parking lot on the south bank of the river. Locate the Gunpowder South Trail, which is blazed with blue dots and crosses the road a few yards uphill from the parking lot. The route described here follows the blue-blazed trail upstream to Falls Road, then turns downstream along the north bank.

With your back to the river and the parking lot, turn right off Bunker Hill Road and follow the blue-blazed Gunpowder South Trail obliquely uphill and straight through a stand of pines at the top of the slope. Cross the Bunker Hill Trail (pink dots) and continue straight downhill on the blue-blazed trail. Cross a stream (Mingo Branch) and turn left. Zigzag uphill, then continue along the top of a broad ridge between the valley of Mingo Branch on the left and the valley of Big

MAP 11 — Hereford Hike

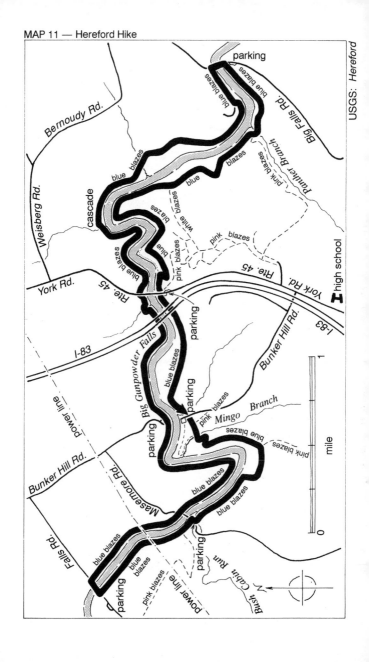

USGS: *Hereford*

Gunpowder Falls on the right. Pass a trail junction where Mingo Forks Trail (pink dots) intersects from the left. Continue downhill on the blue-blazed trail and along a ravine. Cross a stream and continue on the blue-blazed trail to the edge of Big Gunpowder Falls. With the river on your right, follow the blue-blazed path upstream. Be alert for places where the path is being undermined by erosion. Just before reaching Masemore Road, bear right to cross Bush Cabin Run on stepping stones (but do not cross if the water is flowing over the stones).

From the south (or near) end of the Masemore Road bridge, continue upstream with the river on your right. At a junction with the pink-blazed Highland Trail, fork right to continue along the river on the blue-blazed trail and across a small stream. Follow the riverside path upstream to Falls Road.

Cross the bridge at Falls Road and turn downstream on the riverside path. Again, be alert for places where the path is being undermined by erosion or animal burrows. Pick you way across a slope of jumbled boulders, where the path is sometimes obscure. With the river on your right, continue for nearly 3 miles downstream past Masemore Road and Bunker Hill Road and under the Interstate 95 bridges. At York Road turn away from the river and climb obliquely up the road embankment. With great caution, cross the road.

Continue downstream from York Road on the blue-blazed Gunpowder North Trail, which for the first two hundred yards is difficult and obscure, but then descends to the river's edge. After nearly a mile, the trail passes the foot of a long cascade. As the blue-blazed trail continues downstream, it is sometimes distant from the river. After crossing a stream at the bottom of a wide ravine, the trail climbs steeply up a slope covered with mountain laurel, then descends, climbs again, and eventually zigzags down to the river's edge. Continue downstream. Eventually the trail joins a gravel road. With the river on your right, follow the gravel road to Big Falls Road.

With caution, cross the bridge at Big Falls Road, then turn upstream on the blue-blazed Gunpowder South Trail. Be alert for places where the path is being undermined by erosion. At times the trail climbs away from the river in order to avoid difficult or even impassable terrain next to the stream, so stick to the blue-blazed path, which winds its way for 2 miles to York Road, along the way passing junctions with the pink-blazed Panther Branch Trail and the white-blazed Sandy Lane Trail.

With caution, cross York Road and continue upstream next to the river on the blue-blazed trail. After passing under the Interstate 83 bridges, the trail climbs obliquely high up the side of the valley, then descends to the meadow and parking lot at Bunker Hill Road.

8

GUNPOWDER FALLS STATE PARK

East Hereford

Walking—4.0 miles (6.4 kilometers). The route shown by the bold line on Map 12 on page 120 follows a well-marked footpath from York Road downstream along a wild and winding stretch of river to Panther Branch. Return through woods and farmland above the valley.

The park is open daily from sunrise to sunset. Dogs must be leashed. The park is managed by the Department of Natural Resources, Maryland Forest, Park and Wildlife Service; telephone 592-2897.

IN COMMON PARLANCE in these parts, Baltimore is "Bawlamer." A brief lexicon of other Bawlamer locutions, such as "Merlin" for Maryland, "Naplis" for our state capital, "Anna Runnel" and "Harrid" for two of our nearby counties, and "Droodle" for Druid Hill, is contained in the urban guidebook *Bawlamer*, published by the Citizens Planning and Housing Association. Less well-known, however, is that our Baltimore dialect is marked by other geographic expressions that are peculiar not for pronunciation but for usage.

Heading the list is *falls*, as in Big Gunpowder Falls. The focus of the present chapter, of course, is not a local Niagara or even a waterfall at all. Indeed, during dry periods or at other times when water is not being released from Prettyboy Reservoir or Loch Raven, the Gunpowder not only does not *fall* but scarcely even *flows*.

According to William B. Mayre, a Maryland historian who made a specialty of place-names, court records, and old documents of every variety, Baltimore City and Baltimore County are the only area in the United States where there are whole freshwater rivers and streams called *falls*. Apparently early settlers along the tidal shores of the Gunpowder River and the Patapsco River (or rather "Patapsico," in our local patois) called the swift and rocky freshwater streams above tidewater the falls of those rivers. And, of course, compared to tidewater, they do fall and were often dammed and harnessed for waterpower. Hence Big Gunpowder Falls and, for the smaller stream to the north, Little Gunpowder Falls, both of which empty into the tidal Gunpowder River. Jones Falls is the freshwater portion of the Northwest Branch of the tidal Patapsco River. Gwynns Falls is the falls of the tidal Middle Branch. Similarly, old maps and other documents call the main branch of the Patapsco that flows through the state park Patapsco *Falls*. For example, an early nineteenth-century print in the possession of the Maryland Historical Society depicts the original mill at Oella and states on its face: "Union Manufactories of Maryland on Patapsco Falls, Baltimore County."

If a major freshwater stream in Baltimore is a *falls*, a middling stream is a *run* and a minor one is a *branch*. Hence in the city there are Charles Run, Moores Run, Chinquapin Run, and Herring Run, this last turning into Back Creek when it reaches tidewater. As noted in the last chapter, two of the tributary runs and branches feeding Big Gunpowder Falls are Bush Cabin Run and Mingo Branch, and the present walk passes Panther Branch.

With the exception of the various tidal arms of Baltimore Harbor, the saltwater counterpart to a tributary run or branch is a *creek*, unless the saltwater appendage is so small and serpen-- tine as to be a *gut*. Thus, off the north side of the Patapsco River we have in rapid succession North Point Creek, Jones Creek, Bear Creek, Bullneck Creek, and Colgate Creek. In Baltimore City and Baltimore County, there are only a few exceptions (notably Deer Creek) to the reservation of *creek* for a small tidal river. And off the creeks branch myriad *coves*.

Finally, perhaps you are wondering about the word *brook*. Mr. Mayre dismisses the term as "literary" and utterly foreign to our parts. It is virtually never seen in old deeds or other documents and appears only in the contrived names given in recent years to housing subdivisions and suburban cul-de-sacs.

So much for *falls* and other riverine terms, but what about "Gunpowder"? The name occurs not only in Big and Little Gunpowder Falls but also in Gunpowder Neck and Gunpowder Island (now Carroll Island). Although most accounts assume that the name originated with mills where charcoal was ground to make gunpowder, *The Traveller's Directory*, or *A Pocket Companion to the Philadelphia-Baltimore Road*, published in 1802, gives a more entertaining even if legendary explanation:

> Great Gunpowder River—Between this and Bush River is Gun- powder Neck, so named from a tradition that the Indians, who formerly lived in this tract, when first acquainted with the use of gunpowder, supposed it to be a vegetable seed; they purchased a quantity and sowed it on this neck, expecting it to produce a good crop.

AUTOMOBILE: The section of Gunpowder Falls State Park explored by this walk is located north of Baltimore a few miles east of Prettyboy Reservoir. Park your car on York Road 1.7 miles north of Hereford.

From Interstate 695 (the Beltway) north of Baltimore, take Exit 24 for Interstate 83 north toward Timonium and York, PA. Follow Interstate 83 north 12.4 miles,

MAP 12 — East Hereford

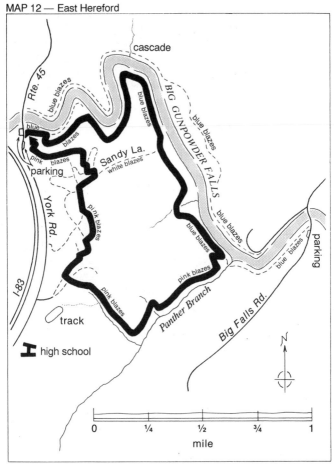

USGS: *Hereford*

then take Exit 27 for Route 137 (Mt. Carmel Road) and Hereford. At the top of the exit ramp, turn right (east) onto Route 137 and go 0.4 mile to a T-intersection with Route 45 (York Road). Turn left onto Route 45 and go 1.7 miles. Just before the road crosses the bridge over Big Gunpowder Falls, park in one of the small lots on either side of the road.

WALKING: (See Map 12 opposite.) The walk starts from the meadow east (or downstream) from York Road. Pick up the trail where it crosses a small stream about 40 yards from the river's edge. Nearby is a stone fireplace. Fork left onto the Gunpowder South Trail, which is blazed with blue dots. You will return later by the other fork (that is, by Panther Branch Trail, blazed with pink dots).

Follow blue-dot Gunpowder South Trail through the woods to the river's edge. After only 60 yards or so, fork right uphill away from the river on the blue-blazed trail. Zigzag uphill along the side of the valley. Continue along the crest of the slope, then descend to the bottom of the valley.

With the river on your left, follow the path downstream, usually near the water but sometimes farther up the side of the valley. Be alert for places where the path is being undermined by erosion. After about a mile, you will reach a trail intersection with Sandy Lane Trail (white dots).

Continue to follow the blue-blazed Gunpowder South Trail through the woods and along the foot of the bluff at a distance from the river. Eventually, follow the path to the right up a ravine, across a stream, then up and to the left above the river. With the river downhill on your left, continue along the side of the valley. Descend gradually to the river's edge and continue downstream.

Twenty yards before a stream (Panther Branch) joins the river from the right, turn very sharply right onto the Panther Branch Trail, which is a narrow footpath blazed with pink dots. The trail zigzags uphill over a shoulder and down to the right. For the rest of the walk, follow the pink dots of the Panther Branch Trail. As you will see if you have sharp eyes, the ravine at Panther Branch contains some old stone foundations that may be the ruins of a gristmill and its companion gunpowder mill that blew up on July 7, 1874.

With Panther Branch on your left, follow the pink-dot path up a ravine. Eventually, climb to the right (look for traces of an old millrace on the right) and follow a smaller ravine for a short distance before turning left to cross a rivulet. Continue above Panther Branch. Bear right again up another side ravine. With a very small stream on your left, follow the pink dots up the ravine and past several paths intersecting from the left. Follow the pink dots to a weedy field dotted with scrub at the head of the ravine. Continue uphill through the brush and then straight across a cultivated field. Cross a rutted road, then (after just a few yards) turn right onto a wide track. Continue with a pine plantation on your left and a hedgerow (and field beyond) on your right.

Follow the track into the woods, still with a pine plantation on your left. Jog left, then right, and continue through deciduous woods. Sixty yards after the path turns downhill to the left, leave the dirt road and turn right on the pink-dot footpath. Follow the pink dots downhill through the woods, then up through weeds, brush, and saplings to a grassy path in front of another pine plantation. Follow the path right. After passing a grassy track intersecting from the left, go straight for 15 yards, then turn right at another trail intersection.

Follow the pink dots as the trail veers left at the next intersection (instead of proceeding straight downhill on Sandy Lane Trail). Turn left again immediately on a narrow footpath through the woods (instead of proceeding straight downhill on the fire lane around the edge of the pines). Follow the footpath for 50 yards, then turn right. Go 30 yards, then bear left onto a narrow footpath. Follow the pink dots down a ravine, across a gully, along the side of the valley, and back to the meadow by York Road and Big Gunpowder Falls.

Further reading: William B. Mayre's discussion of *falls* is contained in "A Commentary on Certain Words and Expressions Used in Maryland," which appeared in *Maryland Historical Magazine* for June 1951. Mr. Mayre discusses "Gunpowder" in the March 1958 issue.

9

NORTHERN CENTRAL RAILROAD TRAIL

Walking and bicycling—up to 39 miles (63 kilometers) round-trip. This old railroad—or at least the section between Cockeysville and the state line with Pennsylvania—now forms a hiker's highway through forest and farmland. The route is shown by the bold line on Map 13 on page 137. The rails and ties have been removed and the roadbed has been paved with finely crushed limestone, making a hard-packed surface that is suitable for bicycling as well as for walking. If you do not want to retrace your steps, a car shuttle is necessary. In addition to Ashland and Freeland at each end of the trail, several other access points are described under the automobile directions, making possible a series of shorter trips.

The trail is open daily from sunrise to sunset. Dogs must be leashed, and bicycles must have bells or horns. Cyclists should yield to other trail users, pass with care, and keep their speed to a moderate, safe pace. The trail is managed as part of Gunpowder Falls State Park by the Department of Natural Resources, Maryland Forest, Park and Wildlife Service.; telephone 472-3144 or 592-2897.

HIKE OR RIDE TO PENNSYLVANIA. From Ashland near Cockeysville, a hiker/biker trail follows the old roadbed of the Northern Central Railway for 20 miles north to the Mason-

Dixon line, where the trail abruptly ends. (Pennsylvania may soon extend the trail as far north as York.) If I may editorialize for a moment, writing my various *Country Walks* books has made me familiar with a number of Rails-to-Trails projects, and this is the best that I have ever seen. For mile after mile the trail follows the banks of Big Gunpowder Falls, Little Falls, and Beetree Run across Maryland's rolling Piedmont landscape, passing through Glencoe, Corbett, Monkton, White Hall, Parkton, and other small towns and hamlets that originally were spawned by the railroad.

The Northern Central Railway was chartered in Maryland as the Baltimore & Susquehanna in 1828, one year after incorporation of the nation's first railroad, the Baltimore & Ohio. Plans for the B&S called for the railway's northern terminus to be located at the Susquehanna riverport of York Haven, which was near the projected route of Pennsylvania's Main Line Canal. The new railroad would thus tap the commerce of the entire Susquehanna basin and bring to Baltimore trade that might otherwise go to Philadelphia. Not surprisingly, enthusiasm for the venture was high in Baltimore (sales of stock were oversubscribed within the first few days), but for three years legislators in Harrisburg refused to grant authority for the line to enter Pennsylvania.

Construction of the railroad began anyway at Baltimore in 1829. Progress was slow and more costly than anticipated, partly because there was no American railroad expertise on which the B&S could draw. Just building the first few miles up the Jones Falls Valley to what is now Lake Roland (the reservoir did not then exist) took until 1831. Using horse-drawn cars, the railroad earned what income it could by hauling chromium and copper ore from Isaac Tyson's mines at the Bare Hills. Textile mills in the lower Jones Falls Valley also provided traffic. From Lake Roland the B&S extended its line northwest through the Greenspring Valley to Owings Mills, which was reached in 1832. That same year the company imported a small steam locomotive from England, and the railroad started hauling flour from Owings Mills and Rockland Mills.

The Greenspring line, however, was unprofitable. Even before it was finished, it was relegated to branch status when Pennsylvania finally accepted the Baltimore & Susquehanna—or actually, a Pennsylvania company called the York & Maryland Line Railroad that was to be operated by the B&S. (As a *quid pro quo,* Maryland allowed the southward extension of Pennsylvania's Tidewater Canal along the Susquehanna.) From a junction with the Greenspring tracks at Lake Roland, the B&S resumed building northward, reaching the limestone and marble quarries at Texas and Cockeysville in 1834 and '35 and John Weise's White Hall paper mill in 1836. The spread of industrial development up the Jones Falls Valley as far as Mt. Washington also gave business to the B&S. Even so, huge loans, a moratorium on interest payments, and increased subscriptions of stock by Maryland and Baltimore were necessary to keep construction of the railroad going.

In 1838 the B&S reached York. Abandoning for the time being its original plan to go to York Haven, the company financed construction through York of an east-west subsidiary railroad linking Wrightsville on the Susquehanna with Gettysburg. After 1840, coal, lumber, and pig iron that were transshipped from the Susquehanna at Wrightsville greatly increased tonnage carried by the B&S to Baltimore.

For about a dozen years Wrightsville served as the northern terminal of the B&S, but in 1850 the company began construction of a subsidiary railroad to York Haven, and from there on to Harrisburg. Baltimore & Susquehanna trains started serving Harrisburg in 1851—the same year that the B&O completed its line to the Ohio River at Wheeling. Also in 1851, the B&S created yet another subsidiary to build a railroad still farther north along the Susquehanna to the anthracite fields in the vicinity of Sunbury, Pennsylvania.

Before the line to Sunbury was completed, however, the Baltimore & Susquehanna and its associated railroads in

Pennsylvania were insolvent. By the standards of the day, they had developed an extensive regional system, but in doing so they had taken on more debt and more construction expense than they could handle. In 1854 the Baltimore & Susquehanna merged with its Pennsylvania subsidiaries and was rechartered as the Northern Central Railway. The new company was still saddled with all the old debts but was granted authority to issue more stock and to borrow more money from Maryland and Pennsylvania in order to finish the line to Sunbury. Even before the Sunbury extension was completed in 1858, the company's precarious financial condition improved as it entered coal country and started hauling anthracite south to Baltimore. From then on the railroad prospered.

The Northern Central Railway figured tangentially in a curious incident in February 1861, when President-elect Abraham Lincoln traveled in a zigzag route from Illinois to New York, then south to Washington. In the presidential election, Lincoln had carried every free state and no slave states (of which Maryland was one). By mid-February seven states in the deep South had already seceded from the Union and formed the Confederate States of America. In Baltimore Lincoln had received only about a thousand votes from the minuscule Republican faction, some of whose leaders—highly unpopular in the city—thought it would be a fine thing to have a parade or at least a small procession when Lincoln arrived. The city government itself declined to plan an official reception or to send a delegation to meet Lincoln ahead of time in Harrisburg, to which he had gone from Philadelphia in order to address the Pennsylvania legislature. Lincoln's itinerary called for him to take the Northern Central Railway from Harrisburg to Baltimore on February 23, then proceed to Washington the same day.

For the trip down from Harrisburg, the Northern Central supplied a special express train, pulled by one of its best locomotives and equipped with spare pieces of machinery in case of a breakdown. According to the *Baltimore Exchange*, flagmen were posted every half-mile along the line, and watchmen guarded every bridge. On the morning of the 23rd, Mrs. Lincoln and her two children took this train—but President-elect Lincoln did not. Warned by detective Allan Pinkerton, Senator William Seward, and General Winfield Scott that there was a conspiracy to kill him in Baltimore, Lincoln had left Harrisburg for Philadelphia secretly the prior evening. From Philadelphia he took a sleeping car to Baltimore, through which he passed in the middle of the night, and in this way arrived unannounced in Washington at 6 o'clock in the morning. When the story got out, newspapers hostile to Lincoln heaped ridicule on the president-elect, depicting him in cartoons as a quaking figure in a nightcap or even disguised in a Scotch-plaid cap and a long cloak, which according to some stories he had borrowed from his wife. Newspapers and magazines sympathetic to Lincoln took a different line, and it was not long before they were trumpeting sensational and contradictory accounts of the Baltimore assassination conspiracy that had been cleverly foiled. However, no evidence of a plot to kill Lincoln in Baltimore ever turned up, and no one was ever arrested in connection with the matter.

As for Mrs. Lincoln, convinced that her husband had been given bad advice, she reached Baltimore without incident. Her travel arrangements, however, included the precaution of getting off the Northern Central train a stop before it pulled into the Calvert Street station, where it was met by nearly the entire Baltimore City police force and an immense crowd that groaned and hooted.

During the Civil War the Northern Central Railway was repeatedly a target of saboteurs and Confederate raiders. After Virginia seceded from the Union on April 17, 1861, Southern sympathizers in Maryland vehemently objected to the transit across their state of Northern troops rushing to secure Washington, D.C. Following the confrontation of April 19 between a Baltimore mob and the Sixth Massachusetts Regiment on its way to Washington, Mayor Brown and the

Baltimore board of police commissioners (and possibly also Governor Hicks) authorized destroying the railroad bridges leading from the north into Baltimore in order to prevent the arrival of more troops and the outbreak of more rioting. Over a period of four days, parties of police and militiamen burned the Northern Central's bridges all the way to the border with Pennsylvania. Telegraph lines were cut and some bridges of the Philadelphia, Wilmington & Baltimore Railway were also destroyed.

The officer in charge of wrecking the Northern Central was Lieutenant John Merryman of the Baltimore County Horse Guards. A prominent landowner residing at Hayfields, Merryman more than once waved his sword in front of crowds of cheering onlookers and shouted something to the effect that "We'll stop them from stealing our slaves." After federal troops gained control of Baltimore in May, Merryman was imprisoned in Fort McHenry and charged with treason—but not tried. In *Ex-Parte Merryman,* his appeal for judicial help became the subject of the ruling by Roger B. Taney, Chief Justice of the Supreme Court of the United States, that President Lincoln's suspension of the writ of *habeas corpus* was unconstitutional—a decision that Lincoln and the military authorities simply ignored until they were confident that danger was passed.

The railroad spans into Baltimore were rebuilt over a period of a month, but in 1863, nearly three dozen Northern Central bridges in York County, Pennsylvania, were wrecked during Robert E. Lee's invasion culminating at Gettysburg in the first three days of July. The damage was repaired at government expense by four hundred laborers from the United States Military Railroad Corps. Working day and night and using prefabricated wooden trusses, these men rebuilt the bridges and put the line back in service in just two weeks. Four months later Lincoln took a Northern Central train for part of his journey to Gettysburg to deliver his address dedicating the battlefield cemetery.

In 1864 the Northern Central bridge over the Gunpowder Falls north of Cockeysville and ten bridges south of the town were burned by a detachment of Confederate raiders during Jubal Early's march through Maryland to the outskirts of Washington. From Cockeysville Confederate cavalry led by Colonel Harry Gilmor were sent still farther east to destroy the railroad bridge of the Philadelphia, Wilmington & Baltimore Railway over the Gunpowder. Gilmor succeeded in damaging the bridge and in burning two trains—acts which did not prevent him from becoming police commissioner of Baltimore in 1877.

Finally, the Northern Central Railway saw the Civil War close when, twelve days after Lee's surrender at Appomattox and a week after Lincoln's assassination, the president's body was transported by train to Illinois for burial. According to *The Sun* for April 22, 1865, "The front of the Calvert Station of the Northern Central Railway was very beautifully trimmed with mourning, as were also the windows communicating with the ticket office. The funeral train provided by this company consisted of eight first-class passenger cars and a baggage car, all appropriately decked in the habiliments of mourning." At small stations and road crossings along the Northern Central line, silent crowds gathered to see the train pass.

Although the Northern Central repeatedly suffered damage during the Civil War, the conflict nonetheless brought prosperity to the railroad. One large Northern Central shareholder was Simon Cameron, briefly Lincoln's Secretary of War in 1861. Described by one historian as "a man who always stood ready to combine his personal business with the public's," Cameron gave military traffic to the Northern Central in the opening months of the war before his scandalous conduct caused Lincoln to send him out of the way (to Russia, in fact, as ambassador). More significantly, over the long course of the war, the Northern Central was strategically located between the industrial cities of the North and what came to be the main theater of action in Virginia. Hauling war material helped the railroad to boost its revenue by 186 percent during the war and to pay its old debts.

Following the Civil War, the Northern Central gradually became an adjunct of the Pennsylvania Railroad, which had started to acquire Northern Central stock in 1861. From its junction at Harrisburg with the Pennsylvania Railroad's main line between Pittsburgh and Philadelphia, the Northern Central provided the shortest route to tidewater. By 1863 the Pennsylvania Railroad had purchased nearly 34 percent of the Northern Central's shares, which was enough to exercise working control. Starting in 1874 the president of the Pennsylvania Railroad also served as president of the Northern Central, and finally in 1914 the Northern Central executed a 999-year lease and became an integral part of the vast Pennsylvania Railroad system.

The late nineteenth and early twentieth centuries were the glory years of the Northern Central. From the 1870s to 1913, annual revenue increased by more than 400 percent, chiefly from traffic in coal, lumber, and grain. Passenger traffic also boomed, and by 1893 the Northern Central had 32 weekday trains out of Baltimore, including seven non-stop runs to Harrisburg, one local to York, five locals to Parkton, eleven locals to Cockeysville, and eight trains on the Greenspring Branch.

By the late 1920s, however, the Pennsylvania Railroad was in decline. Coal provided less and less traffic as industries switched to petroleum and natural gas. Obsolete factories in Pennsylvania began to close and to relocate in the South and in other low-wage regions. Business shrank further during the Depression. Although World War II provided a temporary surge in rail traffic, the postwar boom in automobile and truck transport left the railroad weaker than ever. In the 1950s the Pennsylvania Railroad began to abandon unprofitable branches and segments.

People who knew the Northern Central as a working railroad

remember it chiefly as a commuter line from Parkton southward into Baltimore's old Calvert Street station, a site now occupied by the Sunpapers building. From Parkton to Baltimore the railroad had two sets of tracks. Termed collectively the Parkton Local, the commuter trains were running only three times daily by the late 1950s. Commenting on the trains' arrival downtown at 7:30, 8:30, and 10:00 A.M., Ralph Reppert of the Sunpapers said that the schedule accommodated "the workers, the clerkers, and the shirkers." After complaining for years of its financial losses from operating commuter trains on the Northern Central, the Pennsylvania Railroad was allowed to terminate local passenger service in 1959. Long-distance passenger service over the Northern Central line ended in 1971. Finally, freight service was halted abruptly and permanently—at least for the section between Cockeysville and York—when the railroad was severely damaged by flooding from three days of rain during Tropical Storm Agnes in 1972. Having declared bankruptcy in 1970, the Penn Central Corporation (created in 1968 by the merger of the Pennsylvania Railroad and the equally-shaky New York Central) refused to repair the Northern Central north of Cockeysville. The abandoned line was eventually purchased from Penn Central by the state of Maryland in 1980, two years after the U.S. Department of Interior had approved a Rails-to-Trails grant to the state of $450,000. Now the Northern Central line from Ashland northward is an immensely successful hiker/biker trail, and the line from Timonium southward is used by the Mass Transit Administration's light-rail commuter trains that started running in 1992. Plans call for the extension of the light-rail line northward to Hunt Valley by the end of 1994.

AUTOMOBILE: The Northern Central Railroad Trail is located north of Baltimore. The access points described below are easily reached from the various exits off Interstate 83. If you do not want to retrace your steps, a car shuttle is necessary. Obviously, a shuttle involves either two cars and two driver-hikers, or a driver who drops you off at the start (after you have left your car at the end) or who simply meets you at the end. As shown on Map 13 on page 137, Interstate 83 and York Road (which run more or less parallel to each other) provide good linkage for shuttling cars between the access points described below.

Ashland is located at the southern end of the Northern Central Railroad Trail. From Interstate 695 (the Beltway) north of Baltimore, take Exit 24 for Interstate 83 north toward Timonium and York, PA. Follow Interstate 83 north 5.5 miles, then take Exit 20A for Shawan Road east toward Cockeysville. Follow Shawan Road 0.7 mile, then turn right (south) at an intersection with Route 45 (York Road). Follow Route 45 south 0.3 mile, then turn left onto Ashland Road. Go 0.4 mile, then head half-right on Ashland Road into a housing development called Ashland at Hunt Valley. Continue straight on Ashland Road for a quarter of a mile to a parking lot for the Northern Central Railroad Trail.

Ashland was a very substantial iron-making town founded next to the railroad in 1844. By 1867 the company had three furnaces that used a pre-heated blast of air to smelt iron with Pennsylvania anthracite. In 1870 the work force numbered about a hundred men. The long stone building to the left of the parking lot formerly housed workers. Some of the brick houses at Ashland also were part of the company village. The furnaces, formerly located east of the railroad, operated until 1884, then again briefly in 1887. The works were torn down in 1893 and most of the houses were demolished in 1984, when the village was re-developed.

If there is no room to park at Ashland, you can try parking 2.0 miles up the trail at a lot located on Phoenix Road just north of the intersection with Carroll Road. (See Map 13.) Many people also park where Papermill Road crosses the trail, but there is no lot there and parking on the road shoulder may eventually be prohibited. (Papermill Road, incidentally, will someday be linked directly westward to the intersection of Shawan Road and York Road.)

Monkton is located 7.5 miles north of Ashland and 5.4 miles south of Parkton on the railroad trail. From Interstate 83 about 12.4 miles north of the Beltway, take Exit 27 for Route 137 (Mt. Carmel Road) and Hereford. At the top of the exit ramp, turn right (east) onto Route 137 and go 0.4 mile, then turn right (south) at an intersection with Route 45 (York Road). Follow Route 45 south 100 yards, then turn left onto Route 138 (Monkton Road). Follow Route 138 for about 3.0 miles, then (after crossing Big Gunpowder Falls) turn left into a parking lot for the Northern Central Railroad Trail.

If there is no room to park at the lot in Monkton, you probably can find room on the shoulder of Old Monkton Road, located back west a few hundred yards on the other side of the river. Another alternative is the large lot in White Hall, located 3.2 miles up the trail and reached via Weisberg Road (also called Wiseburg Road) off York Road. (See Map 13.)

Parkton is located 5.4 miles north of Monkton and 5.7 miles south of Freeland. From Interstate 83 about 15.8 miles north of the Beltway, take Exit 31 for Middle

MAP 13 — Northern Centrail Railroad Trail

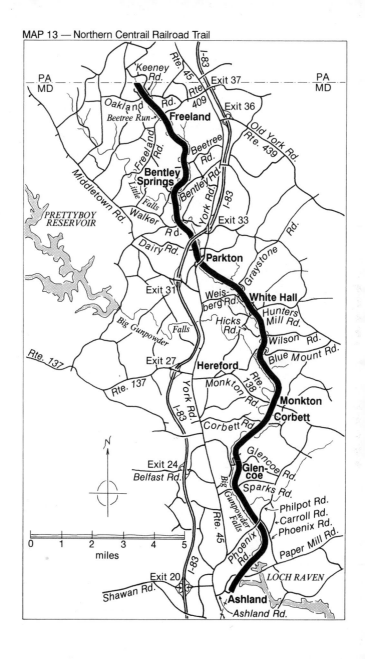

town Road and Parkton. At the top of the exit ramp, turn right (east) and follow Middletown Road 0.6 mile, then turn left (north) at an intersection with Route 45 (York Road). Follow Route 45 north 1.2 miles, then turn very sharply left and go 0.1 mile across a stone bridge. Park on the left next to the Northern Central Railroad Trail. (There is also another small lot in Parkton where Dairy Road crosses the trail.)

Freeland is located 5.7 miles north of Parkton along the railroad trail. From Interstate 83 about 21.7 miles north of the Beltway, take Exit 36 for Route 439, Maryland Line and Bel Air. At the top of the exit ramp, turn right (west) to follow Route 439 toward Maryland Line. Go 0.3 mile, then turn right (north) onto Route 45 (York Road). Follow Route 45 north 1.0 mile to a crossroads with Route 409 (Freeland Road). Turn left (west) onto Route 409 and go 1.8 miles to the parking lot on the right for the Northern Central Railroad Trail.

If there is no room to park at Freeland, you probably can find room in the large lot at Bentley Springs, located 2.8 miles south along the trail and reached via Bentley Road off York Road. (See Map 13.)

WALKING and BICYCLING: The trail is shown by the bold line on Map 13 on page 137. The route is unmistakable throughout its entire length. Occasionally, however, you must cross roads and parking lots, so use caution at all places where cars may be present.

From the parking lot in Ashland, there is only one way to go on the railroad trail: north.

From Monkton or Parkton, you can go north or south.

From Freeland, you can walk or ride north 1 mile to the boundary with Pennsylvania or south 19 miles to Ashland.

Finally, in case you are wondering about the stanchions located at intervals along the trail and bearing the letter W, they signaled the train's engineer that he should blow his whistle in advance of reaching a station or crossing a road. The white posts with black numbers show the distances to the railroad's southern terminus at Baltimore and northern end at Sunbury, Pennsylvania. The wooden posts with incised numbers show mileage along the railroad trail from Ashland northward.

Further reading: A book-length treatment of the Northern Central is Robert L. Gunnarsson's *The Story of the Northern Central Railroad* (Greenberg Publishing). In their respective histories of the Civil War, Bruce Catton and Shelby Foote indicate—perhaps because there is no real way of knowing otherwise—that the danger to Lincoln in Baltimore may have been real, but Thomas J. Scharf, a Marylander and Southern sympathizer, devotes fourteen pages to the subject in his *History of Maryland*, where he is at great pains to say that the conspiracy story was an invention of Northern outsiders eager to attract the president-elect's attention.

10

ROBERT E. LEE MEMORIAL PARK

Lake Roland

Walking—5.5 miles (8.9 kilometers) round-trip. A footpath shown by the bold line on Map 14 on page 152
borders Lake Roland, Jones Falls, and Roland Run.
Walk from the dam at the lake's southern end to the
marsh and meadow at the northern end, then return by
the way you came. Although the trail is not well maintained, it gets a lot of use and is easily followed. The area
is also popular with mountain bikers.

The park is open daily from 6 A.M. to 9 P.M. Dogs must
be leashed. Swimming and wading are prohibited.
Although located in southern Baltimore County, the area
is managed by the Baltimore City Department of Recreation and Parks; telephone 396-6106. In 1862 the
Jones Falls was dammed and Lake Roland created as a
reservoir for Baltimore City's water supply—a function it
no longer serves.

NOTICE: The dam at Lake Roland is being repaired
during 1993, and the area is a muddy mess, so you may
want to stay away until work is completed early in 1994.

BECAUSE OF THE VARIETY of its habitats—bottomland
woods, meadows, freshwater marsh, dry piney highlands, and
open water—Robert E. Lee Park (better known as Lake Ro-

land) is particularly popular with bird watchers, although most of the areas described in this book, even those well within the city, are also good for birding.

About 650 species of birds live and breed in the United States and Canada, but many of these are not found east of the Rocky Mountains. The 1986 edition of the *Field Checklist of Maryland & D.C. Birds*, co-published by the Maryland Ornithological Society and the Audubon Naturalist Society of the Central Atlantic States, lists 311 regularly occurring species. Another seventy are "rarities and accidentals" in our area.

Even for fledgling birders, identifying the many species that nest in the Baltimore area or pass through during migration is easier than might at first be thought. Shape, size, plumage, and other physical characteristics are distinguishing field marks. Range, season, habitat, song, and behavior are other useful keys to identifying birds.

Range is of primary importance for the simple reason that many birds are not found throughout North America or even the eastern United States, but only in certain regions such as the Atlantic and Gulf coasts. For example, cedar waxwings and Bohemian waxwings closely resemble each other, so it helps to know that the latter are not seen in Maryland. A good field guide provides range maps based on years of reported sightings and bird counts. Of course, bird ranges are not static: some pioneering species, such as the glossy ibis and house finch, have extended their ranges during recent decades. Other birds, such as the ivory-billed woodpecker, have lost ground and died out.

Season is related to range, since migratory birds appear in different parts of their ranges during different times of year. The five species of spot-breasted thrushes, for instance, are sometimes difficult to distinguish from each other, but usually only the hermit thrush is present in eastern Maryland during winter and only the wood thrush is found here during summer. Again, the maps in most field guides reflect this sort of information.

Habitat is important in identifying birds. Even before you spot a bird, the surroundings can tell you what species you are likely to see. Within its range a species usually appears only in certain preferred habitats, although during migration some species are less particular. (In many cases, birds show a degree of physical adaptation to their preferred environment.) As its name implies, the marsh wren is seldom found far from cattails, rushes, sedges, or tall marsh grasses; if a wrenlike birds is spotted in such a setting, it is unlikely to be a house wren or Carolina wren or one of the other species commonly found in thick underbrush or shrubbery. Ducks can be difficult to identify unless you tote a telescope; but even if all you can see is a silhouette, you can start with the knowledge that shallow marshes and creeks normally attract few diving ducks (such as oldsquaw, canvasbacks, redheads, ring-necked ducks, greater and lesser scaup, common goldeneye, and buffleheads) and that large, deep bodies of water are not the usual setting for surface-feeding puddle ducks (American black ducks, gadwalls, mallards, common pintails, America widgeons, wood ducks, northern shovelers, and blue-winged and green-winged teals).

Some of the distinctive habitats that different bird species prefer are open oceans; beaches; salt marsh; mud flats; meadows; thickets; various types of woods; and creeks, ponds, and lakes. The area where two habitats join, called an *ecotone*, is a particularly good place to look for birds because species peculiar to either environment might be present. For example, both meadowlarks and wood warblers might be found where a hay field abuts a forest. All good field guides provide information on habitat preference that can help to locate a species or to assess the likelihood of a tentative identification.

Song announces the identity (or at least the location) of birds even before they are seen. Although some species, such as the red-winged blackbird, have only a few songs, others, such as the mockingbird, have an infinite variety. Some birds, most notably thrushes, sing different songs in the morning and evening. In many species the basic songs vary among individuals and also from one area to another, giving rise to regional "dialects." Nonetheless, the vocal repertory of most songbirds is sufficiently constant in timbre and pattern to identify each species simply by its songs.

Bird songs, as distinguished from calls, can be very complex. They are sung only by the male of most species, usually in spring and summer. The male arrives first at the breeding and nesting area after migration. He stakes out a territory for courting, mating, and nesting by singing at prominent points around the area's perimeter. This wards off intrusion by other males of his species and simultaneously attracts females. On the basis of the male's display and the desirability of his territory, the female selects her mate. Experiments suggest that female birds build nests faster and lay more eggs when exposed to the songs of males with a larger vocal repertory than others of their species, and the relative volume of their songs appears to be a way for males to establish status among themselves.

In a few species, including eastern bluebirds, "Baltimore" orioles, cardinals, and white-throated sparrows, both sexes sing, although the males are more active in defending their breeding territory. Among mockingbirds, both sexes sing in fall and winter, but only males sing in spring and summer. Some birds, such as canaries, have different songs for different seasons.

Birds tend to heed the songs of their own kind and to ignore the songs of other species, which, after all, do not compete for females nor, in many cases, for the same type of nesting materials or food. In consequence, a single area might include the overlapping breeding territories of several species. From year to year such territories are bigger or smaller, depending on the food supply. Typically, most small songbirds require about half an acre from which others of their species are excluded.

Bird calls (as distinguished from songs) are short, simple, sometimes harsh, and used by both males and females at all times of year to communicate alarm, aggression, location, and existence of food. Nearly all birds have some form of call. Warning calls are often heeded by species other than the caller's. Some warning calls are thin, high-pitched whistles that are difficult to locate and so do not reveal the bird's location to predators. Birds also use mobbing calls to summon other birds, as chickadees and crows do when scolding and harassing owls and other unwanted visitors. Birds flying in flocks, like cedar waxwings, often call continuously. Such calls help birds migrating by night to stay together.

The study of bird dialects and experiments with birds that have been deafened or raised in isolation indicate that songs are genetically inherited only to a very crude extent. Although a few species, such as doves, sing well even when raised in isolation, most birds raised alone produce inferior, simplified songs. Generally, young songbirds learn their songs by listening to adult birds and by practice singing, called *subsong*. Yet birds raised in isolation and exposed to many tape-recorded songs show an innate preference for the songs of their own species.

Probably the easiest way to learn bird songs is to listen repeatedly to recordings and to refer at the same time to a standard field guide. Most guides describe bird vocalizations with such terms as *harsh, nasal, flutelike, piercing, plaintive, wavering, twittering, buzzing, sneezy,* and *sputtering.* Played slowly, bird recordings demonstrate that the songs contain many more notes than the human ear ordinarily hears.

Shape is one of the first and most important aspects to notice once you actually see a bird. Most birds can at least be placed in the proper family and many species can be identified by shape or silhouette, without reference to other field marks. Some birds, such as kestrels, are distinctly stocky, big-headed, and powerful-looking, while others, such as catbirds and cuckoos, are elegantly long and slender. Kingfishers, blue jays, tufted titmice, Bohemian and cedar waxwings, and cardinals are among the few birds with crests.

Bird bills frequently have distinctive shapes and, more than any other body part, show adaptation to food supply. The beak can be chunky, like that of a grosbeak, to crack seeds; thin and curved, like that of a creeper, to probe bark for insects; hooked, like that of a shrike, to tear at flesh; long and slender, like that of a hummingbird, to sip nectar from tubular flowers; or some other characteristic shape depending on the bird's food. Goatsuckers, swifts, flycatchers, and swallows, all of which catch flying insects, have widely hinged bills and gaping mouths. The long, thin bills of starlings and meadowlarks are suited to probing the ground. In the Galapagos Islands west of Ecuador, Charles Darwin noted fourteen species of finches, each of which had evolved a different type of beak or style of feeding that gave it a competitive advantage for a particular type of food. Many birds are nonetheless flexible about their diet, especially from season to season when food sources change or become scarce. For example, Tennessee warblers, which ordinarily glean insects from foliage, also take large amounts of nectar from tropical flowers when wintering in South and Central America.

In addition to beaks, nearly every other part of a bird's body is adapted to help exploit its environment. Feet of passerines, or songbirds, are adapted to perching, with three toes in front and one long toe behind; waterfowl have webbed or lobed feet for swimming; and raptors have talons for grasping prey.

Other key elements of body shape are the length and form of wings, tails, and legs. The wings may be long, pointed, and developed for swift, sustained flight, like those of falcons. Or the wings may be short and rounded for abrupt bursts of speed, like those of accipiters. The tail may have a deep fork like that of a barn swallow, a shallow notch like that of a tree swallow, a square tip like that of a cliff swallow, or a rounded tip like that of a blue jay.

Size is difficult to estimate and therefore not very useful in identifying birds. The best approach is to bear in mind the relative sizes of different species and to use certain well-known

birds like the chickadee, sparrow, robin, kingfisher, and crow as standards for mental comparison. For example, if a bird resembles a song sparrow but looks unusually large, it might be a fox sparrow.

Plumage, whether plain or princely, muted or magnificent, is one of the most obvious keys to identification. Color can occur in remarkable combinations of spots, stripes, streaks, patches, and other patterns that make even supposedly drab birds a pleasure to see. In some instances, like the brown streaks of American bitterns and many other species, the plumage provides camouflage. Most vireos and warblers are various shades and combinations of yellow, green, brown, gray, and black, as one would expect from their forest environment. The black and white backs of woodpeckers help them to blend in with bark dappled with sunlight. The bold patterns of killdeers and some other plovers break up their outlines in much the same manner that warships used to be camouflaged before the invention of radar. Many shore birds display countershading: they are dark above and light below, a pattern that reduces the effect of shadows and makes them appear an inconspicuous monotone. Even some brightly colored birds have camouflaging plumages when they are young and least able to avoid predators.

For some species, it is important *not* to be camouflaged. Many seabirds are mostly white, which in all light conditions enables them to be seen at great distances against the water. Because flocks of seabirds spread out from their colonies to search for food, it is vital that a bird that has located food be visible to others after it has landed on the water to feed.

To organize the immense variation in plumage, focus on different basic elements and ask the following types of questions. Starting with the head, is it uniformly colored like that of the red-headed woodpecker? Is there a small patch on the crown, like that of Wilson's warbler and the ruby-crowned kinglet, or a larger cap on the front and top of the head, like that of the common redpoll and American goldfinch? Is the crown striped like the ovenbird's? Does a ring surround the eye, as with a Connecticut warbler, or are the eye rings perhaps even joined across the top of the bill to form spectacles, like those of a yellow-breasted chat? Is there a stripe over or through the eyes, like the red-breasted nuthatch's, or a conspicuous black mask across the eyes, like that of a common yellowthroat or loggerhead shrike? From the head go on to the rest of the body, where distinctive colors and patterns can also mark a bird's bill, throat, breast, belly, back, sides, wings, rump, tail, and legs.

Finally, what a bird *does* is an important clue to its identity. Certain habits, postures, ways of searching for food, and other behavior characterize different species. Some passerines, such as larks, juncos, and towhees, are strictly ground feeders; other birds, including flycatchers and swallows, nab insects on the wing; and others, such as nuthatches and creepers, glean insects from the crevices in bark. Woodpeckers bore into the bark. Vireos and most warblers pick insects from the foliage of trees and brush.

All of these birds may be further distinguished by other habits of eating. For example, towhees scratch for insects and seeds by kicking backward with both feet together, whereas juncos rarely do, although both hop to move along the ground. Other ground feeders, such as meadowlarks, walk rather than hop. Despite the children's song, robins often run, not hop. Swallows catch insects while swooping and skimming in continuous flight, but flycatchers dart out from a limb, grab an insect (sometimes with an audible smack), and then return to their perch. Brown creepers have the curious habit of systematically searching for food by climbing trees in spirals, then flying back to the ground to climb again. Woodpeckers tend to hop upward, bracing themselves against the tree with their stiff tails. Nuthatches walk up and own trees and branches head first, seemingly without regard for gravity. Vireos are sluggish compared to the hyperactive, flitting warblers.

Many birds divide a food source into zones, an arrangement

that apparently evolved to ensure each species its own food supply. The short-legged green heron sits at the edge of the water or on a low overhanging branch, waiting for its prey to some close to shore. Medium-sized black-crowned and yellow-crowned night herons hunt in shallow water. The long-legged great blue heron stalks fish in water up to two feet deep. Swans, geese, and many ducks graze underwater on the stems and tubers of grassy plants, but the longer necks of swans and geese enable them to reach deeper plants. Similarly, different species of shore birds take food from the same mud flat by probing with their varied bills to different depths. Species of warblers that feed in the same tree are reported to concentrate in separate areas among the trunk, twig tips, tree top, and ground. Starlings and cowbirds feeding in flocks on the ground show another arrangement that provides an even distribution of food: those in the rear fly ahead to the front, so that the entire flock rolls slowly across the field.

Different species also have different styles of flight. Soaring is typical of some big birds. Gulls float nearly motionless in the wind. Buteos and turkey vultures soar on updrafts in wide circles, although turkey vultures may be further distinguished by wings held in a shallow V. Some other large birds, such as accipiters, rarely soar but instead interrupt their wing beats with glides. Kestrels, terns, and kingfishers can hover in one spot. Hummingbirds, like oversized dragonflies, can also hover and even fly backward. Slightly more erratic than the swooping, effortless flight of swallows is that of swifts, flitting with wing beats that appear to alternate (but do not). Still other birds, such as the American goldfinch and flickers, dip up and down in wavelike flight. Some species, including jays and grackles, fly dead straight. Among ducks, the surface-feeding species launch themselves directly upward into flight, seeming to jump from the water, but the heavy diving ducks typically patter along the surface before becoming airborne.

Various idiosyncrasies distinguish yet other species. The spotted sandpiper and northern waterthrush walk with a teetering, bobbing motion. Coots pump their heads back and forth as they swim. The eastern phoebe regularly jerks its tail downward while perching, but wrens often cock their tails vertically. Herons and egrets fly with their necks folded back; storks, ibises, and cranes fly with their necks outstretched. Still other birds have characteristic postures while sitting or flying or other unique habits that provide a reliable basis for identification.

AUTOMOBILE: Robert E. Lee Memorial Park (better know simply as Lake Roland) is located just north of Baltimore. The entrance is on Falls Road a few yards north of the intersection with Lake Avenue.

From Interstate 83 (the Jones Falls Expressway) inside the Beltway, take Exit 10A for Northern Parkway eastbound. Follow Northern Parkway east only a few hundred yards to a four-way intersection with Falls Road, and there turn left. Follow Falls Road 0.9 mile. Just before the long bridge over Jones Falls, turn right and then right again onto Lakeside Drive, which is the entrance road to Robert E. Lee Memorial Park. Go. 0.4 mile to an intersection with Hollins Avenue (which provides an alternative means of approach from Lake Avenue). Continue straight to the parking lot.

WALKING: (See Map 14 on page 152.) Cross the bridge just below the dam, then follow an asphalt path uphill to the right. Fork right along the water's edge. After circling along the shore, continue gradually uphill past a picnic shelter at the top of the knoll. Just beyond the shelter, turn right onto a rough, eroded dirt path leading downhill and along the shore to the tracks of the MTA's light rail line connecting Baltimore and Cockeysville. With caution, cross the tracks on the established walkway. Incidentally, the light rail line

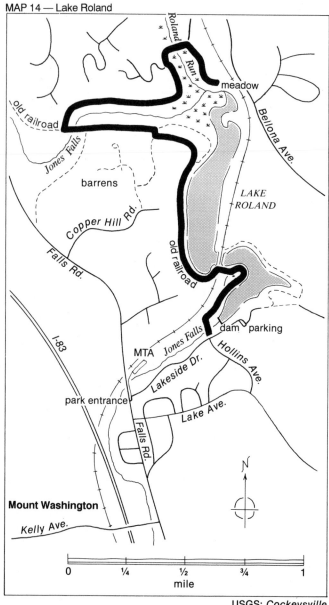

MAP 14 — Lake Roland

Roland Run

old railroad

Jones Falls

barrens

Copper Hill Rd.

Falls Rd.

I-83

park entrance

meadow

Bellona Ave.

LAKE ROLAND

old railroad

MTA   Jones Falls   dam   parking

Lakeside Dr.   Hollins Ave.

Falls Rd.   Lake Ave.

Mount Washington

Kelly Ave.

N

0   ¼   ½   ¾   1
mile

USGS: *Cockeysville*

follows the roadbed of the old Northern Central Railway, which north of Cockeysville is now a hiker/biker trail, as described in Chapter 9. And for the next half mile at Lake Roland, the trail follows the old, abandoned roadbed of the Northern Central's Greenspring Valley branch. The rails, cuts, embankments, stone culverts, and a railroad bridge are still evident. The junction of the Greenspring line with the Northern Central's main line used to be located a few hundred yards south of Lake Roland.

After crossing the light rail tracks, continue straight along the shore with the lake on you right. Where an earth ridge appears on the right—and where a mountain-bike trail climbs right—continue straight along a trough that gradually curves left. At a trail junction, turn sharply right for 30 yards, then bear left at another intersection. Continue more or less straight through the woods to an old railroad bridge over Jones Falls.

Cross the bridge, then immediately turn right and descend steeply from the railroad embankment. With Jones Falls on your right, follow the path (which is sometimes obscure and often muddy) through the streamside jungle. Continue as the path passes below houses on the left. Eventually, the trail reaches a road. Bear right across a bridge over Roland Run; be alert for cars. About 40 yards beyond the bridge, turn right at a gate. Follow a grassy track several hundred yards to a large meadow overlooking the marsh at the northern end of Lake Roland.

Return to the dam at the southern end of Lake Roland by the way you came.

Further reading: Roger Tory Peterson, best known for *A Field Guide to the Birds* (Houghton Mifflin), has also written the small *How to Know the Birds* (Mentor Books). Roger F. Pasquier's *Watching Birds* (Houghton Mifflin) is a good introduction to bird life.

11

LOCH RAVEN

Southeast Narrows and Southern Shore

Walking and bicycling—up to 10.0 miles (16.1 kilometers) round-trip. This walk starts by following the shore of the reservoir along a portion of Loch Raven Drive that is closed to cars on Saturday and Sunday between 10 A.M. and 5 P.M. With its sweeping views over the water, the roadway provides a pleasant walk totaling 3.5 miles round-trip. For the full hike shown by the bold line on Map 15 on page 161, continue on a dirt fire road that winds around wooded hillsides and ravines. The trail eventually ends by the water's edge at the tip of a peninsula . Return by the way you came.

If you are looking for a country setting in which to push your child in a stroller, Loch Raven Drive makes an excellent promenade during the period it is closed to cars. It is also a good place for roller-skating or for bicycling with a young child. Conversely, the dirt fire road along the southern shore is popular with mountain bikers. Mountain bikers should note, however, that riding at Loch Raven and at other Baltimore City watershed areas is subject to ongoing review and may be prohibited because many bikers refuse to stay on the various fire roads or to avoid areas where there are obvious problems with erosion.

Watershed lands are open from sunrise to sunset. Dogs must be leashed. Swimming and wading are prohibited. The reservoir and watershed areas are managed by the Baltimore City Bureau of Water and Waste Water; telephone 795-6151.

LOCH RAVEN IS ONE of Baltimore City's three major reservoirs. The others are Prettyboy Reservoir, located upstream from Loch Raven on Big Gunpowder Falls, and Liberty Reservoir on the North Branch of the Patapsco River. Both Loch Raven and Liberty Reservoir are the last impoundments on their rivers before the water is removed and treated for drinking. Prettyboy Reservoir simply provides additional storage within the Gunpowder watershed. A more or less steady flow of water is released from Prettyboy to keep Loch Raven full and also to promote trout fishing within the Hereford section of Gunpowder Falls State Park, located immediately downstream from Prettyboy Dam. (See Chapters 7 and 8.) As a result, the level of Prettyboy Reservoir fluctuates widely between wet and dry periods. Baltimore also has the right to pump water from the Philadelphia Electric Company's Conowingo Dam on the Susquehanna River, but the city does so only during droughts or in other emergencies.

To protect its water supply, Baltimore City owns about 9 square miles of forested land surrounding each of its three reservoirs. In managing these buffer areas, the city has adopted a multiple-use policy that allows a wide variety of recreational activities as long as they are compatible with the chief priority of maintaining high water quality. Permitted activities include fishing, hiking, horseback riding, and—on a trial basis— mountain biking. Rowboats can be rented at the Loch Raven Fishing Center off Dulaney Valley Road. Eighteen hundred boat permits are distributed annually, but no gasoline motors or sailboats are allowed on the reservoirs. Moreover, boaters must sign a pledge agreeing not to use their boats elsewhere. In this way the watershed managers hope to prevent the spread to the reservoirs of zebra mussels, which are thought to cling to the hulls of boats and which have become a major problem in some places because they clog waterworks intake pipes. Also, an eighteen-hole golf course has long existed at Pine Ridge on the western shore of Loch Raven, and the feasibility of developing another adjacent eighteen-hole course, plus a three-hole course for the disabled, was being studied in 1993.

The idea of building additional golf courses at Loch Raven is not new. The proposal was put forward in 1987 and rejected as likely to add to the flow of fungicides, weed killers, fertilizers, and sediments into the reservoir. However, by commissioning a new study of the issue, golf proponents hope to demonstrate that the proposed courses can improve rather than degrade water quality in Loch Raven. Some of their arguments are merely environmental cant. Golf proponents extoll the virtues of "increasing biodiversity" (translation: cutting some fairways through the woods and landscaping with a variety of deciduous trees) and "improving wildlife habitat" (building birdhouses). More substantively, the golf proponents say that the new courses could help to mitigate pollution from small streams that currently drain rainwater away from nearby subdivisions into the reservoir. The golf consultants plan to evaluate the possibility of intercepting this less-than-pristine stormwater by building several ponds, where sediments could settle out and from which water could be drawn for sprinkling the golf courses in summer. In this way, they anticipate, more stormwater would ultimately seep into the ground or evaporate, and less dirty runoff would enter the reservoir. Buffer strips of forest along the water's edge would also intercept runoff.

Opponents counter that chemically tainted runoff would be increased rather than diminished by replacing about a hundred acres of forest with fairways and greens that are regularly treated with lawn chemicals. Research conducted at Liberty Reservoir by Edward Corbett of Pennsylvania State University indicates that an evergreen forest like that at Pine Ridge is superior to turf if the object is to absorb rain and reduce runoff. Also, city watershed managers and other officials point out that Baltimore owns only 6 percent of the Big Gunpowder watershed and should anticipate widespread development and continuing deterioration of environmental conditions on the remaining 94 percent over which it has little or no control. Under these circumstances, many people question whether it makes sense to experiment with the city's limited watershed land—its last line of defense against pollution—by converting a hundred acres of forest to new golf courses that might themselves be a source of continuing pollution. Ultimately the issue will be decided by Baltimore's Board of Estimates, headed by the mayor (to whom you may want to write a letter if you have an opinion on the matter).

Regardless of the ultimate outcome of the golf course controversy, the range and intensity of recreation allowed on Baltimore's watershed lands is already liberal compared to what is permitted at other municipal reservoirs in the East. Although boating on reservoirs and hiking, riding, and picnicking in the adjacent buffer areas do not significantly impair water quality, these activities nonetheless present Baltimore's watershed managers with other tiresome problems. For example, because crowds and drinking were getting out of hand, Baltimore has closed its picnic area at Loch Raven and has curtailed use of the Liberty Dam overlook. Also, litter is pervasive, thrown overboard from boats, scattered at fishing spots along the shore, and heaped at focal points such as the trailhead below Prettyboy Dam. Another bane is off-road motorcycles. Even horseback riding and mountain biking have become a nuisance in some places as dirt fire roads have been churned into quagmires and gullied by erosion.*

Recreational use of reservoirs and adjacent watershed lands also increases administrative burdens. Areas popular with visitors have to be patrolled more often to enforce regulations. (Incidentally, watershed police have full power to issue citations and to arrest offenders.) Although much of the responsibility for overseeing the wide range of programs at Baltimore's reservoirs has fallen on the city's Watershed Section, some of the administrative duties have been shifted to other agencies with a more immediate interest in public recreation. The Baltimore Municipal Golf Corporation operates Pine Ridge Golf Course at Loch Raven (but a logbook listing lawn chemicals applied to the course is reviewed by watershed staff). The Baltimore County Department of Recreation and Parks runs the Loch Raven boat rental and fishing concession (telephone 252-8755). And the state's Department of Natural Resources manages the reservoir's fisheries.

In summary, the residents of the Baltimore region are very fortunate that the city's reservoirs and watershed lands are open to the public for a wide variety of recreational activities. The continuation of this policy, however, depends on the cooperation and reasonable behavior of those who use these areas.

---

*   I am all for mountain biking (I sometimes ride rather than walk many of the trails in this book), but the actions of some bikers at Loch Raven and elsewhere have put them in bad odor with the public and with watershed and park managers. Obnoxious behavior includes spray-painting trees with big arrows and trail messages, playing chicken with hikers, and scarring the woods with mazes of sinuous, muddy, and sometimes heavily eroded pathways which, as they become impassable, are bypassed by new tracks a few dozen yards away.

Baltimore-area mountain-biking clubs should take concerted action to educate bikers—both members and nonmembers alike—and to establish and maintain trails that are acceptable to the managers of our local parks and watershed areas.

AUTOMOBILE: Loch Raven is located north of Baltimore. The walk described here starts on Loch Raven Drive at the intersection with Morgan Mill Road.

From Interstate 695 (the Beltway) north of Baltimore, take Exit 27B for Route 146 (Dulaney Valley Road) north. Follow Route 146 north about 4.2 miles. Immediately after crossing a bridge over Loch Raven, bear right on Dulaney Valley Road where Jarrettsville Pike heads left. Continue on Dulaney Valley Road 1.7 miles. Where Dulaney Valley Road turns left at Peerce's Plantation Restaurant, go straight on Loch Raven Drive and follow it 1.0 mile to the intersection of Loch Raven Drive and Morgan Mill Road. South of this intersection, Loch Raven Drive is closed to automobile traffic between 10 A.M. and 5 P.M. on Saturday and Sunday. Park near the intersection; pay close attention to signs indicating where parking is permitted and where (and when) it is not.

WALKING and BICYCLING: (See Map 15 opposite) From the intersection of Loch Raven Drive and Morgan Mill Road, pass the orange gate and follow Loch Raven Drive, with the reservoir on your right. Follow the road along the edge of the reservoir, across a bridge, and gradually uphill to another orange gate at the intersection of Providence Road and Loch Raven Drive.

Immediately beyond the orange gate, turn right past a green gate and enter the woods on a fire road. From here to the water's edge, the route shown by the bold line on Map 15 follows fire roads, which are wide enough to accommodate a Jeep; ignore narrow side trails that have been worn by mountain bikers.

Follow the fire road though the woods, then through a clearing and back into the woods. For the next half mile, the trail is often muddy, but it improves after that.

MAP 15 — Loch Raven: southeast narrows and southern shore

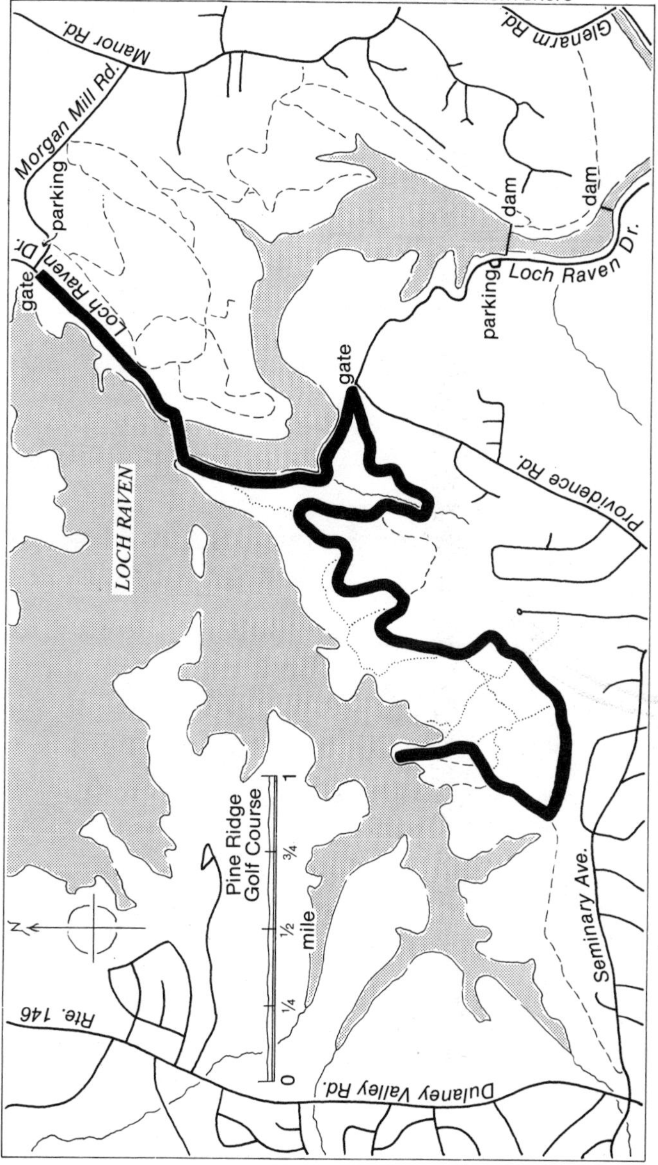
USGS: Towson
Manor Rd.
Morgan Mill Rd.
Glenarm Rd.
parking
gate
Loch Raven Dr.
dam
dam
parking
Loch Raven Dr.
gate
Providence Rd.
LOCH RAVEN
Pine Ridge Golf Course
0
1/4
1/2
3/4
1
mile
N
Rte. 146
Seminary Ave.
Dulaney Valley Rd.

Eventually, the fire road climbs obliquely along the side of a large ravine. Part way up the hill, fork right. Continue obliquely uphill, with the slope falling off to your right. Follow the fire road along the contour of the hill, then gradually around to the left. During the leaf-less season, Loch Raven is visible to the right. Continue as the fire road winds, dips, climbs, and curves along the hillside.

After about 1.5 miles, the terrain becomes less hilly and the woods less mature—or that is, the trees get smaller and the understory becomes choked with vines and scrubby growth. Eventually, after passing a long series of houses visible one after another through the woods to the left, turn right at a major intersection.

Continue through the woods. At a fork in the trail, bear right. Continue as straight as possible on the wide trail past a series of paths intersecting from right and left. Continue down to the water's edge near the tip of a promontory.

Return to the starting point by the way you came.

12

LOCH RAVEN

Southeast Highlands

Walking—up to 5.0 miles (8 kilometers) round-trip. Follow fire roads through the woods overlooking Loch Raven. The route shown by the bold line on Map 16 on page 172 climbs, dips, and winds around the hillsides and eventually leads to a remote promontory north of the dam. Some of these trails are popular with mountain bikers, but the long spur ending at the water is used mainly by hikers.

Watershed lands are open from sunrise to sunset. Dogs must be leashed. Swimming and wading are prohibited. The reservoir and watershed areas are managed by the Baltimore City Bureau of Water and Waste Water; telephone 795-6151.

ALTHOUGH BALTIMORE CITY owns about nine square miles of watershed land surrounding each of its three reservoirs, its property amounts to less than 6 percent of the 303 square miles in the Big Gunpowder Falls drainage area above Loch Raven Dam and also less than 6 percent of the 164 square miles in the Patapsco watershed above Liberty Dam. No part of these two drainage areas is within the city. The resulting lack of control over the watershed greatly complicates protection of Baltimore's water supply, which also serves much of the metropolitan region.

Sedimentation, for example, is a major problem largely traceable to erosion on land that is not controlled by the city. According to a study of the Baltimore region conducted in 1977 by the Soil Conservation Service, annually cultivated cropland contributed about half of the nearly one million tons of sediment—the equivalent of 20,000 freight cars full—that were estimated to wash into the waters of the Baltimore area annually. Yet various conservation measures—such as no-till planting, strip cropping along hillside contours, and gully control—that in 1977 were used on only 32 percent of the farmland in the Baltimore region, reduced soil loss on that land by 80 percent. Even if only very approximate, these figures at least give some idea of the magnitude of Baltimore's interest in what happens on the surrounding farmland, since much of the sediment ends up in the metropolitan area's reservoirs, as indicated by periodic depth surveys. Erosion from farmland not only clogs streams and reduces the storage capacity of the reservoirs, but also increases turbidity and pollution from fertilizers, animal wastes, and pesticides with which the mud is permeated. The high level of nitrogenous chemicals in the reservoirs encourages the growth of algae, which in turn makes the process of water purification more difficult.

Since the 1977 report, erosion from farmland in the Baltimore region is thought to have been reduced significantly, in part because there are fewer farms, but also because crops on the overwhelming majority of farms that remain are planted without plowing. Similarly, where drainage swales cross fields, standard practice is now to line the depression with grass in order to retard erosion and to catch sediments.

Another major source of sediments is large-scale residential and commercial development entailing the stripping and grading of huge tracts of land. Again, according to the 1977 report of the Soil Conservation Service, the amount of soil loss per acre on land undergoing development is about fifteen times greater than on land in cultivated row crops, forty-four times greater than on land in pasture, and sixty-three times greater than on land in timber. Even if only a small percentage of land is undergoing development at any time, these figures show that erosion from construction sites contributes disproportionately to stream sedimentation.

To reduce erosion and sedimentation, Maryland adopted a Sediment Control Law in 1970 requiring that all construction projects be carried out in accordance with a grading and sediment control plan approved by the local Soil Conservation District. City and county development permit agencies are supposed to inspect construction sites and to enforce the required sediment control measures, such as dikes to divert stormwater runoff around the sites, straw mulch and cellulose fiber to cushion the impact of rain and to slow runoff, holding ponds to allow sediments to settle, and gravel sediment traps and low, fence-like barriers of permeable fabric to filter rain water before it flows from the site. At first, enforcement of such measures was lax, but government agencies and development contractors have been more observant of the law in recent years, so that now, in the law's third decade, the required procedures have finally become a normal and accepted part of the development process. If installed and maintained properly, the various control measures are estimated to reduce the outflow of sediments from construction sites by about 70 percent.

The dependence of Baltimore City on the cooperation of county Soil Conservation Districts and development permit agencies to encourage soil conservation practices and to enforce sediment control laws is typical of the economic and environmental dilemma faced by Baltimore's watershed managers. Several jurisdictions are involved, and often a cheap solution for one area's wastewater problem imposes injury and expense on a neighboring area. For example, in 1972 tests conducted by the federal Environmental Protection Agency indicated that algae growth in Loch Raven was rampant, stimulated in part by phosphates in the effluent from the Manchester and Hampstead sewage treatment plants in Carroll County. Equipment to remove some of the phosphorus was not installed until five years later, after Baltimore City, Baltimore County, Carroll County, and the state contributed the necessary funds.

A comprehensive and coordinated program to combat water pollution is the object of an agreement reached in 1984 among Baltimore City, Baltimore and Carroll counties, and the state. The program of action that has grown out of this agreement stresses several approaches to reduce chemical pollution and sedimentation. At the state level, the Department of the Environment is supposed to use its system of discharge permits to tighten control over municipal and industrial effluents from point sources of pollution—that is, pollution that comes from specific major sources, such as sewage treatment facilities and manufacturing and food processing plants. The sewage treatment plant at Hampstead has been upgraded still further, and at Manchester sewage effluent will be sprayed onto land instead of dumped into Big Gunpowder Falls.

As significant as pollution from point sources is, on a cumulative basis it is thought to be exceeded by pollution from nonpoint sources—that is, from a myriad of smaller sources such as stormwater runoff from fertilized fields, dairy pastures, livestock feedlots, and urban streets. Because of its widespread nature, nonpoint pollution is a particularly intractable problem.

Regarding agricultural pollution in Maryland, the county Soil Conservation Districts are supposed to take the lead toward reducing erosion and stormwater runoff from farm fields, pastures, and feedlots by encouraging the use of so-called Best Management Practices—or anti-pollution measures tailored to each farm. But as of 1993, plans to reduce runoff laden with manure and commercial fertilizers have been implemented on only about 10 percent of farmland in Maryland. The cooperation of farmers is sought with a carrot-and-stick approach. The carrot is the lure of financial assistance from state and federal agriculture departments to implement better farming practices, such as contour strip cropping, terracing, the construction of concrete pits for storing animal wastes, and the development of springs and erection of fences so that livestock are watered at drinking troughs rather than by wading into streams. The stick is the threat of legal action by the state Department of the Environment against farmers whose operations are egregiously bad—although in reality sanctions are never applied. Some environmentalists have urged that pollution-control planning be made mandatory for all farms that receive assistance from the Maryland Department of Agriculture or that have large numbers of animals or that apply manure to crops, but so far the formulation and implementation of best management plans is voluntary.

In more developed areas, the county health departments are charged with the responsibility to correct sanitation problems found in many old subdivisions and once-rural areas—problems such as failing septic systems, overburdened sewers, and pumping stations that sometimes leak or overflow into local streams.

In Baltimore County and to a lesser extent in Carroll County, policies have also been adopted to steer development away from sensitive areas, such as stream banks, flood plains, wetlands, and steep slopes. These policies are implemented by a process of reviewing construction projects on a case-by-case basis, and also by zoning. For example, in 1976 Baltimore County established a new Watershed Protection Zone covering areas near reservoirs and large tributaries. As of 1993 the requirements applicable in the Watershed Protection Zone specified a maximum density of 0.2 houses per acre. Thus, a hundred-acre tract can have no more than 20 houses, but the houses can be clustered on lots as small as 1 acre. Also, 70 percent of the overall site has to be maintained according to conservancy standards, meaning that fragile areas, forests, productive farmland, and other natural or at least rural features are to be left undisturbed.

As urban and suburban development spreads, stormwater runoff from roofs, streets, and parking lots becomes a major source of pollution. Not only is surface runoff from such areas contaminated with oil residues, toxic metals, and other wastes, but also the sheer volume of runoff is increased by the development of land. Comparisons of different kinds of environments show that forested areas account for the lowest volume of runoff per acre, in part because during light rains, much of the water never reaches the ground but instead is intercepted by leaves and bark, from which it later evaporates. Also, rain is absorbed by the thick layer of duff on the forest floor. Meadows yield the next lowest volume of runoff, followed by lawns and then by cultivated farm fields. Pavement and roofs, of course, result in substantial and immediate runoff, even during a light rain. During showers in the city and suburbs, storm sewers quickly flush the water into streams, loading the rivers with filth, swelling peak volumes, and increasing erosive energy.

To moderate this surge of stormwater runoff into local streams (some of which, of course, feed into the metropolitan reservoirs), regulations in Baltimore County aim to limit the amount of runoff that occurs after development to the same volume it was before. A developer of a small or low-density project may be allowed to build curb-less roads and grassy or rock-filled drainage swales that are sufficient to slow stormwater runoff, filter out dirt and debris, and increase percolation into the ground. But if these measures are not totally effective, infiltration basins and holding ponds may be required, fed in some cases by curbed roads and storm sewers.

AUTOMOBILE: Loch Raven is located north of Baltimore. The walk described here starts near the intersection of Loch Raven Drive and Morgan Mill Road.

From Interstate 695 (the Beltway) north of Baltimore, take Exit 27B for Route 146 (Dulaney Valley Road) north. Follow Route 146 north about 4.2 miles. Immediately after crossing a bridge over Loch Raven, bear right on Dulaney Valley Road where Jarrettsville Pike heads left. Continue on Dulaney Valley Road 1.7 miles. Where Dulaney Valley Road turns left at Peerce's Plantation Restaurant, go straight on Loch Raven Drive and follow it 1.0 mile to the intersection of Loch Raven Drive and Morgan Mill Road. Park near the intersection; pay close attention to signs indicating where parking is permitted and where (and when) it is not.

WALKING: (See Map 16 on page 172.) Start your walk on a fire road that leaves Morgan Mill Road 160 yards uphill from the intersection of Morgan Mill Road and Loch Raven Drive. With the reservoir downhill to your right, enter the woods on the fire road and follow it along the hillside, passing (after only 90 yards) a trail intersecting from the left. Continue along the hillside, with the reservoir visible downhill to the right through the trees. Follow the fire road as it gradually descends and passes another trail intersecting from the left—and by which you will return at the end of the walk. Continue straight on the wide path as it passes within a dozen yards of Loch Raven Drive. Follow the path up a ravine for about 200 yards, then turn right at the first trail junction. Follow a wide path up and then around to the left, with the land sloping off to the right toward the reservoir.

Follow the path as it eventually climbs away from Loch Raven to a four-way trail junction marked A on Map 16, and there turn right. After only 50 yards, pass

MAP 16 — Loch Raven: southeast highlands

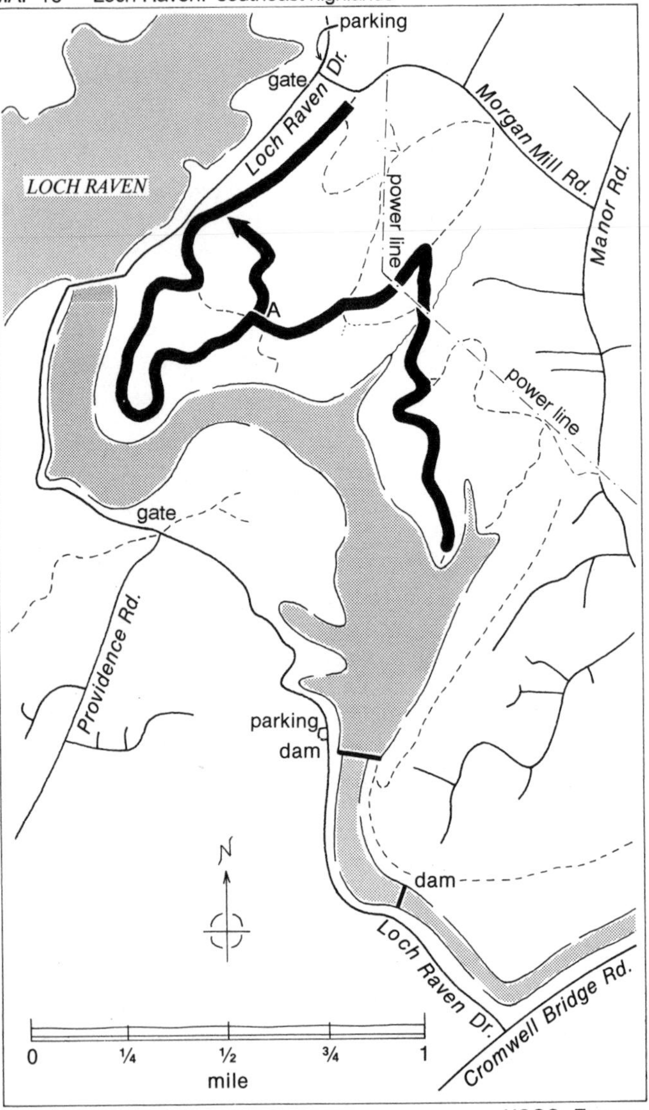

LOCH RAVEN

parking

gate

Loch Raven Dr.

Morgan Mill Rd.

Manor Rd.

power line

A

power line

gate

Providence Rd.

parking
dam

N

dam

Loch Raven Dr.

Cromwell Bridge Rd.

0   ¼   ½   ¾   1
mile

USGS: Towson

a trail intersecting from the right. Continue straight gradually uphill, then along a plateau. At an intersection by a gravelly clearing, bear right downhill. Pass under high power lines as you descend obliquely along the eroded, gullied path. Near the bottom of the ravine, turn sharply right and continue gradually downhill. Cross a stream under the power lines, then continue along the side of the valley and obliquely uphill. Just as the fire road reaches the top of the slope, fork right, then again bear right in a dozen yards. Follow the trail to the water's edge at the tip of a promontory.

To return to your car, go first back to the four-way trail junction at point A on Map 16, and there turn right. Follow the trail through the woods and downhill. At an intersection, turn sharply right and follow the path back to your starting point at Morgan Mill Road.

13

GUNPOWDER FALLS STATE PARK

Belair Road to Harford Road

Walking and mountain bicycling—up to 9.0 miles (14.5 kilometers) round-trip. The route shown by the bold line on Map 17 on page 181 follows the riverbank of Big Gunpowder Falls through a deep, wooded valley. Continue as far as you want, then return by the way you came. Although level and not particularly strenuous, the trail is rough in places. Now surrounded by suburbia, this gorge is a remarkable wilderness enclave.

The park is open daily from sunrise to sunset. Dogs must be leashed. The park is managed by the Department of Natural Resources, Maryland Forest, Park and Wildlife Service; telephone 592-2897.

THIS WALK IS THE FIRST OF THREE starting at the Belair Road bridge over Big Gunpowder Falls and focusing on the stretch of river below Loch Raven Dam. On the south bank, the riverside path extends upstream to the Harford Road bridge through a deep gorge. On the north bank upstream from Belair Road, the circle path explores the valley slopes and upland. Downstream, the trail follows the river toward the edge of the fall zone where the Gunpowder leaves its Piedmont valley and enters the Coastal Plain. Throughout the length of all three excursions, the valley slopes are covered with woods.

At high water the river is swift, powerful, and sometimes turbulent. At low water (or no water), its bed is a broad, bare swath of cobbles and boulders.

≈ ≈ ≈ ≈

If by now you have taken some of the walks outlined in this book, you probably have noticed a certain sameness in our local landscape. With the exception of Anne Arundel County, the countryside in the Baltimore region is characterized by rolling uplands dissected by an intricate system of ravines, valleys, and gorges. This landscape is as good a place as any to examine the erosional cycle by which running water carves into an elevated region and over the ages reduces it to a lower plain.

Stream erosion is the dominant force shaping the world's landforms. Whenever any part of the earth's crust is raised above sea level, either by uplift of the land or withdrawal of the ocean as water is amassed in continental glaciers and the polar ice caps, the newly elevated surface is at once subject to the erosive power of running water. Any downward-pitched trough, even though at first shallow or insignificant, is self-aggrandizing, collecting the rainwater that falls on other areas. Initially, many minor watercourses are dry between rains, but others may be fed seasonally by melting snow or even continuously by melting glaciers or the outflow from wetlands where precipitation is stored for a period before continuing its journey to the sea. Gradually, the watercourses deepen with erosion, and once they penetrate the water table, they are fed by a steady seepage of groundwater from the sides of the gullies and ravines.

As a stream extends itself by developing tributaries, its erosive power rapidly increases. The larger drainage area concentrates more water in the channel downstream, where stream energy is swelled by the greater mass of moving water. In consequence, the speed of the river increases and so does its ability to carry fine clay, silt, and sand in suspension, to abrade and wear down rocks, and to push and roll pebbles and cobbles downstream.

Although the process of erosion is ceaseless, it of course speeds up during periods of peak flow. Annual spring thaws swell our region's rivers, but far more significant are the protracted and spectacular thaws that follow episodes of continental glaciation. The most recent incursion of continental ice to extend southward from eastern Canada into New England, New York, and northern Pennsylvania ended about 12,000 years ago, and during the two or three millennia of melting that followed, rivers like the Susquehanna and Delaware were far more voluminous and more erosive than they are today.

During North America's current interlude from continental glaciation, most erosion in our region is attributable to a relatively few heavy rains each year or two and—even more so— to less frequent but spectacular flood rains. Although these infrequent events may seem freakish, over thousands of years they are commonplace and may even be said to occur with regularity. In Maryland 2 inches of rain in 24 hours is termed a "two-year storm." It fills streams to their banks and causes severe erosion. Five inches of rain in 24 hours is a ten-year storm, and 7 inches is a hundred-year storm. And 27 inches of rainfall in 6 hours is the storm that dams must be built to withstand. During the 1868 Patapsco flood (discussed in Chapter 1), 18 inches of rain fell in half an hour. Confined to a gorge like the Patapsco or Gunpowder valleys, such a torrent can in a few hours do what is normally the erosive work of centuries, moving tremendous amounts of earth in the turbulent floodwater.

Although at first erosion is fastest in the lower reaches of a river where volume is greater, the ocean constitutes a base level below which the stream cannot cut to any significant degree. As downward cutting approaches the base level, the site of the most rapid erosion moves slowly upstream.

Meanwhile, the lower river still possesses great energy. The current erodes the bank wherever the stream is deflected by each slight turn. This tendency to carve wider and wider curves is present along the entire stream but is accentuated in the lower reaches, where downward cutting is no longer possible but where sideward cutting can continue as long as there is flow. Gradually, a meandering course develops as the river snakes back and forth, eroding first one side of the valley and then the other. When sinuosity becomes so extreme that the curves loop back on themselves, the current will intercept the channel farther downstream, cutting off the looping meander. Thus, as millennia pass, the river migrates in an ever-changing course over the bottomland, creating a valley much wider than it is deep and leaving behind abandoned channels here and there.

Another distinctive geologic feature develops at the mouth of the river where it empties into an ocean, estuary, or lake. As the current dissipates in the standing water, the capacity of the stream to carry material in suspension is reduced and then eliminated, so that the river's load of gravel, sand, and silt is dropped and forms a delta, as has occurred where Big Gunpowder Falls flows into Chesapeake Bay. Because the current slows gradually, the deposits tend to be sorted, with larger, heavier particles dropped first (all very convenient for the sand and gravel companies that mine these areas). After the delta has extended itself a considerable distance in one direction, a flood may cut a new and shorter channel to open water, causing the former course to be abandoned, at least for a period. Deltas typically have several channels or sets of channels among which the stream shifts as deposits are concentrated first in one and then in another.

Examining the variables of stream gradient, valley depth, valley width, and number of meanders will indicated the state of development that has been reached by any stretch of river. In the earliest stage, gullies and ravines eat into the elevated land surface. Because the dominant direction of cutting is downward, the gullies and ravines are steep-sided and V-shaped, eventually becoming major valleys, such as those of Big Gunpowder Falls and the Patapsco River. The gradient of the stream bed is steep compared to navigable waterways. Rapids are common. There are only minor flats in the valley bottom. Valley depth relative to width is at its maximum. Such a stream is said to be in *youth*.

As the stream approaches base level, its gradient diminishes and downward cutting slows. Bends in the course of the stream become accentuated, and the width of the valley increases relative to its depth. At the point where sideward cutting becomes significant and a flat valley floor starts to develop, the stream is said to be in *maturity*.

Finally, when downward cutting has ceased and the stream is at base level, sideward cutting produces a nearly flat and featureless valley, much wider than it is deep, across which the river meanders from side to side. Such an eroded surface is called a *peneplain*. The gradient is low and the broad bottom-land is marked only by the scars, swamps, and lakes left by former channels. Perhaps a few rock hummocks and hills— more resistant to erosion than were their surroundings—are left rising above the plain. This stage of river development is *old age*. Meanwhile, the countless gullies and ravines at the river's headwaters remain youthful as they continue to fan outward like the roots of a growing tree, so that the watershed becomes larger and larger, perhaps even intercepting and diverting to itself (or *capturing*) streams that previously took a different course to the sea.

The terms *youth, maturity,* and *old age* can also be applied to an entire landscape or region to describe the extent to which it has been acted upon by stream erosion. As an upland region experiences the headward erosion of a stream system, more and more of the landscape is given over to a branching network of steep-sided gullies, ravines, and valleys, which gradually widen and develop flat valley bottoms. An area is said to be in youth until about half of the original upland is consumed by valley slopes and the streams are just beginning to develop flats at the valley bottoms. As the percentage of upland diminishes and the portion in the valley flats increases, the area is in maturity. At some point the upland lying between different stream systems is cut away until the divide changes from a wide, flat summit to a sharp-crested ridge that in turn is worn down to a low, rounded rise. Old age is said to start when more than half of the region is in valley bottom, and it continues as the whole region is gradually reduced to a peneplain. Thus, in general, youth is the time of dominant upland, maturity the time of dominant valley slope, and old age the time of dominant valley bottom.

Such, at any rate, is the general model. Of course, the terms *youth, maturity,* and *old age* do not describe the actual age of a stream or landscape, but only its stage of erosional development. Also, the appearance of any particular stretch of river is determined largely by the durability and structure of the materials through which the stream flows, and the terrain along even a single river can reflect different stages of erosion in no particular sequence, depending on the resistance of the underlying materials.

Turning to the Maryland landscape at hand, as you approach Big Gunpowder Falls and walk along the river or through any of the other stream valleys discussed in this book, study the landscape to determine the degree to which it conforms to the pattern outlined above.

AUTOMOBILE: The section of Gunpowder Falls State Park explored by this walk is located northeast of Baltimore. The walk starts where Belair Road crosses Big Gunpowder Falls.

From Interstate 695 (the Beltway) northeast of Baltimore, take Exit 32B for Route 1 north toward Bel Air. Follow Route 1 (Belair Road) about 5.4 miles to the bridge over Big Gunpowder Falls. Immediately after crossing the bridge, turn right into the parking lot for

MAP 17 — Belair Road to Harford Road

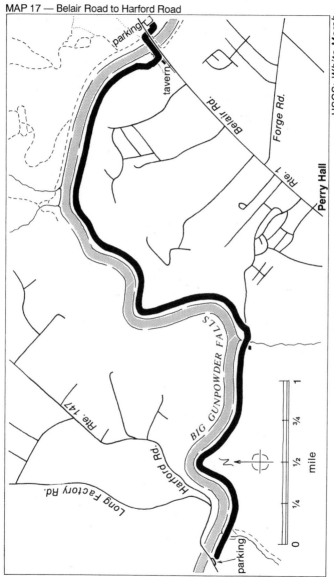

USGS: *White Marsh*

parking

tavern

Belair Rd.

Forge Rd.

Rte. 1

Perry Hall

Rte. 147

Harford Rd.

Long Factory Rd.

BIG GUNPOWDER FALLS

parking

N

0   ¼   ½   ¾   1

mile

Gunpowder Falls State Park, Central Area, Big
Gunpowder Trail.

WALKING and MOUNTAIN BICYCLING: (See
Map 17 on page 181.) From the parking area, descend
to the tunnel at the near end of the bridge. Go under
Belair Road, then immediately turn left to follow the trail
that crosses the bridge on the upstream side.

At the far end of the bridge, bear right and follow a
gravel ramp downhill next to a tavern. Continue
straight across a grassy area. Cross a stream and
continue into the forest on a narrow footpath that
winds though the woods and eventually reaches the
river's edge. For the first quarter mile, the trail does not
amount to much, but conditions improve once the trail
reaches the river.

With the water on your right, follow the riverside
footpath for as long as you care to walk, keeping in
mind that you will return by the same route. Be alert for
places where the trail is undermined by erosion or
animal burrows. The path stretches 4.5 miles to
Harford Road. At 3.0 miles, the trail reaches a road and
passes to the right of a brick sewage treatment building, then continues along the river's edge. Near
Harford Road the trail fords a stream that during high
water can be more easily crossed on the rocks a few
dozen yards upstream; do not cross, however, if the
water is flowing over the rocks.

The headquarters for Gunpowder Falls State Park is on the
north bank of the river a short distance downstream from the
Harford Road bridge—although plans call for the headquarters
to be moved to Jerusalem Mill (Chapter 16) after the mill is
restored. Also along Harford Road north of the bridge are

several stone structures (some of them have been converted to private residences) that were originally part of the Gunpowder Copper Works. The copper works were constructed in the first decade of the nineteenth century by Levi Hollingsworth, who supplied the United States Navy with copper sheathing for ships during the War of 1812. His plant also rolled the copper for the dome of the national Capitol when it was rebuilt after the original building had been burned by the British in 1814. Hollingsworth's dome lasted until the 1860s. The copper works remained in operation until the 1860s or '70s.

Further reading: My discussion of the cycle of erosion is based on Robert M. Garrels *A Textbook of Geology* (Harper & Brothers) for general theory and *Maryland Geological Survey: Baltimore County* (Johns Hopkins Press) for local specifics. Martin F. Schmidt, Jr. has written *Maryland's Geology* (Tidewater).

14

GUNPOWDER FALLS STATE PARK

Stockdale Road and valley rim

Walking and mountain bicycling—3.5 miles (5.6 kilometers). The route is shown by the bold line on Map 18 on page 189. From Belair Road head upstream along the river's edge on old Stockdale Road, now a gravel and dirt path closed to cars. The path eventually climbs the side of the valley. Return on dirt roads and paths through former farmland now planted in pines.

For a slightly longer excursion, you can also explore the spur trail that continues upstream along the river to Long Green Creek. Yet other trails lead downstream from the parking lot, as described in Chapter 15 and shown on Map 19 on page 197.

The park is open daily from sunrise to sunset. Dogs must be leashed. The park is managed by the Department of Natural Resources, Maryland Forest, Park and Wildlife Service; telephone 592-2897.

IN TERMS OF THE STAGES of stream development discussed in the preceding chapter, the stretch of Big Gunpowder Falls traversed by this walk is still young. The river flows in a steep-sided valley. Only narrow strips of bottomland flats border the river, and there are some places where the sides of the valley slope directly into the water. Although the gorge itself twists and turns, the channel does not meander but rather is confined by the valley walls.

However, 3 miles below the Belair Road bridge the river leaves its rocky Piedmont valley and flows out over the Coastal Plain, composed of gravel, sand, silt, and clay deposited either as marine or delta sediments during periods when the region was submerged beneath the ocean. Since the beginning of the Pleistocene epoch (or Ice Age) in North America about a million years ago, the sea has advanced and receded across the Coastal Plain many times, depending on how much of the planet's water was amassed in continental glaciers. As would be expected, the relative ease of erosion in the soft marine and deltaic sediments has enabled the rivers that now cross the coastal zone to advance rapidly into maturity and even old age. For example, when Big Gunpowder Falls reaches the Coastal Plain, the valley walls dwindle and disappear. The river flows slowly within mud and gravel banks over a broad lowland marked by former channels that now are located far from the present course of the river. The Gunpowder has even had time to develop a large delta in the vicinity of Day's Cove.

Marking the transition between Piedmont and Coastal Plain is the so-called fall line, which is not really a sharp line but rather a zone of considerable width. Within the fall zone, the uplands are covered by a tapering layer of Coastal Plain sediments, but the stream channels penetrate to the underlying Piedmont rocks. Also, waterfalls and rapids are not confined to the fall zone but frequently extend dozens of miles upstream, as is the case on the Gunpowder Falls and Patapsco River. In Maryland, the railroad tracks linking Philadelphia, Baltimore, and Washington follow the eastern edge of the fall zone because the route combines level terrain with narrow river crossings.

Although in most respects Big Gunpowder Falls conforms to the pattern of stream development discussed in the preceding chapter, several anomalies exist. One curiosity is that some of the Gunpowder's tributary valleys, such as the Dulaney and Cockeysville valleys, have smooth, broad (in other words, *old*) profiles compared to the relatively youthful main gorge farther downstream, even though the tributaries necessarily are of more recent origin than the section of river below them. The tributaries, it turns out, flow through areas underlain by Cockeysville marble, which (because it is limestone) dissolves more easily than the gneiss, serpentine, granite, gabbro, and other hard crystalline rocks that predominate throughout the region. Thus, the terrain along a river can reflect different stages of erosional development in no particular sequence, depending on the underlying rock.

The variety of rock types, their different degrees of resistance to erosion, and complications in their structure may also have contributed to some of the abrupt twists and turns that occur in the valley of Big Gunpowder Falls. For the most part, however, the Gunpowder and its many tributaries show the spreading, rootlike pattern of a dendritic stream system, as is typical in areas where there is no systematic rock structure that dictates the pattern of erosion.

Another anomaly is evident in Maryland's Piedmont upland, which consists of gentle, rounded hills characteristic of a mature stream system. Yet the rolling landscape is further dissected by a youthful system of gorges and ravines. This combination of features suggests that the entire Piedmont, after being shaped by erosion into a region of moderate, rounded ridges and broad valleys, was uplifted. The rise of the land increased stream gradients and renewed the ability of rivers to erode downward. As a result, youthful gorges were cut into the old surface, producing the present landscape in which the gentle slopes and broad bottomlands of the former valleys remain as elevated shoulders above the entrenched gorges. In the terminology of geologists, such a process of regional uplift and renewed erosion is called *rejuvenation*.

There is evidence in Maryland and along the East Coast that

the uplift of the Piedmont has not progressed at a steady rate relative to sea level, which itself has fluctuated. After each uplift, the land along the coast was exposed to the horizontal cutting action of waves and meandering rivers. In consequence, on a regional scale the topography of both the Piedmont and the Coastal Plain roughly forms a flight of terracelike surfaces that parallel the coast and even extend upstream in the major river valleys.

AUTOMOBILE: The section of Gunpowder Falls State Park explored by this walk is located northeast of Baltimore. The walk starts where Belair Road crosses Big Gunpowder Falls.

From Interstate 695 (the Beltway) northeast of Baltimore, take Exit 32B for Route 1 north toward Bel Air. Follow Route 1 (Belair Road) about 5.4 miles to the bridge over Big Gunpowder Falls. Immediately after crossing the bridge, turn right into the parking lot for Gunpowder Falls State Park, Central Area, Big Gunpowder Trail.

WALKING and MOUNTAIN BICYCLING: (See Map 18 opposite.) From the parking area, descend to the tunnel at the near end of the bridge. Go under Belair Road, then continue straight into the woods on a path. With the river on your left, follow the track (Old Stockdale Road) for about 0.7 mile, then fork slightly right—and slightly uphill—away from the river on the old road. (The footpath that continues along the river crosses Sweathouse Branch after about half a mile and from there goes on for a few hundred yards to Long Green Creek, where there is a minor but pleasant cascade. If you want to lengthen your excursion, you can take this spur, then return for the rest of the walk described below.)

MAP 18 — Stockdale Road and valley rim

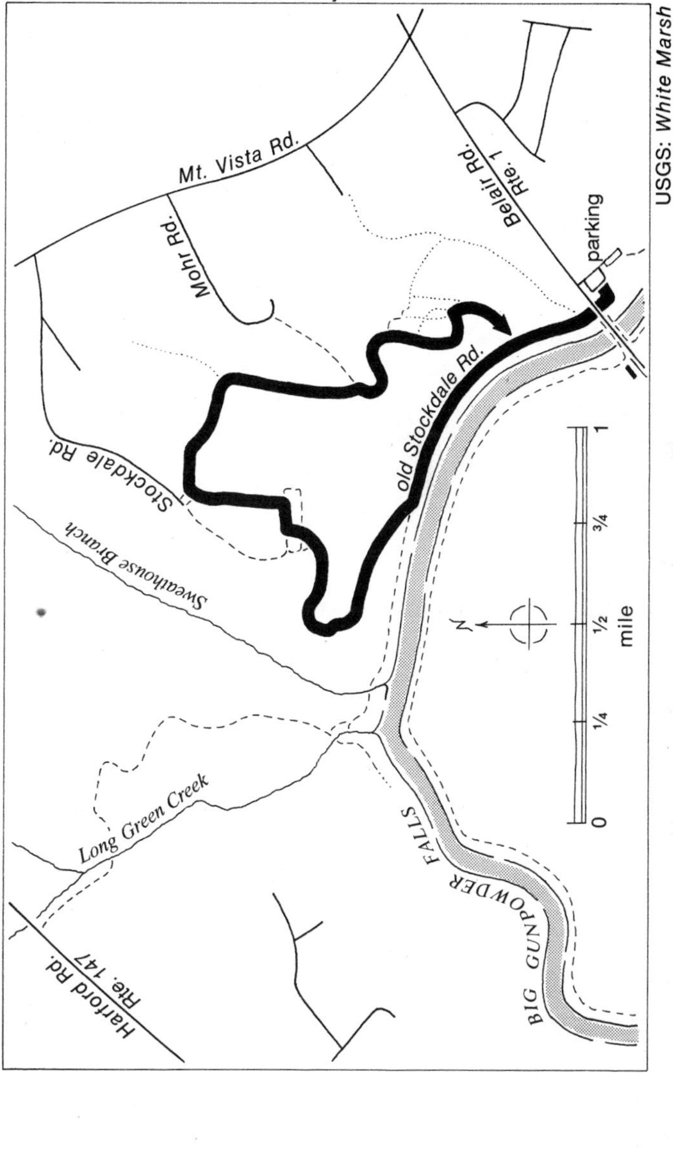

USGS: *White Marsh*

Mt. Vista Rd.

Mohr Rd.

Belair Rte. 1

parking

old Stockdale Rd.

Stockdale Rd.

Sweathouse Branch

Long Green Creek

Harford Rd.
Rte. 147

FALLS

BIG GUNPOWDER

N

0   ¼   ½   ¾   1
mile

After forking right away from the river, follow the main track as it climbs obliquely along the side of the valley and curves to the right. Continue uphill to the rim of the valley. Go through a pine plantation, passing trails that intersect from either side. At a T-intersection, turn right to follow the main track, then turn left in 170 yards to continue on the main path.

As you approach two houses located on a gravel road, turn right back into the woods on a wide path starting next to a log cribbing. Continue through the woods on the wide path, passing a trail intersecting from the left. Eventually, after passing a pine plantation on the left, turn right at a T-intersection. Pass through areas that are relatively unwooded and sunny; here the trailside brush sometimes grows so rapidly that it obscures the path. Plow straight ahead. (If you look closely, you will see traces of fences, gateposts, and foundations indicating that this area was once a farmyard; the pine plantations occupy former fields.)

Follow the path to the right of a cement-block shed, now in an advanced state of ruin and so overgrown with brush that you might not even notice it. Continue downhill with a pine plantation on your left, at one point passing a trail intersecting from the left. Follow the main track as it curves left around the end of the pine plantation and climbs a small rise. Fifty-five yards past the top of the rise, turn right downhill onto a narrow and obscure footpath. Follow the footpath downhill and gradually to the right along the side of the ravine. (You can help to maintain this trail by breaking off twigs that grow out into the path.)

Eventually, cross a stream, then turn left onto the riverside trail. With the river on your right, follow the path to Belair Road.

15

GUNPOWDER FALLS STATE PARK

Belair Road to Route 40

Walking—up to 8.0 miles (12.9 kilometers) round-trip. As shown by the bold line on Map 19 on page 197, a footpath extends along the south bank of Big Gunpowder Falls from Belair Road downstream past Philadelphia Road to Route 40 (Pulaski Highway). Hike as far as you want along the rocky river and return by the way you came. As you approach Route 40, the landscape changes from Piedmont to Coastal Plain. Although level and not particularly strenuous, the trail is rough in places.

As shown on the map, a horse trail (sometimes very muddy) extends downstream from Belair Road along the north bank of the river for about 2 miles.

The park is open daily from sunrise to sunset. Dogs must be leashed. The park is managed by the Department of Natural Resources, Maryland Forest, Park and Wildlife Service; telephone 592-2897.

THIS RIVERSIDE WALK passes the sites—and in a few cases, the relics—of some of the iron furnaces, forges, nail factories, and other industrial operations that were located along Big Gunpowder Falls above and below Philadelphia

Road during the eighteenth and nineteenth centuries. The early ironworks needed waterpower just like any other mill. Low rock and wooden dams created a fall of water that turned a water wheel; through a series of gears and cams, the wheel operated the bellows for the smelting furnaces and forges, and also the mechanical hammers that beat the white-hot pig iron to remove impurities and to flatten it into plates and bars that could later be worked or cast into useful objects.

In 1719 Maryland's colonial legislature established a legal procedure to encourage the development of water power for the production of iron. The law stated in part: ". . . . be it Enacted that if any person or persons shall desire to set up a forging mill or other convenience for carrying on Iron Works on land not before cultivated adjoining a stream, he may get a writ *ad quod damnum*"—that is, a writ of land condemnation. If the owner of the land refused to build a forge himself, the petitioner was granted a deed for 100 acres, "the owner being paid for it." The law further provided: "If pig iron is not run in seven years, the grant is void." Not fewer than twenty-three of these writs of private condemnation were granted between 1733 and 1767, most of which resulted in ironworks being built.

One forge site on Big Gunpowder Falls was the Long Calm, where Philadelphia Road used to ford the stream. (The Long Calm is located upstream from the present-day Interstate 95 bridge.) A forge was built here in 1757 by the Nottingham Company. Because the owners of the Nottingham Company were either British or Loyalists, their property was expropriated during the Revolution by the state Office of Confiscated Effects, whose ledgers show the site to have included "Forges, Sawmill, Gristmill, Forge Dam, Water Courses, and Many Improvements." In 1781 the state auctioned the Nottingham works to Charles Ridgely and Company. Under Ridgely's ownership the forge manufactured a variety of products, as indicated by a newspaper advertisement:

Cannon (from Nine to Two-pounders), Bar-Iron, pig iron, pots from 15 gallons to three quarts, kettles from 45 to 15 gallons; Dutch-ovens, tea-kettles, skillets, salt-pans, flat irons, mortars and pestles, wagon-boxes, stoves, dripping pans and bakers. . . . N. B. Castings of any sort made on the shortest notice.

In 1795 Ridgely's Nottingham Forge burned to the ground, but was rebuilt. Forty years later, when David Ridgely tried unsuccessfully to sell the property, it was described in the advertisement as including a new dam and two forges, one new and the other built in 1827 for rolling out iron strapping to make barrel hoops.

By 1840 the plant was operated under lease by Horace Abbott and Company, which had a subcontract to make engine parts for the *Kamchatka*, a steam frigate being built in New York for the Russian navy. A reporter for the *American* visited the forges at the Long Calm and wrote:

I proceeded to the other works on the Falls of the Great Gunpowder River, 14 miles from Baltimore near the Philadelphia Turnpike. This establishment was fitted up by these gentlemen for the purpose of making a heavier kind of work. The hammer which they have erected is driven by a powerful water wheel, 22 feet in diameter, with 14.5-foot buckets, assisted by a fly wheel of 18 tons weight. There are two air furnaces besides several large fires for heating. When I was there, the workmen had just completed the main center shaft for the Russian steam frigate above alluded to. This shaft is the largest ever made in this country, being 14.5 feet in length and 18.5 inches in diameter, and is estimated to weigh *thirteen thousand* pounds.

In 1845 David Ridgely sold the forges at the Long Calm to Robert Howard, who the next year built an iron-smelting furnace farther downstream just west of Philadelphia Road. In 1856 this furnace produced 1,100 tons of iron during thirty weeks of continuous blast. Two years later, however, Howard's forges and furnace on Big Gunpowder Falls were put out of operation permanently by a flood that destroyed the dam and cracked the furnace.

AUTOMOBILE: The section of Gunpowder Falls State Park explored by this walk is located northeast of Baltimore. The walk starts where Belair Road crosses Big Gunpowder Falls.

From Interstate 695 (the Beltway) northeast of Baltimore, take Exit 32B for Route 1 north toward Bel Air. Follow Route 1 (Belair Road) about 5.4 miles to the bridge over Big Gunpowder Falls. Immediately after crossing the bridge, turn right into the parking lot for Gunpowder Falls State Park, Central Area, Big Gunpowder Trail.

WALKING: (See Map 19 opposite.) From the parking area, descend to the trail that crosses the bridge on the downstream side. After crossing the bridge, turn left. With the river on your left, follow the footpath downstream though the woods and along the bank. Be alert for places where the path is being undermined by erosion or animal burrows. Now and then the trail splits but soon rejoins. Also, sometimes the trail is obscure, but you cannot get lost; simply keep the river on your left.

Approximately 200 yards upstream from the Interstate 95 bridge, the path abruptly rises a few feet and passes above—and to the right of—the stone abutment of what was once a wooden dam. There is a matching abutment on the opposite bank. The dam supplied water to power Robert Howard's nineteenth-century ironworks at the Long Calm. The low earthen ridge extending from the abutment away from the river toward

Map 19 — Belair Road to Route 40

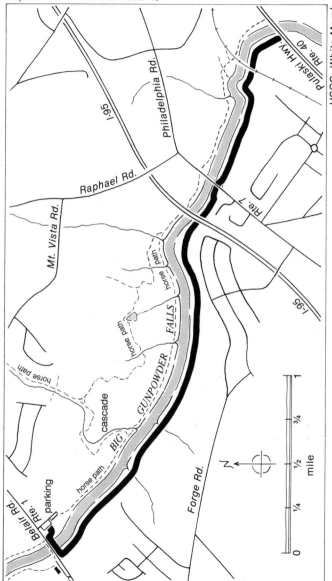

USGS: White Marsh

higher land was, of course, part of the dam. Presumably Howard's millrace ran along the side of the valley to his forge farther downstream at the Philadelphia Road. The intake for the race appears to have been located about 25 yards in from the dam abutment. The land in the vicinity of the I-95 bridge has been completely regraded, but starting about 50 yards downstream from the concrete apron below the bridge, the path is unusually level for 75 yards, and for part of that distance it is supported by a stone retaining wall, all of which may indicate that the path there follows the route of the millrace.

Continue under the Interstate 95 bridge, then follow the path toward another bridge at Philadelphia Road.

A bridge—the Forges Bridge—was first built at Philadelphia Road in 1822, a few years after the road itself was moved from the ford at the Long Calm.

Pass under the bridge at Philadelphia Road, then bear obliquely up the embankment to an old road, now closed to cars. With the river on your left, continue downstream on the old road, which eventually reaches an area now overgrown with weeds and brush.

An expanse of rocks and gravel next to the river (and just upstream from the railroad bridge) is a good place to stop if you do not want to continue downstream 0.2 mile to Route 40—although if you stop here, you will miss the transition to the visibly different terrain and substance of the Coastal Plain. To continue to Route 40, follow the path under the railroad bridge and along the muddy, sandy embankment, then return by the way you came.

As noted above, downstream from the present-day Philadelphia Road bridge, the asphalt path leads 0.5 mile to a circular area of weeds and brush. This was the site of the Joppa Iron

Works, also known as Big Gunpowder Mills or the Patterson Iron Works. The works were constructed in 1817, and by 1820 fifteen men and six boys were employed producing sheet iron, barrel hoops, spikes, cut nails, and brads. By 1850 the Patterson Iron Works employed 130 hands producing 36,000 kegs of nails annually. The following year the works were rebuilt on a larger scale to include six puddling furnaces, one heating furnace, one water-driven hammer, two trains of rolls to produce sheet iron, and thirty-seven nail machines to cut nails from the sheets. The works continued in operation until the 1860s, after which they were dismantled. In 1913 a distillery was built on the old ironworks foundations. The distillery buildings survived until the property was acquired for park purposes in 1970.

On the opposite bank of the river, a small cut-stone puddling furnace is built into a cleft in the rock back a few dozen yards from the river's edge next to the rapids. These rapids, incidentally, are the last on Big Gunpowder Falls.

Return to Belair Road by the way you came. Although it is possible to cross the river at Route 40 and to follow the north bank back to Belair Road, I do not recommend it. For one thing, there is not presently any sidewalk on the bridge, so using it to cross the river on foot is unsafe. Also, the riverside path along the north bank is in very poor condition for more than half a mile downstream from the Interstate 95 bridge. Nor is there any good way to cross the apron of concrete that slopes steeply into the river under the Interstate 95 bridge.

However, if you do not mind the sometimes muddy conditions, the horse trail along the north side of the river between Belair Road and Interstate 95 is pleasant. About 200 yards upstream from the Interstate 95 bridge is the abutment of Robert Howard's dam at the Long Calm.

16

GUNPOWDER FALLS STATE PARK

Little Gunpowder Falls: Jerusalem Mill and Jericho Bridge

Walking—5.5 miles (8.8 kilometers) round-trip. This is one of our region's best opportunities to walk back in time. As shown by the bold line on Map 20 on page 205, a footpath extends from Belair Road downstream along the northeast side of Little Gunpowder Falls to the old mill at Jerusalem Road, and from there follows the river's southwest bank to the covered bridge at Jericho Road. Return by the way you came. Although the trail is rough in a few spots, particularly where it fords Wildcat Branch, it is well-marked with blazes and is easily passable. For much of the way it follows the streambank, but at times ascends the side of the valley high above the river.

The park is open daily from sunrise to sunset. Dogs must be leashed. The park is managed by the Department of Natural Resources, Maryland Forest, Park and Wildlife Service; telephone 592-2897.

MAKE A PILGRIMAGE to Jerusalem along Little Gunpowder Falls, which forms the boundary between Baltimore and Harford counties. A predilection for alliterative biblical place-names is also evident in nearby Jericho and Joppa (a variant of Jaffa).

Like the Big Gunpowder Falls, the Little Gunpowder formerly was bordered by a succession of water-powered mills, including the eighteenth-century Jerusalem Mill. Shown in the photograph on page 200, this old mill still stands, although its restoration—scheduled to start in 1993—may entail dismantling the building and rebuilding it with mostly new materials. When restoration is complete, the Park Service plans to relocate the headquarters of Gunpowder Falls State Park from Harford Road to Jerusalem, and also to open part of the mill as a museum.

Jerusalem Mill was founded in 1772 by David Lee, a Quaker who—like the Ellicotts—moved here from Bucks County Pennsylvania. Lee bought Jerusalem from Isaiah Linton, who already operated a sawmill and perhaps also a gristmill at the site. For its day the new structure erected by Lee was a large mill, which Lee operated on a merchant basis, buying wheat outright in large quantities from farmers and selling the flour on his own account, rather than merely grinding grain for a share of the product, as was done at smaller country mills. Lee also ran a farm, and during the Revolution he manufactured gunstocks and (according to some accounts) assembled flintlock guns. For this less-than-pacifistic enterprise, the Fallston Friends Meeting reprimanded him in 1776.

Lee's son Ralph and grandson David (he built the large house that still stands near the mill) carried on the milling business. Ralph Lee's customers included Baltimore's Jewish community, which annually sent a representative to the mill to oversee the grinding of wheat and to certify, by stamping the barrels, that the flour was fit for use at Passover. One object of this inspection was to make sure that the flour had minimal moisture content (moisture causes flour to ferment slightly) and was therefore suitable for making unleavened bread.

Owned by the Lee family for at least 125 years, the mill continued in operation under other owners until the death of the last miller in 1961, when it was bought by the state. During the middle third of this century, the mill ground feed for farmers in Baltimore and Harford counties and produced buckwheat flour and cornmeal. The miller also sold gasoline, beer, soft drinks, cigarettes and candy. Even as late as mid-century, the works were powered by an overshot waterwheel, but in the final years of operation, the mill ran on electricity after a flood breached the dam.

The plan for Gunpowder Falls State Park has from the beginning included restoration of Jerusalem Mill, but for thirty years after the state acquired it the building was allowed to deteriorate to the point where much of it can no longer be saved. The cost of tearing down the upper floors, salvaging what is still in good condition (such as its beams measuring 2 feet square in cross section), and rebuilding with new materials is expected to approach $2 million.

Isaiah Linton (who had sold the Jerusalem tract to David Lee) also sold a site downstream in 1772 to Elisha Tyson, another Quaker miller. Tyson operated Jericho Mill before moving to Baltimore, where he became a locally prominent abolitionist. Jericho covered bridge was built in 1865. Its present structure includes artfully-concealed steel reinforcement installed in 1983. Such bridges were originally covered to prevent the wooden trusses from rotting.

AUTOMOBILE: The section of Gunpowder Falls State Park explored by this walk is located northeast of Baltimore. The walk starts where Belair Road crosses Little Gunpowder Falls at the boundary between Baltimore and Harford counties.

From Interstate 695 (the Beltway) northeast of Baltimore, take Exit 32B for Route 1 north toward Bel Air.

Follow Route 1 (Belair Road) 9.4 miles. Just before crossing the bridge into Harford County at Little Gunpowder Falls, turn left into a roadside parking area paved with gravel.

WALKING: (See Map 20 opposite.) With caution, cross Belair Road, then cross the bridge. About 20 yards beyond the bridge, turn right into the woods at a sign declaring, "Harford County Welcomes You." With Little Falls on your right, head downstream on a path marked with white blazes.

Follow the white-blazed trail to Wildcat Branch, a tributary that joins Little Gunpowder Falls from the left. Follow Wildcat Branch upstream about 15 yards. Because the level of the water fluctuates widely, you will have to judge for yourself whether conditions are safe for you to cross Wildcat Branch here. If you feel uncomfortable about crossing, look for a better place or turn back.

After crossing, continue on the white-blazed trail. With Wildcat Branch downhill on your left, follow the side of the valley gradually uphill, then eventually bear right away from Wildcat Branch. Climb through the woods, then—with Little Gunpowder Falls downhill on your right—follow the side of the valley downstream. Descend past a junction with a blue-blazed trail on the right. Pass under a power line and follow the white blazes uphill through the woods, then downhill and across a small stream. Again pass the blue-blazed trail where it intersects from the right. After skirting a clearing, turn right downhill on the narrow, white-blazed trail. With the river toward your right, descend to the bottomland and continue downstream, then along a trough that is the old Jerusalem Mill headrace. Turn right out of the race and follow the path to Jerusalem Mill at Jerusalem Road.

MAP 20 — Jerusalem and Jericho

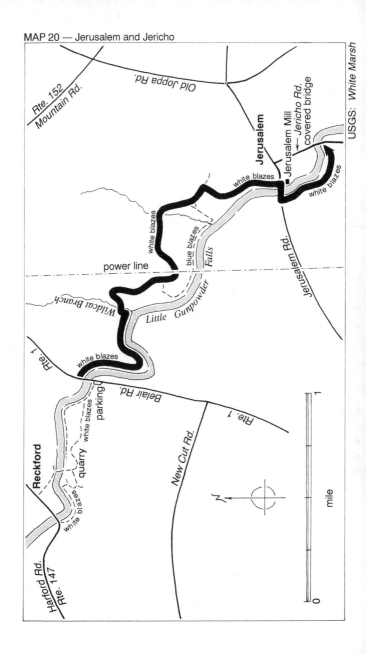

USGS: *White Marsh*

From Jerusalem Mill, cross Little Gunpowder Falls with caution on the road bridge, then turn left across the guardrail and descend the embankment. With the river on your left, follow the white-blazed trail downstream to the covered bridge at Jericho Road.

Return to Belair Road by the way you came—except that you may want, for the sake of variety, to follow the blue-blazed trail shown on Map 20 for part of the distance.

17

NORTH POINT STATE PARK and FORT HOWARD PARK

Walking—up to 5.0 miles (8 kilometers) at North Point State Park. Map 21 on page 221 shows the park as of 1993, and Map 22 on page 223 shows the park as the Department of Natural Resources proposes to develop it as time goes on. Many people (I am one of them) think that the state's plan overdevelops the waterfront area at the jetty; you may want to think about the issue, which is discussed on pages 216 through 220, when you visit this remarkable bayside park.

North Point State Park offers pleasant walking through woods and past farm fields to the shore of Chesapeake Bay, where there is a small beach and a long jetty providing views up and down the coast. The beach is never lifeguarded, so people who want to go wading (the water is too shallow for swimming) do so at their own risk. Also, a spur trail leads north through the woods to the heart of Black Marsh, which is best visited during late fall, winter, and early spring, when mosquitoes and flies are absent. The terrain is level, the walking easy, the scenery varied, and the atmosphere thoroughly tranquil and low-keyed.

North Point State Park is open Wednesday through Sunday (plus Monday holidays) from 8 to 4 in winter and from 10 to 6 during the period that daylight saving time is in effect. It is closed Thanksgiving and Christmas. Dogs must be leashed. The park is managed by the Department of Natural Resources, Maryland Forest, Park and Wildlife Service. For information about North Point State

Park, telephone Gunpowder Falls State Park at 592-2897.

Just 1.5 miles south of North Point State Park at the end of Route 20 is Fort Howard Park. This is more of a picnic park than a walking park, but the waterfront fortifications are an unusual feature worth exploring, as is made easy by a network of paved paths shown on Map 23 on page 226. The park is located at the absolute tip of North Point, from which there are sweeping views east over Chesapeake Bay, south across the mouth of the Patapsco River, and west to Sparrows Point.

Fort Howard Park is open daily from sunrise to sunset, except during October, when it is altogether closed. Dogs must be leashed. The park is managed by the Baltimore County Department of Recreation and Parks; telephone 887-7529.

NORTH POINT is where five thousand British troops landed in the fall of 1814 for their abortive march on Baltimore. Major General Robert Ross, commander of the British land forces, had announced his intention to use Baltimore—that "nest of privateers"—as his headquarters during the coming winter. He said that with the city as his base, his army would go where it pleased through Maryland.

Two years previously, the youthful United States had declared war on England. In a petition to President Jefferson, Baltimore had urged war with France also, on the grounds that her conduct was "scarcely less atrocious than that of England." Since 1793 Great Britain and France, at that time the world's two most powerful nations, had been locked in a protracted global war, and both countries regularly confiscated American merchant ships and cargoes in an attempt to prevent supplies from reaching the enemy. The United States itself engaged in the same practice during the Civil War, but in the early 1800s most Americans saw the seizures as a piratical violation of their neutrality.

Ire toward England was intensified starting in 1805 by the British navy's practice of stopping passenger vessels in United States coastal waters and removing all sailors whom the English determined or merely surmised were British subjects. (Great Britain did not recognize the process by which Englishmen might become naturalized Americans, and in any case, the Royal Navy was sorely in need of seamen.) Also, the "war hawks," a group of congressmen from the frontier states, openly urged that war with Great Britain would provide the opportunity for the United States to seize Canada and its lucrative fur trade, to end the Indian menace in the Ohio Valley (where massacres and conspiracies were said to be incited by British agents), and to throw open more land for settlement.

The War of 1812, however, did not go as planned by the Americans. Successive attempts to invade Canada failed miserably. At Baltimore, the British blockade of Chesapeake Bay reduced the export trade to almost nothing. Among shipowners, only the privateersmen made substantial profits through the seizure and sale of English merchant ships. Commissioned by the federal government as private warships operated as money-making ventures, Baltimore's privateers captured about a third of all enemy vessels that were taken during the war. After being seized, the ships were sailed to American ports, where they and their cargoes were sold through judicial condemnation by admiralty courts.

In the spring of 1814, Great Britain and its allies finally forced the abdication of Napoleon. England then turned its attention to the United States. The London newspapers announced that an expeditionary force of seasoned troops and sailors was being readied. "The seat of the American government, but more particularly Baltimore, is to be the immediate object of attack. . . . Terms will be offered to the American government at the point of the bayonet."

In mid-August the British force appeared in Chesapeake Bay, where the English had already seized Tangier Island as a base of operations. Baltimore gained time while the British marched from Benedict on the Patuxent River to Washington, which they captured on August 24, 1814. This event was enormously exaggerated in England, where the brief occupation of the national capital—a straggling, swampy place of 8,000 inhabitants—was said by the British press to be equivalent to the fall of London. *The Times* of London declared, "The world is speedily to be delivered of the mischievous example of the existence of a government founded on democratic rebellion." After only one day in Washington, where they burned the government buildings, the "modern Goths"—as one indignant American writer called the British—marched back to their ships.

Meanwhile, Baltimore dug in. The previous year a half-million dollars had been raised by subscription among the residents for the defense of the city because no aid came from Washington. Fort McHenry had been strengthened and other shore batteries constructed. A line of earthworks over a mile long was thrown up to the east of the city at Hampstead Hill, across land now occupied by Highlandtown, Patterson Park, and Johns Hopkins Hospital. This was to be the main line of resistance.

Work on the fortifications continued until Sunday, September 11, when three alarm guns in the courthouse square and the ringing of bells announced the arrival of the British squadron of fifty ships at North Point, 14 miles east of Baltimore at the mouth of the Patapsco River. After the militia had mustered, Major General Samuel Smith, to whom the city had assigned its defense, sent General John Stricker with 3,185 men out Philadelphia Road to reconnoiter and to delay the enemy's advance. By that evening Stricker had reached the narrow neck of land between the head of Bear Creek and the Back River, about halfway between Baltimore and North Point. He deployed his men there, except for a contingent of cavalry and riflemen who were sent farther ahead toward a farm owned by Robert Gorsuch.

At three o'clock the following morning, five thousand British soldiers rowed ashore in the dark at North Point. Their landing place at the tip of the peninsula was chosen because the Patapsco was thought to be too shallow for the larger ships to go farther upstream. The battle plan called for the smaller boats to push past Fort McHenry and to attack the city at the same time as the assault by land.

As light came on, the British army advanced up North Point Road toward Baltimore. Eventually, they stopped to rest while General Ross and his retinue left the road in order to get something to eat at the Gorsuch farm. According to Robert Gorsuch's grandson, the elder Gorsuch was forced not only to provide breakfast for General Ross and eight other officers but also to eat and drink a sample of every dish that he served before the British would touch it. Talking of the coming battle while he ate, General Ross purportedly boasted that he would "eat his supper in Baltimore, or in Hell."

Meanwhile, John Stricker (according to his account of the 12th of September) learned from his horse scouts that "the enemy in small force was enjoying itself at Gorsuch's farm." Two hundred and thirty infantry, some cavalry, and a cannon were immediately pushed forward. Stricker reported:

> This small volunteer corps had not proceeded scarcely half a mile before the main body of the enemy showed itself, which was immediately attacked. The infantry and riflemen maintained a fire of some minutes and returned with some loss in killed and wounded; the cavalry and artillery, owing to the disadvantageous ground, not being able to support them.

The skirmish was more critical than the Americans thought. On the British side, an eyewitness account was provided by the

Reverend Mr. Gleig, the military chaplain. He had been waiting with the main British force while General Ross breakfasted at the Gorsuch farm. After an hour the troops started to move again, but they had not traveled more than a mile when the "sharp fire of musketry was heard in front, and shortly afterward a mounted officer came galloping to the rear, who desired us to quicken our pace for that the advance guard was engaged." Gleig continued:

At this intelligence the ranks closed, and the troops advanced at a brisk rate, and in profound silence. The firing still continued, though from its running and irregular sound, it promised little else than a skirmish; but whether it was kept up by detached parties alone, or by the outposts of a regular army, we could not tell because, from the quantity of wood with which the country abounded, and the total absence of all hills or eminences, it was impossible to discern what was going on at the distance of a half a mile from the spot where we stood.

We were already drawing near the scene of action, when another officer came at full speed toward us, with horror and dismay in his countenance, and calling loudly for a surgeon. Every man felt within himself that all was not right, though none was willing to believe the whispers of his own terror. But what at first we would not guess at, because we dreaded it so much, was soon realized; for the aide-de-camp had scarcely passed when the General's horse, without its rider, and with the saddle and housing stained with blood, came plunging onwards. In a few moments we reached the ground where the skirmishing had taken place, and beheld General Ross laid by the side of the road, under a canopy of blankets, and apparently in the agonies of death. As soon as the firing began he had ridden to the front, that he might ascertain from whence it originated and, mingling with the skirmishers, was shot in the side by a rifleman. The wound was mortal; he fell into the arms of his aide-de-camp, and lived only long enough to name his wife, and to commend his family to the protection of his country. He was removed towards the fleet, but expired before his bearers could reach the boat.

It is impossible to conceive the effect which this melancholy spectacle produced throughout the army. . . . All eyes were turned upon him as we passed, and a sort of involuntary groan ran from rank to rank from the front to the rear of the column.

Nonetheless, the British pushed on until they ran into General Stricker's main force. A battle of an hour and a half followed. As the British troops advanced at a walking pace, the Americans fired what Gleig described as a "dreadful discharge of grape and canister shot, of old locks, pieces of broken muskets, and everything else which they could cram into their guns." After firing one volley, part of the American line retreated without orders. As the lines of British soldiers approached nearer and nearer, firing as they came, General Stricker was forced to pull his troops back to the main line of fortifications outside the city.

The next day, after a bivouac at the North Point battlefield, the British continued slowly toward Baltimore, hindered by the trees which the retreating Americans had cut down across the road during the night. Rain fell all day and it was not until evening that the British covered the 7 miles to Hampstead Hill, where they stopped in front of the American fortifications. Gleig reported:

It now appeared that the corps which we had beaten yesterday was only a detachment, and not a large one, from the force collected for the defense of Baltimore. . . . Upon a ridge of hills which concealed the town itself from observation stood the grand army, consisting of twenty thousand men. Not trusting to his superiority in numbers, their general had there entrenched them in the most formidable manner, having covered the whole face of the heights with breastworks, thrown back his left so as to rest it upon a strong fort, erected for the protection of the river, and constructed a chain of field redoubts which covered his right and commanded the entire ascent. Along the line of the hill were likewise fleches and other projecting works, from which a cross fire might be kept up; and there were mounted throughout this commanding position no less than one hundred pieces of cannon.

The new British commander, Colonel Arthur Brooke, tried to outflank the defenses by moving his troops to the north, but the Americans kept between the British and the city. Brooke then decided to try a night attack, provided he could receive support from the navy. But, as reflected in our national anthem, the English ships were repulsed at Fort McHenry, and Brooke eventually determined that attack would be futile. In the early morning, while their ships continued the unsuccessful bombardment of Fort McHenry, the British began their retreat, which was not discovered by the Americans until daylight. The American troops were so worn out from the two days of watching and waiting, much of it in the rain, that General Smith decided not to counterattack. By the next day, the British had returned to their ships and were gone.

After the retreat, the Baltimore newspapers dubbed the British the "night-retrograders." In England, however, *The Times* of London described the repulse at Baltimore and the contemporaneous naval defeat of the British at Plattsburg on Lake Champlain as a "lamentable event to the civilized world."

≈   ≈   ≈   ≈

When you visit **North Point State Park**, you may wonder how this waterfront site could have remained undeveloped up to the present day. The fact is, however, that the area near the jetty was formerly occupied by the Bay Shore Amusement Park, which operated from 1906 to 1950 and was served by a United Railways & Electric Company trolley running to and from Baltimore. The amusement park was in fact built by United Railways in order to induce people to ride the streetcar. A large open-sided trolley shed where passengers got on and off still stands a few dozen yards inland from the jetty, and part of the trail north into Black Marsh follows the former trolley roadbed, which at one point passes an old reinforced-concrete power station that supplied electricity to the trolley line and the amusement park.

In 1947 Bethlehem Steel Corporation, reacting to rumors that U.S. Steel was looking for a tidewater site for a steel mill that would compete with Sparrows Point, bought the amusement park, which it operated briefly but then shut down. Bethlehem Steel held the site until the state of Maryland purchased the 1,310-acre tract for $5.4 million in 1987.

The fact that there was once an amusement park at North Point has, unfortunately, inspired the Department of Natural Resources to prepare an overblown plan for intensive use and development of the waterfront area near the jetty. According to the draft plan, the jetty itself is to become a sort of grand promenade featuring a brick walkway lined with rows of benches and trees (if the trees can be made to live). On the north side of the jetty there would be floating docks where visiting boaters could tie up. (For boats to reach the docks, a long channel would have to be dredged and maintained. Also problematic is whether the floating docks could survive storms at this exposed site.) The plan also calls for a temple-like pergola at the end of the jetty, and a wide brick piazza where the jetty meets the shore. The piazza would fan out to a width of about 60 feet and also would extend inland 60 feet to the trolley shed, which is to be restored. (I am in favor of this restoration. The trolley shed will make a handsome pavilion for some purpose or other. If nothing else, picnic tables can be put there.) About another 60 feet inland from the trolley pavilion, there is an old fountain left over from the amusement park. According to the state's plan, the fountain is to be restored as the centerpiece of a formal garden. And another 60 feet inland—on the same long axis as the jetty, the trolley pavilion, and the fountain—the state's plan calls for a large multi-purpose building containing a visitor center with the

usual exhibits, toilets, and park offices, plus a kitchen and cafeteria-style food concession. There would also be classrooms, an environmental research center, and a dormitory for visiting students. Behind the multi-purpose building would be a stage facing a grassy amphitheater. Nearby would be a parking lot for 150 cars, reached by a road that would bring virtually all park visitors directly and immediately to the waterfront. Between the parking lot and the beach would be several acres of lawn with picnic tables.

Is this the sort of thing that park visitors want to see or use when, after driving from throughout the metropolitan region, they finally reach the Chesapeake shore at North Point? When you visit North Point, you can contemplate the Department of Natural Resources' $6 million plan and decide for yourself whether it would enhance or diminish your enjoyment of the park. The entire plan is shown on Map 22 on page 223; there are larger drawings at the park office and also a visitors' logbook where you can record your comments.

Critics of the state's plan have suggested various alternatives, and the common theme behind all of them (besides being far less expensive) is to locate the main parking lot and visitor center near Route 20 in order to maintain the park's southern peninsula and shore in a more natural condition than is provided by the state's plan. Perhaps my views are merely those of an inveterate walker, but I have the impression that most park visitors welcome the opportunity to walk to the beach and jetty and not find a 600-foot-long axis of festival architecture—a sort of Tivoli on the Bay—when they get there. As of the beginning of 1993, visitors park their cars in the large lot just inside the park entrance, then walk along the cinder road to reach the water's edge and the jetty; handicapped people, however, may drive to the parking area near the water. This simple and inexpensive arrangement is working very satisfactorily, and I personally feel that it should be continued indefinitely while the state's planners take the time to learn from actual public use of North Point State Park what it is that visitors want and need.

AUTOMOBILE: North Point State Park and Fort Howard Park are located southeast of Baltimore at North Point, where the Patapsco River joins Chesapeake Bay. The access route described below is not the most direct, but it involves very little extra distance and avoids the confusing snarl of highway ramps and loops in the vicinity of Sparrows Point.

From Interstate 695 (the Beltway) southeast of Baltimore and north of the Key Bridge, take Exit 41 for Cove Road toward Route 20 (and Route 151). Follow Cove Road to an intersection with Route 151 at a traffic light, then turn left onto Route 151 southbound. Follow Route 151 south 2.2 miles, then bear left onto Route 20 south toward Edgemere and Fort Howard; this intersection is poorly marked and occurs at a yield sign just before Route 151 passes under the Interstate 695 bridge.

Follow Route 20 south 2.5 miles, then turn left into the entrance for **North Point State Park**. Follow the entrance road only a few hundred yards, then turn left into the parking lot.

NOTE: The state's plan for North Point State Park calls for relocating the entrance 0.4 mile farther north off Route 20; you may find that this has been done by the time you visit the park. Also, the state may have relocated the main parking lot to the waterfront area.

For **Fort Howard Park** simply continue on Route 20 for less than 2 miles. The park entrance is on the left at the end of the road.

WALKING AT NORTH POINT STATE PARK: Map 21 opposite shows the park as of early 1993,

MAP 21 — North Point State Park as of 1993

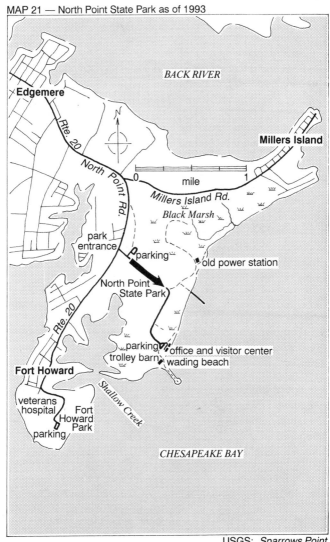

BACK RIVER

Edgemere

Millers Island

Rte 20

North Point Rd.

0   mile   1

Millers Island Rd.

Black Marsh

park
entrance

parking

old power station

North Point
State Park

Rte 20

parking
trolley barn

office and visitor center
wading beach

Fort Howard

veterans
hospital   Fort
Howard
Park

parking

Shallow Creek

CHESAPEAKE BAY

USGS: *Sparrows Point*

and Map 22 opposite shows the park as the Department of Natural Resources proposes to develop it as time goes on.

Assuming that conditions are still as they were early in 1993, follow the cinder road to the water's edge and jetty. There is some automobile traffic on this road, so be alert. The best thing to do is to walk on the left, facing any cars that may come along.

After about 0.5 mile you will pass the Black Marsh spur trail on the left (just before the main road curves right). Black Marsh is well worth visiting. The trail is broad and dry, but you should be prepared for mosquitoes and flies during the warmer part of the year.

Return to the parking lot by the way you came.

≈   ≈   ≈   ≈

Just south of North Point State Park is **Fort Howard Park**, located at the actual tip of North Point. Like Mayan ruins overrun by jungle, several massive structures lie half-buried in the tangled brush and woods. All are of concrete, empty, strangely abstract, like the imaginary buildings in the drawings of M. C. Escher. These are the fort's old bunkers and huge amphitheater-like gun pits, which during the first two decades of this century helped to guard the water approach to Baltimore.

Built at the end of the nineteenth century during the Spanish-American War, Fort Howard never saw combat then, nor did it during World War I, when Forts Smallwood, Armistead, and Howard formed Baltimore's line of coastal defense against attacks that never came. The Fort Howard garrison, however, was said to maintain a high standard of proficiency. The *Baltimore Sun* for October 14, 1908, reported that the Howard gunners had been credited with hitting, nine times out of ten, a

BACK RIVER

Edgemere

Millers Island

Rte. 20

parking

new access road

hiker/biker trail

park entrance

0   1

mile

Millers Island Rd.

Black Marsh

parking
North Point
State Park

old power station

North Point Rd.

Rte. 20

group picnicking

maintenance area

ranger residence

multi-purpose center

parking, picnicking, and wading

trolley barn pavilion

dock

gazebo

Fort Howard

veterans hospital

Fort Howard Park

Shallow Creek

parking

CHESAPEAKE BAY

USGS: *Sparrows Point*

target that was being towed in the shipping channel nearly 3 miles away. The fort's guns included two batteries of 12-inch mortars that fired projectiles weighing 1,000 pounds. The mortars were housed in the largest firing pits. Another emplacement held two 12-inch disappearing rifles (i.e., modern rifled guns—not smoothbores) that were raised for firing and lowered behind the revetment walls for loading. Four other emplacements (only three of which survive) housed 6-inch, 5-inch, and 4.7-inch rifles and 3-inch rapid-fire guns.

In 1941, long after the guns had been removed, the fort was decommissioned as obsolete. The bunkers, barracks, officers' houses, parade ground, and other land were turned over to the Veterans Administration for development of the present-day hospital. Twenty-five years later, the area occupied by the concrete revetments was returned to the Army for use by the intelligence school at Fort Holabird. During the Vietnam War, a mock Vietnamese village was constructed in the underbrush and vines among the old coastal batteries.

Fort Holabird was closed in 1972, and the next year its 62-acre parcel at North Point was deeded to Baltimore County by the General Services Administration under the federal government's Legacy of Parks program, by which surplus federal property is donated to local governments with the provision that the land be used for recreation. The hospital grounds, however, are not part of the park and are not open to visitors.

AUTOMOBILE FROM NORTH POINT STATE PARK TO FORT HOWARD PARK: Turn left out the entrance at North Point State Park and follow Route 20 south less than 2 miles to the end of the road, where Fort Howard veterans hospital is on the right and Fort Howard Park is on the left. Fork left for the park and follow the curving entrance drive to the parking lot.

MAP 23 — Fort Howard Park

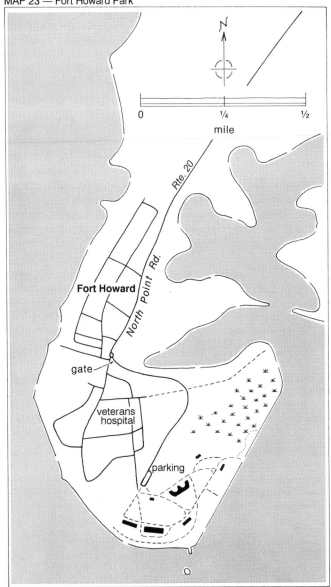

N

0   ¼   ½

mile

Rte. 20

North Point Rd.

Fort Howard

gate

veterans hospital

parking

USGS: *Sparrows Point*

WALKING AT FORT HOWARD PARK: The park has a network of paved paths shown by dashed lines on Map 23 opposite.

From the parking lot, follow any of several paths that lead to the various gun emplacements and to the water's edge. Fort Howard Park is so small that you can easily explore the entire installation of scattered gun sites.

Further reading: Some of the older histories, such as Thomas J. Scharf's *The Chronicles of Baltimore* and Matthew Page Andrews' *History of Maryland* and *Tercentenary History of Maryland*, devote a lot more space to the War of 1812 and the British attack on Baltimore than do more recent histories.

18

BALTIMORE & ANNAPOLIS TRAIL PARK

Walking and bicycling—up to 26.6 miles (42.8 kilo-meters) round-trip. The old Baltimore & Annapolis Railroad now serves as a hiker/biker trail, providing a cross-sectional view of suburban Anne Arundel County, from Glen Burnie in the north, past Marley Station Mall and Severna Park, to wooded ravines and even a few horse farms in the south near the Severn River. The route is shown by the bold line on Map 24 on page 237. The asphalt surface is suitable not only for walking and bicycling but also for roller-skating and for pushing young children in strollers.

The trail is open daily from sunrise to sunset. Dogs must be leashed. Cyclists should yield to other trail users, pass with care, and keep their speed to a moderate, safe pace. The trail is managed by the Anne Arundel County Department of Recreation and Parks, which has a ranger station in a handsome old country store located where the trail crosses Earleigh Heights Road at milepost 7; telephone 222-6244.

THE BALTIMORE & ANNAPOLIS RAILROAD was chartered in 1880 under the name Annapolis & Baltimore Short Line Railroad. The route crossed the Severn River on a long bridge, then followed the river's north shore through what are now Arnold, Severna Park, Pasadena, Harundale, Glen Burnie, Ferndale, Linthicum, Baltimore Highlands, and Westport to Baltimore. The sobriquet "Short Line" was a piece of self-promotion, intended to inform customers that the new railroad provided a shorter, faster route than the Annapolis & Elk Ridge Railroad, which since 1840 had operated along the Severn's south shore, linking Annapolis, Crownsville, and Odenton with Annapolis Junction north of Laurel, where passengers transferred to and from the Baltimore & Ohio line to Washington.

After a period spent raising capital and acquiring the right-of-way, the Short Line company started construction in 1886, at times employing more than a thousand black and immigrant laborers to grade the roadbed and lay tracks. Pulled by steam locomotives, trains started running in March 1887, traversing a region between Baltimore and Annapolis that was wholly rural in character. There were no towns: just scattered churches, schools, and country stores that served as the focal points of loose farm communities. Most agricultural products—chiefly vegetables and fruit—were transported by boat to market in Baltimore. Much of the region was not even cultivated. Its sandy soil had been exhausted by tobacco during the eighteenth century, and since then large areas had reverted to piney woods.

The railroad helped gradually to change all that. Before automobiles came into widespread use in the 1920s and '30s, the railroad served as the main locus of commercial activity and transportation in this part of Anne Arundel County. Trains carried mail and groceries, dry goods, coal, kerosene, and feed to general stores that were established at sidings up and down the line. Truck farmers shipped fresh produce by train to Baltimore. Canneries and lumber yards were built along the railway. In the vicinity of the Patapsco River and at Pasadena, pits were established from which sand and gravel were shipped out by railroad. The line helped to bring into being a variety of small hotels and taverns—some with dance floors—located on the Severn and Magothy waterfront or by the railroad. Owners of vacation homes also came and went by train.

The A&B Short Line—reorganized in 1894 as the Baltimore & Annapolis Short Line Railroad Company—promoted excursions to Annapolis and to Bay Ridge on the Chesapeake, reached by an extension of the rail line eastward from the state capital. Escaping the summertime miasma of Baltimore, passengers enjoyed the breeze and scenery of the train ride, especially as the coaches crossed the half-mile-long bridge over the Severn River. The railroad company also promoted excursions to the small turn-of-the-century resort of Round Bay on the Severn, which was owned by the railroad's principal shareholder. A short spur ran to the resort, which later was converted into a waterfront residential community.

Construction of the railroad fueled land speculation up and down the line. Areas near the railway were bought and subdivided by real-estate companies. Although lots sold slowly at first, some new towns were successful. In 1889 a development that became Glen Burnie was platted by the Glenn family, which over the course of the nineteenth century had acquired extensive holdings in northern Anne Arundel County. Glen Burnie became a commuter town that by 1925 had about two thousand residents. The small summer community of Briarcliff on the Severn was established in 1896. The Severn River Company started selling lots at Severna Park in 1906. (The brick station at Severna Park was built in 1919.) Commuting to work by train became a way of life both for year-round suburbanites and for those who seasonally closed their houses in Baltimore and moved to summer cottages on the Magothy and Severn rivers. South of Severna Park, the land for Pines-on-the-Severn was subdivided in the early 1920s. Many modest summer cottages, long since converted to year-round residences, are now pricey waterfront or water-view homes. At some early subdivisions, however, only a few houses were built, and at others the streets and dwellings altogether failed to materialize.

In 1907 The Maryland Electric Railways Company (which owned no other railroad) acquired control of the Baltimore & Annapolis Short Line and by the following year completed installation of overhead wires from which self-propelled cars drew power. An electric substation was built at Jones Station Road next to the railway. (Painted white, the boxlike brick structure now houses a shop run by the Ann Arrundell County Historical Society—that's how they prefer to spell the name—where browsers are welcome.) In 1914 the railroad was converted from alternating to direct current, which entailed building a larger power house that still stands next to the trail a few hundred feet north of Jones Station Road. Electrification enabled the railroad to provide a smoother, quieter, cleaner ride for its growing clientele of passengers. The steel cars had large windows with shallowly-arched stained glass transoms, plus a second tier of elliptical clerestory windows. Inside, the cars were paneled with mahogany, and the seats were covered with green plush.

In 1921 the Short Line merged into the Washington, Baltimore & Annapolis Electric Railroad Company, which since 1908 had operated trains between Baltimore and Washington with a spur to Annapolis that in part followed the old Annapolis & Elk Ridge right-of-way. The WB&A was a model of modern efficiency. According to one newspaper account, its operations were studied by a delegation of Japanese engineers who were preparing to build electric railroads in their own country. At its peak the railroad system carried more than 5 million passengers annually (1,750,000 on the former Short Line). Up to seventy trains a day left Baltimore for either Washington or Annapolis. On the Short Line route, passenger coaches ran hourly throughout the day and evening and more frequently during rush hours.

By the end of the 1920s, however, the number of riders was declining as automobile use increased. In 1931, after the Depression was already two years old, the WB&A entered receivership. Granted a tax exemption by the state and a voluntary reduction in wages by its employees, the company continued in business until 1935, when the tax exemption was terminated and the Maryland Public Service Commission authorized the receiver to auction the company's assets for scrap. The Washington-Baltimore route and the line along the south shore of the Severn were abandoned, but the former Short Line along the Severn's north shore was salvaged by a group of investors newly incorporated as the Baltimore & Annapolis Railroad.

Although the B&A survived the Depression and even prospered during World War II, when rationing of gasoline and tires restricted automobile use, the railroad quickly lost riders to automobiles and buses in the postwar years. Ritchie Highway had been completed in 1939, and by 1948 the Baltimore & Annapolis Railroad was itself operating buses that supplemented its worn out, money-losing trains. The buses were not significantly slower than the train, which took 55 minutes and made thirty stops during the 22-mile trip to Annapolis. (Today's MTA buses take about an hour.) Convinced that the company could not make money by operating passenger trains and that bus service provided an adequate alternative to the railroad, the Maryland Public Service Commission allowed the B&A—by then rechristened by some riders as the Bumble & Amble or the Bounce & Agitate—to terminate passenger rail service in 1950. In its decision, the commission wrote that the B&A had "not been maintained as a first-class railroad; the roadbed needs constant attention; the rails are worn and would have to be replaced if passenger service is continued; the cars or trains are antiquated, decrepit and unattractive as a means of travel; schedules are slow, and there is no inducement, save that of necessity, for anyone to travel by rail. While not yet dead, it is moribund."

What was noxious to some, however, was nostalgic to others. After the discontinuation of passenger service was announced, newspapers ran evocative valedictions. In the *Baltimore Evening Sun* for December 14, 1949, Richard K. Tucker wrote that the "ancient, rattling electric train suddenly became like an old friend, more valued despite a myriad of faults than something new and strange."

> The deep Anne Arundel County woods in the springtime and autumn somehow didn't look the same from the windows of a cramped and speeding bus. Grown men who had recalled shooting imaginary Indians from the open windows of the B.& A. as small boys somehow couldn't find any nostalgia in a tangle of auto traffic. And traversing the broad Severn River at sunset over the old wooden B.& A. trestle was an experience ten times more memorable than crossing the bridge in a parade of honking automobiles.
>
> More than that, there was a comforting old country store atmosphere to the worn leather seats, the ancient overhead lamps with their scallop-edged white glass shades, the dark wood fittings rubbed by generations of county travelers, and (something the buses will never have) the roughed metal strips beside the window for striking the big wooden matches carried from country kitchens. The cars, more often than not, were pungent with the odor of cigar and pipe smoke.

Did B&A commuters really miss the train? They had a chance to demonstrate their preference anew in 1961, when passenger service from Harundale north into Baltimore was resumed on an experimental basis for a few weeks, then dropped because of lack of riders.

Freight service, however, continued on the Baltimore & Annapolis line. During the 1950s and '60s, a lone 70-ton diesel switcher making at most one trip each weekday hauled boxcars and gondolas to and from factory sidings and sand and gravel pits. Occasionally the train delivered coal to the Naval Academy—until, that is, the old trestle over the Severn, with a swing-span drawbridge at the middle, was condemned in 1968. Freight service from Baltimore to Jones Station south of Severna Park stopped in 1969. After the flood rains of Tropical Storm Agnes in 1972 fragmented the line by damaging bridges at the Patapsco River, Saw Mill Creek, and Marley Creek, the B&A sought permission from the Interstate Commerce Commission (which had jurisdiction because the B&A handled freight that traveled among states) to shut down the railroad altogether. The petition was first denied and then, in 1976, granted only for the section of the line south of Dorsey Road at the northern edge of Glen Burnie. In the meantime, no trains ran. But after the Patapsco River bridge was rebuilt in 1976, freight service resumed from Baltimore to Dorsey Road, and in 1987 the old Short Line—by then *very* short—celebrated its 100th anniversary. At that time, the company operated one train three days a week over 6.5 miles of track. It had six full-time employees, six part-time employees, and the same diesel locomotive (now at the Baltimore & Ohio Railroad Museum) that the B&A had bought new in 1950. But the railroad company also had a gold mine in its right-of-way, which in 1991 the Mass Transit Administration purchased for $9 million for its new light rail line terminating at Dorsey Road. In 1973, incidentally, the MTA also took over the old B&A's bus service to Annapolis, although B&A Charter Tours, Inc. carries on the name and the charter-bus aspect of the business. As a corporate entity, the Baltimore & Annapolis Railroad, Inc. also lives on, although it is no longer engaged in railroading. Now the Canton Railroad Company operates diesel-powered freight trains on the new MTA tracks in the middle of the night in order to serve various industries along the old B&A line north of Dorsey Road.

Abandoned and derelict, the B&A right-of-way south of Dorsey Road was purchased in 1980 for just $1.3 million by the Anne Arundel County Department of Recreation and Parks.

Between 1985 and 1993 the county spent $10.5 million on new bridges, parking lots, grading, landscaping, paving, fences, and other work (including restoration of the Earleigh Heights ranger station) to create the very popular linear park seen today. There are plans to link the northern end of the trail at Dorsey Road with another 8-mile trail extending west then north around BWI Airport to Patapsco Valley State Park. The old roadbed of the Annapolis & Elk Ridge Railroad along the south shore of the Severn River is also being converted to a linear park stretching from Annapolis Mall to Odenton.

AUTOMOBILE: The Baltimore & Annapolis Trail Park is located south of Baltimore. The two access points described below are easily reached from Route 2 (Ritchie Highway), which runs parallel to the trail immediately to its east.

Earleigh Heights Road crosses the trail at about its midpoint, where the ranger station is located. From Interstate 695 (the Beltway) take Exit 2 for Route 10 south toward Severna Park. (If you are coming from the Key Bridge, take Exit 2-3B for Routes 10-2 south.) Follow Route 10 south 6.5 miles, taking care **not to exit** onto Route 100 eastbound toward Gibson Island. Where Route 10 ends at a T-intersection with Route 2, turn left and follow Route 2 south toward Severna Park. Go only 1.2 miles, then turn right onto Earleigh Heights Road. Follow Earleigh Heights Road for just 0.3 mile, then turn left into the B&A Trail parking lot.

From Earleigh Heights Road, the distance to the trail's southern end near Route 50 is 7 miles, and the distance to the trail's northern end at Dorsey Road is 6.3 miles. Earleigh Heights Road is a good place for bicyclists to start. A round trip to either end of the trail

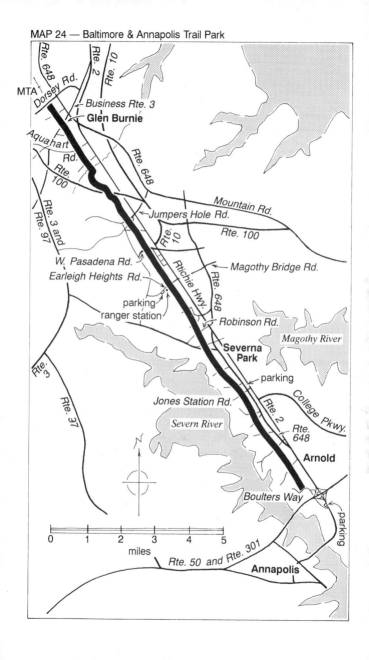

MAP 24 — Baltimore & Annapolis Trail Park

is an easy ride; a round trip to both ends totals 26.6 miles.

Jones Station Road is a good starting point for walkers who want to see the trail's most attractive section first, but parking here in the MTA's commuter parking lot is permitted only on weekends. From Interstate 695 (the Beltway) take Exit 2 for Route 10 south toward Severna Park. (If you are coming from the Key Bridge, take Exit 2-3B for Routes 10-2 south.) Follow Route 10 south 6.5 miles, taking care **not to exit** onto Route 100 eastbound toward Gibson Island. Where Route 10 ends at a T-intersection with Route 2, turn left and follow Route 2 south toward Severna Park. Go 4.7 miles, then turn right onto Jones Station Road, then right again in a hundred feet into the MTA's Severna Park park & ride lot. The trail is located just across Baltimore Annapolis Boulevard behind the boxlike white brick substation, which is visible from the parking lot entrance. The substation is now occupied by the Ann Arrundell County Historical Society's Browse & Buy Shoppe.

From Jones Station Road, the distance to the trail's southern end near Route 50 is 3.4 miles. The distance north to Earleigh Heights Road is 3.6 miles, to Marley Station Mall is 7 miles, and to Dorsey Road is about 10 miles.

WALKING and BICYCLING: The trail is shown by the bold line on Map 24 on page 237. The route is unmistakable throughout its entire length. Frequently, however, you must cross roads, so use caution at all places where cars may be present. Stubby posts show the distance from the trail's southern end at Boulters Way near Route 50. Posts with capital letters are keyed to discussions contained in the excellent *Baltimore & Annapolis Trail Park Guide* on sale at the Earleigh Heights Road ranger station.

From Earleigh Heights Road, I suggest that you head south to see the trail's more scenic half first. To go south, start with the ranger station on your right.

From Jones Station Road, again I suggest that you head south first to see the trail's most attractive section. To go south, start with the white brick substation on your left.

19

CYLBURN ARBORETUM

Walking—1.0 mile (1.6 kilometers). The old Tyson estate, with its Victorian stone mansion, formal gardens, and extensive woods, is now Baltimore's arboretum and horticultural center. Labels identify hundreds of varieties of trees, shrubs, flowers, and other plants. Over 150 species of birds have been seen here. The Circle Trail— shown by the bold line on Map 25 on page 250—follows the rim of the valley and leads to the various demonstration gardens behind the mansion.

The arboretum is open daily from 6 A.M. to 9 P.M. Dogs and mountain bicycling are prohibited. The arboretum is managed by the Baltimore City Department of Recreation and Parks; telephone 396-0180.

SUMPTUOUS CYLBURN ARBORETUM occupies 170 acres of meadows and woods on a high plateau above the Jones Falls Valley just south of Northern Parkway. A wide path follows the top of the bluff around three sides of the park and ends at the formal gardens behind the Cylburn Mansion.

Started in 1863, Cylburn was developed during the decade following the Civil War as the country estate of Jesse Tyson, the son of Isaac Tyson, Jr., Baltimore's chrome king. (See Chapter 5.) The gray stone for the mansion was quarried at the Bare Hills west of Lake Roland, where the Tysons had some of their chromite and copper mines.

In 1888 Jesse Tyson married Edith Johns, a Baltimore debutante who in later years Alfred Jenkins Shriver listed in his will as among the ten most beautiful Baltimore women of his era (and all of whom, therefore, were by his testamentary directions painted together in a mural at Johns Hopkins University's Shriver Hall—each woman "at the height of her beauty"). The Tysons entertained frequently and lavishly at Cylburn, where they, their servants, and weekend guests arrived and departed by the Northern Central Railroad; a private carriage road ran from the mansion to the Cylburn station, located off what was then Belvedere Avenue. Four years after Tyson's death in 1906, his widow married Lieutenant (later Major) Bruce Cotton, and for decades Cylburn continued to be a showplace where Baltimore society gathered for receptions in the large drawing room or wandered the lawns and gardens that were lit with hundreds of Japanese lanterns during summer musicales. Following Mrs. Cotton's death in 1942, Major Cotton sold the property to the city for a low price with the specific intention that the estate be made a city park. The grounds and gardens—cared for in part by the volunteer Cylburn Arboretum Association—are very attractive, but the mansion is in sad condition. Its exterior in particular needs immediate attention if rot is to be arrested before repairs become prohibitively expensive.

≈   ≈   ≈   ≈

If you want to learn to identify trees, the large variety of labeled specimens at Cylburn Arboretum provides excellent practice and an enjoyable excursion at all times of year. Oak, hickory, and tulip trees (also called yellow poplar) and to a lesser extent maple, beech, and ash dominate the scene, as is typical in eastern Maryland. Dogwood, sassafras, and mountain laurel are also widespread in the understory.

Learning to identify trees is not difficult. Every walk or

automobile trip is an opportunity for practice. Notice the overall forms and branching habits of the trees, and also the distinctive qualities of their twigs, buds, bark, leaves, flowers, and fruits or seeds. These factors are the key identification features that distinguish one species from another. Finally, when using a field guide, check the maps or descriptions that delineate the geographic range within which a tentatively-identified tree or shrub is likely to be found.

Some trees, of course, have very distinctive and reliable forms. Familiar evergreens like balsam fir and eastern red cedar have a conical shape, like a dunce cap, although in dense stands the red cedar tapers very little and assumes the columnar form of the Italian cypress, which it somewhat resembles. The deciduous little-leaf linden, imported from Europe and used as a street tree, is also more or less conical in shape, but with wider-spreading lower branches than the evergreens mentioned above. The elm displays a spreading form like a head of broccoli. A full-bodied egg-shape is characteristic of the sugar maple and beech, although both will develop long, branchless trunks in crowded woods, as do most forest trees competing for light. The vertically exaggerated cigar shape of Lombardy poplar—a form called fastigiate—and the pendulous, trailing quality of weeping willow are unmistakable. (Both Lombardy poplar and weeping willow have been introduced to North America from abroad.)

Branching habit, an important clue to some trees, is observable even at a distance. White pine, for example, has markedly horizontal branches with a slight upward tilt at the tips, like a hand turned with its palm up. Norway spruce (another imported species) is often seen as an ornamental tree dwarfing and darkening a house near which it was planted fifty or a hundred years ago; it is a very tall evergreen—sometimes reminding me of a pagoda—with long, evenly-spaced, festoon-like branches. The slender lower branches of pin oak slant downward, while those of white oak and red oak are often massive and horizontal, especially on mature trees growing in the open. The lower branches of the horse chestnut (yet another European import) also droop but then curl up at the tips in chunky twigs. Elm branches spread up and out like the mouth of a trumpet. The trunk of the mature honeylocust diverges into large branches somewhat in the manner of an elm. Even the reviled *ailanthus* or tree of heaven, which springs up in dense groves of spindly, spiky saplings wherever earth has been disturbed, eventually develops a spreading form somewhat like an elm or honeylocust.

A good botanist or forester can identify trees by their twigs alone—that is, by the end portion of the branch that constitutes the newest growth. During winter the shape, color, size, position, and sheathing of buds are important. For instance, beech buds are long and pointed, tan, and sheathed with overlapping scales like shingles. Sycamore and magnolia buds are wrapped in a single scale. The twigs of horse chestnut are tipped with a big, sticky, brown bud, while those of silver maple, and to a lesser extent red maple, end with large clusters of red buds. Some oaks, such as white oak, have hairless terminal buds, while other species, such as black oak, have hairy end buds.

Aside from buds, other characteristics of twigs are color, thorns, odor, hair, pith, and the size, shape, and position of leaf scars marking where the leaf stems were attached. For example, most maple twigs are reddish brown, but the twigs of striped maple and mountain maple are greenish. Thorns and spines are significant because relatively few trees have them, notably honeylocust, black locust, Hercules club, prickly ash, buckthorn bumelia, devil's walking stick, Osage-orange, American plum, some crab apples, and the many varieties of hawthorn. *Ailanthus* twigs, which show huge leaf scars, have a rank odor when broken open. Most oaks have hairless twigs, although some species such as blackjack oak are distinctly hairy. As for pith, it can be chambered, solid, spongy, or of different colors, depending on the species. I noted earlier that oak, hickory, and tulip trees are common forest species near Baltimore, but only the pith of white oak in cross section forms a star. Finally, the location of leaf scars in opposite pairs along the twigs (as with maples) distinguishes a wide variety of trees and shrubs from those with leaf scars arranged alternately, first on one side and then on the other (as with oaks). All these distinguishing features can best be appreciated simply by examining the twigs of different species.

Bark is not always a reliable clue for identifying trees, as the color and texture of bark change with age or from trunk to branches to twigs. Often the distinctive character of bark is seen only in the trunks of large, mature trees. Bark can be smooth, furrowed, scaly, plated, shaggy, fibrous, crisscrossed, or papery. Some trees, of course, may be clearly identified by their bark. The names *shagbark hickory* and *paper birch* speak for themselves. Striped maple has longitudinal, whitish stripes in the smooth green bark of the younger trees. The crisscrossed ridges of white ash, the light blotches on sycamores, and the smooth gray skin of beech are equally distinctive. Birches and some cherries are characterized by horizontal lenticels like random dashes.

Most people notice leaves, particularly their shape. The leaves of the gray birch are triangular; catalpa, heart-shaped; sweetgum, star-shaped; beech, elliptical (or actually pointed at each end); and black willow narrower still and thus lanceolate. Notice also the leaf margin or edge. Is it smooth like rhododendron, wavy like water oak, serrated like basswood, or deeply lobed like most maples? And how many lobes are there? Tulip trees, for example have easily recognized four-lobed leaves; maples have three- or five-lobed leaves. Also, are the lobe tips rounded like white oak or pointed like red oak? Or, maybe, as with sassafras and red mulberry, the same tree has leaves that are shaped differently, the most distinctive being those with a single asymmetrical lobe creating a leaf outline like a mitten. In some trees, such as the large-leaved magnolia with its tobacco-like foliage, the sheer size of the leaves is significant. Similarly, sycamores have leaves resembling sugar maples or red maples, but usually bigger and coarser in texture.

Some leaves such as those of the Japanese maple, horse chestnut, and Ohio buckeye are palmately compound, meaning that they are actually composed of leaflets radiating from the end of the stem like fingers from the palm. In the fall the whole compound leaf may drop off the tree as a unit. Other leaves, such as ash, hickory, and sumac, are pinnately compound, being composed of leaflets arranged in opposite pairs along a central stalk. With pinnately compound leaves growing from the top of a branchless trunk, the saplings of *ailanthus* almost resemble little palm trees. Still other leaves are *bi*pinnately compound, somewhat like a fern. The leaflets grow from stalks that, in turn, spread from a central stalk. Honeylocust, Kentucky coffeetree, and the ornamental imported silktree are examples.

Although the needles of evergreens are not as varied as the leaves of deciduous plants, there are still several major points to look for, such as the number of needles grouped together. White pine has fascicles of five; pitchpine, loblolly pine, and sometimes shortleaf pine have fascicles of three; and jack pine, red pine, Virginia pine, Austrian pine, and sometimes shortleaf pine have fascicles of two. Needles of spruce, hemlock, and fir grow singly, but are joined to the twig in distinctive ways. Spruce needles grow from little woody pegs, hemlock needles from smaller bumps, and fir needles directly from the twig, leaving a rounded pit when pulled off. Spruce needles tend to be four-sided, hemlock flat, and fir somewhere in between. The needles of larch (also called tamarack) grow in dense clusters and all drop off in winter. The needles of bald cypress also drop off—hence its name.

Flowers are a spectacular, though short-lived, feature of some trees and shrubs. Three variables are color, form, and (less reliably) time of bloom. Eastern redbud, with red-purple clusters, and shadbush (also called Allegheny serviceberry), with small, white, five-petaled flowers, are among the first of our native trees to bloom, sometimes as early as late March in the Baltimore region. As members of the rose family, apples, cherries, plums, peaches, and hawthorns all have flowers with five petals (usually pink or white) in loose clusters, typically blooming in April. The blossoms of flowering dogwood, which also appear in April or early May, consist of four white, petal-like bracts, each with a brown notch at the tip, while the flowers of alternate-leaf dogwood consist of loose, white clusters. These are a few of our native species commonly thought of as flowering trees and shrubs, but the blossoms of other native species are equally distinctive, such as the small but numerous flowers of maples or the tuliplike flowers and durable husks of tulip trees. Unlike most trees, witch hazel—which produces small, yellow, scraggly flowers—blooms in fall or winter.

Finally, the seeds or fruit of a tree are a conspicuous element in summer and fall, sometimes lasting into winter and even spring. Even if a tree is bare, the fruits and seeds (or for that matter, the leaves) can often be found littered on the ground around the trunk. Nobody who sees a tree with acorns could fail to know that it is an oak, although some varieties, such as willow oak and shingle oak (also known as northern laurel oak) are deceptive. Distinctive nuts are also produced by beech trees, horse chestnuts, hickories, and walnuts. Some seeds, like ash and maple, have wings; such winged seeds are termed samaras. Others, such as honeylocust, Kentucky coffeetree, and redbud, come in pods like beans and in fact are members of the same general legume family. The seeds of birches, poplars, and willows hang in tassels, while those of sweetgum and sycamore form prickle-balls (as do the shells of horse chestnut and buckeye). Eastern cottonwood produces seeds that are windborne by cottonlike tufts. And, of course, brightly colored berries and fruits are produced by many species, such as crabapples, holly, hawthorn, and hackberry. Among needle evergreens, spruce and pine cones hang from the twigs, while fir cones stand upright like stubby candles, and the small hemlock cones grow from the twig tips.

In conclusion, the trick to tree identification, like bird identification discussed in Chapter 10, is a gestalt approach that entails considering, either simultaneously or in rapid succession, a wide variety of features of which the ones described here—form and branching habit, twigs, buds, bark, leaves, flowers, and fruits or seeds—are the most obvious and the most readily observed. Don't get hung up pondering any single ambiguous or inconclusive feature; move on to consider other clues.

AUTOMOBILE: Cylburn Arboretum is located in north Baltimore. The entrance to the arboretum is on the east side of Greenspring Avenue 0.3 mile south of Northern Parkway and 0.7 mile north of Coldspring Lane.

From Interstate 83 (the Jones Falls Expressway) inside the Beltway, take Exit 10B for Northern Parkway westbound. Follow Northern Parkway west only 0.3 mile, then turn left onto Cylburn Avenue. Follow Cylburn Avenue uphill 0.5 mile to Greenspring Avenue. Turn left onto Greenspring Avenue, then immediately turn left again into Cylburn Arboretum. Follow the entrance road 0.3 mile, then park on the left.

WALKING: (See Map 25 on page 250.) Start your walk on the rutted gravel track that descends from the

MAP 25 — Cylburn Arboretum

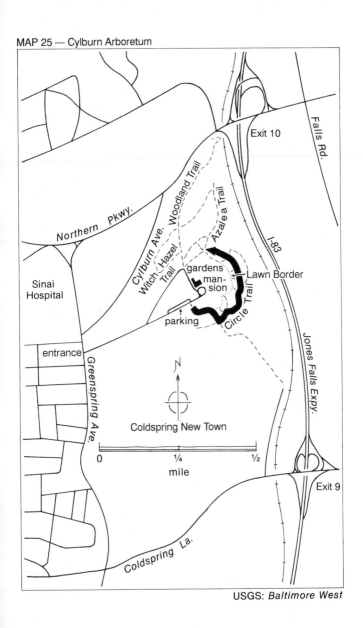

Falls Rd.

Exit 10

Northern Pkwy.

Cylburn Ave. Woodland Trail

Witch Hazel Trail

Azalea Trail

I-83

gardens

man-sion

Lawn Border

parking

Circle Trail

Sinai Hospital

Jones Falls Expy.

entrance

Greenspring Ave.

N

Coldspring New Town

0   ¼   ½

mile

Exit 9

Coldspring La.

USGS: *Baltimore West*

entrance road opposite some parking bays for cars and buses. This spot is located about 100 yards before the entrance road reaches the circular drive in front of the mansion.

Follow the gravel track downhill toward the woods. Just as you enter the woods, turn left onto a wide footpath (the Circle Trail). Follow the Circle Trail along the rim of the bluff. After about 125 yards, turn right to continue on the Circle Trail, which eventually brings you around to the rear of the mansion, where you can explore the various specialty gardens. For a longer walk, you can return to your car by circling back clockwise along a path (the Lawn Border) that follows the edge of the grass next to the woods. Other short trails are shown on the map.

Further reading: Any of the standard field guides will help you to identify trees, but what is mostly necessary is practice at arboretums, where the trees are labeled and where you can see them at different seasons.

20

GWYNNS FALLS • LEAKIN PARK

Millrace Path

Walking—4.5 miles (7.2 kilometers). This walk is pieced together from different byways that together give a good overview of Baltimore's big wilderness park. As shown by the bold line on Map 26 on page 263, the excursion starts at the park's Crimea entrance. (For more on Crimea, see Chapter 21). The route follows Hutton Avenue—now closed to all vehicles except an occasional school bus or staff car—downhill to a footpath that cuts through the woods to Windsor Mill Road. Here the route follows Windsor Mill Road for about 200 yards (there is no sidewalk) before reaching the Millrace Path, which is a level track that winds along the side of Gwynns Falls Valley for more than a mile, providing views out over the stream to the opposing hillsides. This is one of my favorite places. Return by the way you came.

The park is open daily from sunrise to sunset. Dogs must be leashed. The park is managed by the Baltimore City Department of Recreation and Parks; telephone 396-0010.

GWYNNS FALLS PARK is the eastern, older half of Baltimore's largest park complex. The other half is Leakin Park. Together totaling about 1,120 acres, Gwynns Falls • Leakin

Park includes the steep valleys of Gwynns Falls and its tributary Dead Run at the western edge of the city. Here it is possible to take a walk in a forest of immense oak, hickory, ash, sycamore, beech, and tulip trees entirely within the city limits.

Part of the route described at the end of the chapter follows the Millrace Path, so-called because it is in fact an old millrace that was filled in to form a walkway. In a photograph from 1915, the Millrace Path is shown as a meticulously groomed promenade about 15 feet wide, along which stroll men and women in their Sunday finery. In our present era of chronic municipal budget crises, however, the only maintenance at the Millrace Path is mowing once annually and occasionally removing giant trees that have fallen across the path. I'm not complaining, however, because still the Millrace Path is a beautiful and restful place for a walk—all the more agreeable for its present unkempt qualities.

Prior to its conversion to a path, the millrace started at a dam upstream from Windsor Mill Road and, maintaining a constant altitude, ran downstream along the side of the valley to a series of flour mills called Calverton Mills or Five Mills. As can still be seen today, the race was in places supported by stone retaining walls high above the river, and in other places its way was blasted past shoulders of rock. Termed the Three Mile Millrace after its overall length, the watercourse was about 80 feet above the level of Gwynns Falls by the time it reached the vicinity of what is now Hilton Parkway, where the first mill was located. The next four mills were sited at progressively lower elevations farther downstream, so that each mill could use water that had passed over the waterwheels of the one next above it. The tailrace of the first mill became the headrace of the next, and so on until the last mill was reached at a site not far upstream from present-day Edmondson Avenue. Built of stone, all five mills were large, merchant operations, meaning that their owners bought wheat and sold flour in great quantities, rather than merely grinding grain for farmers in exchange for a share of the product, as was done at small country mills.

Farther downstream, the Ellicott family had a group of three flour mills at Frederick Road, to which water was fed by a race that started below Edmondson Avenue. (The Ellicott millrace was filled in to create Ellicott Driveway) Still farther downstream were two gristmills belonging to the Carrolls: Millington Mill at present-day Carroll Park Golf Course, and Mount Clare Mill below it. The Baltimore Iron Works, located on Gwynns Falls just before tidewater, also used waterpower in its forging and casting operations. There were yet other mills of various sorts on Gwynns Falls and its tributaries above the Calverton site, notably the Powhatan Woolen Mills near Woodlawn, the Ashland Mill at present-day Dickeyville, the Tschudi Paper Mill, Old Windsor Mill (a flouring mill on present-day Windsor Mill Road) and a gristmill at Franklintown. The Old Holly Mill upstream from Calverton was replaced by Hugh Gelston's Calverton Carpet Factory that operated during the middle of the nineteenth century. And overlooking the valleys of Gwynns Falls and Dead run were the estates and mansions of some of Baltimore's leading citizens.

The many gristmills at Gwynns Falls and the large scale of the Calverton enterprise reflects Baltimore's national preeminence as a grain and flour port at the beginning of the nineteenth century. Wheat from central Maryland and south-central Pennsylvania was brought to mills located within the Fall Zone near the tidewater port. Flour was shipped to other cities along the East Coast and to the Caribbean, South America, and even Europe. Although completion of the Erie Canal in 1825 channeled an immense flow of farm products into New York and enabled its port to surpass Baltimore's in wheat and nearly every other category, flour-milling in the vicinity of Baltimore remained an important industry throughout most of the nineteenth century. Eventually, however, competition from modern mass-production roller mills established in Minneapolis during the 1870s and '80s led to the abandonment of old, water-powered, burr-stone mills at Baltimore and elsewhere.

The Calverton Mills were founded in 1813, and by 1820 all five mills were in operation under different owners. According to the 1820 Manufacturers' Census, the first mill house was four stories tall, measured 50 by 45 feet, and had three pairs of 6-foot burrs powered by two waterwheels, each 16 feet in diameter and 9 feet wide. Operated by nine men, it ground between 35,000 and 50,000 bushels of wheat annually. The other four mills each had four pairs of burrs. All five mills appear to have still been running in 1850, but in 1864 the uppermost one burned. Unable to compete with the "new process mills," the lowermost Calverton mill closed in about 1876 and burned in 1888. The mill on Calverton Lot No. 4 had burned in 1879 while undergoing extensive repairs. An 1899 photograph of Walbrook Mill on Calverton Lot No. 2 shows a massive, austerely handsome structure of four full stories, the bottom level set into the hillside above Franklintown Road, and topped by two levels of dormer windows projecting from a simple gabled roof.

In an article for *The Maryland Monthly Magazine* in 1907, George E. Tack described a walking excursion up the Gwynns Falls valley and mentioned that only two of the Calverton mills still stood: "The mills are built of the gray rock found in these hills, and are now deserted save the lower portion of one. . . . [T]hey seem to look wistfully out of their darkened window frames across the verdant valley, like giants that have outlived their days of usefulness. . . ." Neither mill is shown in the city's 1914 topographic atlas, which labels the millrace as "Mill Race Walk."

Mr. Tack—who is listed as a poet in a 1911 city directory—followed the old millrace upstream to Windsor Mill Road:

It is a beautiful scene, where lofty trees stretch their strong arms over our heads, and through the gold-gleamed aisles the summer birds call in liquid tones to each other. Across the valley the Gelston Hills loom up against the orange sky, and along the stream the woods wear a purple veil. There are several quarries along the winding Franklin road, and during the noon hour blasting is carried on, which at a distance sounds like a bombardment between two hostile armies.

To the left is the Winans estate. . . . All through this section are homes of prominent Maryland families, and the old tulip and oak and maple woods have been the trysting places of the happy lovers of other days. . . .

This is a beautiful old valley, all the year round. The spring and summer seasons have their charms, with their birds and flowers; and autumn, with its gold and russet skies, and haze that hangs like a radiant veil over all the face of nature; and in the winter season, when the fields and woods are draped in ermine robes, . . . we may hear the click of the steel skates as the young people, and their elders move over the frozen surface of the falls.

Although Mr. Tate's flowery prose is no longer fashionable, the interesting fact remains that the Gwynns Falls Valley west of Hilton Parkway has changed little since his day, except to become more wooded and even more quiet than it was.

≈   ≈   ≈   ≈

In 1904 the Olmsted Brothers, Boston's pre-eminent land planning firm and consultants to many eastern cities, presented their *Report upon the Development of Public Grounds for Greater Baltimore*. The Olmsted report recommended development of a comprehensive park system based on stream valleys and adjacent lands in the vicinity of the city, as has since been done at the Patapsco Valley, Gunpowder Falls, Herring Run, and Gwynns Falls, and to a lesser extent at Jones Falls, Stony Run, and other streams within the city. Gradually

Gwynns Falls • Leakin Park has been pieced together by a series of purchases made between 1904 and the present. The last major acquisition was in 1969, when the 100-acre Windsor estate on Windsor Mill and Wetheredsville roads was purchased. A few more acres have been added from time to time since then.

A plan formulated in the early 1990s by Baltimore City and the nationally-active Trust for Public Land calls for the development of a 6-mile trail for bicyclists, walkers, and joggers to link Gwynns Falls • Leakin Park to other parks downstream and ultimately to Middle Branch Park on the Patapsco River. Termed the Gwynns Falls Greenway, the project would make use of at least part of the existing Millrace Path and would refurbish other trail segments—such as Ellicott Driveway and the bikeway past Carroll Park—that have existed at various times in the past but which are now derelict or have been converted to streets. The city already owns more than 90 percent of the land necessary for a continuous right-of-way. If built, the Gwynns Falls trail would link with another planned trail extending upstream along the Patapsco River from its mouth at Reedbird Park. As already mentioned in Chapter 18, the B&A Trail may also link to the Patapsco trail. And there is talk of yet another trail from the upper Gwynns Falls west to the Patapsco River, resulting in a 35-mile loop through the Gwynns Falls and Patapsco valleys.

≈   ≈   ≈   ≈

During the 1960s and '70s the big park at Gwynns Falls and Dead Run was nearly decimated by the eastward extension of Interstate 70 into Baltimore. The plan specified that about 12 percent of the park (130 acres) would be taken by the highway itself. The eight-lane expressway was to slice through the Crimea section in a trench that would be covered for part of its length. Continuing eastward, the highway would follow the

crest of the ridge between the valleys of Gwynns Falls and Dead Run to the confluence of the two streams, would cross the central valley on a long, high bridge, and from there would follow the park's south slope to and across Hilton Parkway before reaching another new highway that was to be built westward from downtown Baltimore along Franklin and Mulberry streets. From the interchange with the Franklin-Mulberry spur, Interstate 70 would continue south to join Interstate 95. Beyond question the sight and sound of such a highway would have completely dominated all of Gwynns Falls • Leakin Park, turning it into little more than something nice to look at from the expressway.

In 1973 and '74, when the highway proposal received city, state, and tentative federal approval, implementation of the plan appeared to be imminent. Interstate 70 was in fact built from the Beltway to the western boundary of Leakin Park, where the highway abruptly ends, as can be seen today. The 1.5-mile Franklin-Mulberry highway, now a grandiose, entrenched segment of Route 40 just west of Martin Luther King Boulevard, was built at a cost of more than $100 million—a sum so stupendous that many people feared that the expenditure would become a compelling justification to finish the job by extending the highway through the park. At Interstate 95 near the exit for Caton Avenue, ramps that now end in air were built to link with Interstate 70. Even the right-of-way through the western part of the city was purchased.

And then the project gradually faded away. The plan to put the highway through the park faced overwhelming opposition from park users and area residents. The project had been delayed by litigation, and more litigation was anticipated. Leaders of Baltimore's business community, who for years had urged that the park highway was needed as a link in the truck route between the port and the Midwest, changed their opinion, concluding that Interstate 95 and the Beltway provided adequate access to Interstate 70 west of the city. Money set aside for the park highway was reallocated to other transportation projects. Even most of the right-of-way was sold.

Is the park highway really dead? Asked about this, highway planners say that the pressure for a highway through the park will never go away and in fact will only increase because of the continuing suburban development of Howard and Carroll counties. In light of the truncated highway segments that have already been built and that approach Gwynns Falls • Leakin Park from both ends, the proposal for a park highway is almost certain to be resurrected some day. And then park partisans will again be called upon to do battle.

AUTOMOBILE: Gwynns Falls • Leakin Park is located at Baltimore's western edge. The Crimea entrance to the park is on Windsor Mill Road directly opposite the intersection with Tucker Lane 0.3 mile east of the junction of Windsor Mill Road and North Forest Park Avenue. Two approaches are described below: the first from downtown and the second from the Beltway.

From downtown Baltimore, follow Route 40 west past Hilton Parkway and Edmondson Village Shopping Center. After passing intersections with Old Frederick Road, Winans Way, and Nottingham Road, turn right onto Cooks Lane. Follow Cooks Lane (which becomes Security Boulevard)1.0 mile to an intersection with North Forest Park Avenue. Turn right onto North Forest Park Avenue and follow it uphill 0.5 mile to an intersection with Windsor Mill Road. Turn right and follow Windsor Mill Road 0.3 mile to the park entrance on the right (opposite Tucker Lane). Enter the park between stone posts surmounted by cast-iron eagles. Follow the entrance road only 100 yards, then turn left into the large parking lot.

Another approach is from Interstate 695 (the Beltway) west of Baltimore. From the Beltway, take Exit 16 for Interstate 70, then fork east toward Park & Ride. Follow Interstate 70 for 1.2 miles to Exit 94 for Security Boulevard. From the bottom of the exit ramp, follow Security Boulevard only a few hundred yards. At the first traffic light, turn right onto North Forest Park Avenue. Follow North Forest Park Avenue uphill 0.5 mile to an intersection with Windsor Mill Road. Turn right and follow Windsor Mill Road 0.3 mile to the park entrance on the right (opposite Tucker Lane). Enter the park between stone posts surmounted by cast-iron eagles. Follow the entrance road only 100 yards, then turn left into the large parking lot.

WALKING: (See Map 26 opposite.) Start at the back corner of the parking lot nearest the woods and tennis courts. With the woods on your left and the courts on your right, follow a path for 65 yards, then turn left onto another path that leads through the woods toward the Carrie Murray Outdoor Education Campus. When you reach a road, turn left, then bear right downhill on Hutton Avenue. (Although this road is closed to most cars, you should still remain alert for occasional vehicles.)

About 100 yards after Hutton Avenue bends right for the first time, the road is crossed by a footpath which is easily spotted as a boardwalk on the right, then—in another 20 yards—as a trail leading uphill into the woods on the left. Turn left here. Follow the trail uphill, then down along what was once a lane bordered by cedars. After passing a clearing on the left, bear right downhill. Follow the trail to the corner of Wetheredsville Road and Windsor Mill Road.

With caution, cross Wetheredsville Road and follow

MAP 26 — Millrace Path

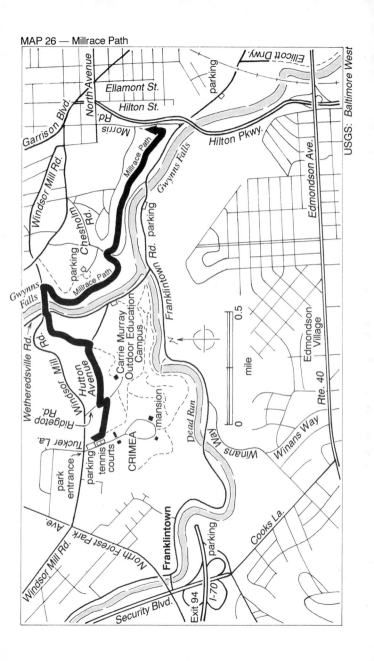

Windsor Mill Road across Gwynns Falls. From the far end of the bridge, follow the shoulder of the road—be very careful here and stay as far off the road as possible—for 120 yards, then turn right into the woods on a wide path.

This is the Millrace Path. It maintains a constant elevation along the hillside. Follow the path for about 1.3 miles. At about the half-way point, you will cross Chesholm Road. Continue along the level path to a shoulder of the valley high above Hilton Parkway, where the path turns very sharply left and descends to Morris Road.

Return by the way you came.

≈   ≈   ≈   ≈

Postscript: Wouldn't it be nice if each weekend the city were to close Franklintown Road and invite the public to turn out for walking, jogging, and bicycling along the length of Gwynns Falls • Leakin Park—about 5.0 miles round-trip? When you recall that the automobile roads at Avalon (Chapter 1) and Loch Raven (Chapter 11) are closed every weekend, and that in consequence those areas have become very popular with walkers and joggers, it seems likely that closing Franklintown Road on a regular schedule would attract many users to Gwynns Falls • Leakin Park. Other cities do this sort of thing—for example, Washington closes Rock Creek Parkway on weekends—so why can't we give it a try here? The cost would be negligible. A relatively minor expenditure for gates would immediately convert the road into a spectacular recreational facility.

Did I hear you ask about parking? It could be handled as follows: For the short term, people could park at the Crimea lot, then walk down Hutton Avenue to Wetheredsville Road, which would be closed south of Windsor Mill Road. Walkers, joggers, and bicyclists could then follow Wetheredsville Road—itself a splendid promenade—along the river to Franklintown Road, which runs from one end of the park to the other. Also, at the eastern end of the park, there is already a large parking area on Franklintown Road about 0.2 mile east of Hilton Parkway. Finally, for about 100 yards east of the intersection with Winans Way, Franklintown Road would have to remain open to provide access to a private residence, but the traffic going to and from one house over this short stretch of road would hardly disrupt things.

If experience showed that closing Franklintown Road was so popular that more parking spaces were needed, the Park & Ride lot at the eastern end of Interstate 70 could be linked to the western end of Franklintown Road by a short footpath and footbridge.

If you care to write a letter of just a few sentences in support of closing Franklintown Road on weekends, the Friends of Gwynns Falls • Leakin Park would be glad to hear from you. Their address is 3819 Clifton Avenue, Baltimore, MD 21216.

Further reading: John W. McGrain has written about the Calverton Mills in the Autumn 1991 and Spring 1992 issues of *Renaissance*, published by the Historic Baltimore Society. The Olmsted Brothers' 1904 *Report upon the Development of Public Grounds for Greater Baltimore* has been republished by the Friends of Maryland's Olmsted Parks & Landscapes. People interested in the park highway controversy can read more about it in prior editions to this book.

21

GWYNNS FALLS • LEAKIN PARK

Crimea

Walking—2.0 miles (3.2 kilometers). Tour Crimea, an imposing nineteenth-century estate that has been preserved (more or less) as part of Baltimore's largest park. The route is shown by the bold line on Map 27 on page 273. At first the trail follows an arborway of Osage-orange trees, then descends along the side of a wooded valley overlooking Dead Run. The blazed trail returns along the edge of the stream, then climbs a broad meadow leading up to the stone Crimea mansion.

For a longer excursion, you can add the walk described in Chapter 20, which is also at Gwynns Falls • Leakin Park.

The park is open daily from sunrise to sunset. Dogs must be leashed. Leakin Park is managed by the Baltimore City Department of Recreation and Parks; telephone 396-0010.

THIS WALK EXPLORES CRIMEA, the country estate developed with a trainload of rubles by Baltimore's rolling stock magnate, Thomas DeKay Winans. The massive, almost cubic stone mansion was built shortly before the Civil War to overlook the valley of Dead Run at what is now the western edge of the city. Named for the Ukrainian Riviera, Crimea was Winans' dacha—his summer home and winter hunting lodge. His intown residence was Alexandroffsky, formerly located in a private walled park east of present-day Union Square and described in various accounts as "palatial," "magnificent," "exotic," and "fabulous." Two cast-iron lions that used to guard Alexandroffsky were removed when it was razed in 1927 and now stand near the feline cages at the zoo in Druid Hill Park.

The story of Winan's Russianisms and his Russian millions starts with his father, Ross Winans, a prominent inventor in the early days of the Baltimore & Ohio Railroad. After traveling abroad with a group of experts sent by the B&O to study the English railroad system in 1828, Ross Winans worked on the adaptation of English engines and rolling stock to the steep grades and tight curves of the new American railroads. He reduced the friction of railroad wheels by fusing them with the axle so that the entire massive assembly revolved as a unit, with the axle turning in grease-packed boxes. This arrangement, with some modifications, is still in use around the world. Winans put the flange of the wheels on the inside edge and invented the swivel wheel truck and coned wheels with beveled treads to help trains negotiate curves. He was the first to use horizontal pistons on his *Crab* locomotives, and in time he built increasingly powerful engines, such as the *Camel* and the *Mud Digger*, to pull the B&O over the Allegheny Mountains. In 1835 Ross Winans and a partner assumed management of the B&O locomotive and rolling stock shops at Mt. Clare under an arrangement allowing them to sell equipment to other lines, provided that the B&O had first call. Then, in 1844 Ross Winans left the B&O and set up his own shop, where he built the *Carroll of Carrollton*, a locomotive said to be so fast for its day that its full potential speed could never be tested because the railbeds were not sufficiently straight or evenly graded for the engine to be fully opened.

All of which brings us to the Russians, who in the late 1830s were embarking on their own railroad program. Czar Nicholas I had ordered the construction of a line between St. Petersburg and Moscow. Two Russian engineers came to the United States in 1839 to study American railroads and rolling stock, and they eventually recommended to the Russian government that George W. Whistler, a civil engineer trained at West Point (and incidentally father of the artist James McNeill Whistler), be hired to superintend construction of the new Russian line. Major Whistler knew Ross Winans; he and Winans has served together on the B&O commission to England, and Whistler had helped survey the B&O route to the Ohio River. Whistler thought highly of Winans' locomotives and abilities. At Whistler's suggestion, Ross Winans was offered a contract in 1842 to set up a shop in Russia to manufacture rolling stock in partnership with the Philadelphia firm of Harrison and Eastwick, which had been recommended by the two Russian engineers. Ross Winans declined on the grounds that he was too old, but he persuaded Whistler and the Russians to accept his two sons, Thomas and William, both of whom had worked under Ross in position of responsibility.

In 1844 Harrison and Eastwick closed their Philadelphia locomotive shop and shipped their equipment to Alexandroffsky near St. Petersburg, where they were joined by the Winans brothers. A new shop was established and the partners embarked on an immensely lucrative contract to supply two hundred locomotives and seven thousand cars for the new Russian railroad, dubbed "the harnessed samovar" by the local populace. In 1850 the contract was expanded to include more equipment and ongoing maintenance. William Winans also designed and built iron bridges for the railroad, which was being laid out by Major Whistler. The Americans are said to have entertained lavishly, and judging from the estates that the Winans later built here and in England, they became accustomed to life in the grand style.

Thomas Winans returned home in 1854, three years after completion of the railroad. He brought with him a Russian wife of Italian and French ancestry and a fortune estimated at $2 million, which, of course, was a huge sum for those days. William Winans stayed in Europe and never returned to the United States. Nor did Major Whistler, who had encountered constant difficulties and delays in the construction of the railbed. Weakened by cholera, he died in 1849 before the line was completed.

Following his return to Baltimore, Thomas Winans designed and had constructed at his father's shop a streamlined "cigar ship." It was completely cylindrical and tapered to a point at each end like a submarine but was limited to surface travel. This design was intended to increase speed and economy by minimizing water resistance and top-heaviness in high winds and seas. Four of Ross Winans' locomotive engines powered a turbine-like wheel that completely circled the ship's waist, supposedly allowing the application of much more force than the midship paddle wheels of conventional steamers of the day. The ship was launched on October 6, 1858, at Winans Cove in South Baltimore, but despite what newspaper accounts said were successful test runs nothing came of the design.

Another unusual venture of the Winans—in this case Ross Winans—was the repair at the outset of the Civil War of a steam-powered, self-propelled armored cannon—in short, a primitive tank. Invented and built by Charles S. Dickinson of Ohio, the gun was supposed to throw two hundred balls per minute from a revolving set of cupped arms, "just like so many hands throwing baseballs," according to William H. Weaver, a journalist and witness when the gun was tested at the Winans' factory. In less than a minute, according to Weaver (who may just have been making the most of a good story), the weapon demolished a brick wall buttressed with a pile of timbers 3 feet thick. An ardent and outspoken supporter of the Confederacy, Ross Winans attempted to send this gun to the South, but the weapon was intercepted by federal troops, who could not make it work. According to Mr. Weaver, a key piece of the mechanism had been removed before the gun was shipped and was to be sent only if the weapon reached its destination. In any case, Ross Winans was imprisoned briefly at Fort McHenry; after his release he was jailed again when he tried to send a shipload of arms to the Confederacy.

Unlike his father, Thomas Winans was content to let the war take its own course. In the 1850s he had purchased a large tract of land in the vicinity of Gwynns Falls and Dead Run, and in 1860 he built the Crimea mansion, which shows a touch of Russia in its ornate carvings at the corners of the cornice and porch posts. Crimea was one of a number of spacious country estates developed in the Gwynns Falls area by wealthy Baltimore residents during the middle of the nineteenth century. The Crimea mansion was reached by a long entrance drive that climbed the hill from Franklintown Road at the bottom of the valley. A semicircular masonry parapet halfway down the bluff (and now enveloped in woods) was once decorated with a battery of dummy cannons, supposedly erected to resemble the Russian batteries at Balaklava, or according to another story, to deter passing Union troops from molesting the estate. A large undershot waterwheel that is still located on Dead Run near Franklintown Road pumped spring water to the house, and a gasworks manufactured gas for the principal residence. Near the main dwelling is the "Honeymoon House," which Winans built for his daughter when she married. The estate also has a caretaker's house, a wooden Gothic chapel, a large stone stable, and a vegetable cellar and ice house set into the slope at the bottom of the valley. The ground floor of the main house now serves as park headquarters. Although Baltimore City has no money to restore the Crimea mansion (as some have talked of doing), funds should be allocated immediately to arrest deterioration of the exterior.

In 1866 Thomas Winans returned to Russia, where he served

as president of the firm of Winans, Whistler, and Winans, managers of the St. Petersburg and Moscow Railroad under an eight-year contract with the Russian government. The Whistler in the firm's name was the son of the former superintendent and also the Winans' brother-in-law, having married Julia Winans while working in Ross Winans' Baltimore shops. After the management contract had run only two years, however, the Russian government took over the work and released the firm with the payment of a settlement of several million dollars. Thomas Winans returned home and divided his time between his houses (he had one also at Newport), travel, and various charities until his death in 1878.

In 1941 the valley portion of the Crimea estate was purchased for a city park from Thomas Winans' heirs, and seven years later the city brought the balance. In both instances the purchase money was provided from the bequest of J. Wilson Leakin, an attorney who had died in 1922. Leakin had left several downtown properties to the city with the stipulation that the proceeds from their rental and eventual sale be used for the acquisition and improvement of a new city park. For years different neighborhood groups and municipal agencies wrangled about where the park should be located. Even after the first Crimea tract was purchased, Mayor Thomas D'Alesandro favored selling the property in 1947 because he thought it inaccessible, but instead the park was expanded in 1948 by the purchase of the Crimea grounds above the valley.

AUTOMOBILE: Gwynns Falls • Leakin Park is located at Baltimore's western edge. The Crimea entrance to the park is on Windsor Mill Road directly opposite the intersection with Tucker Lane 0.3 mile east of the junction of Windsor Mill Road and North Forest Park Avenue. Two approaches are described below: the first from downtown and the second from the Beltway.

MAP 27 — Crimea

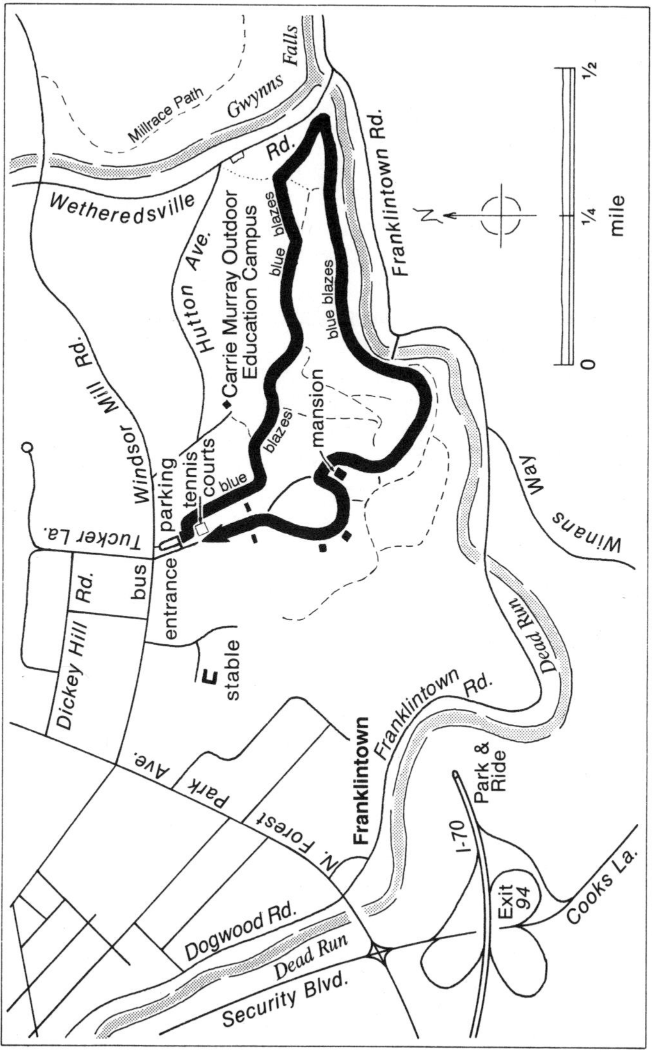

USGS: *Baltimore West*

Gwynns Falls

Millrace Path

Wetheredsville Rd.

Hutton Ave.

Carrie Murray Outdoor Education Campus

blue blazes

blue blazes

Franklintown Rd.

Windsor Mill Rd.

blue blazes

mansion

parking

tennis courts

blue

Tucker La.

bus

entrance

stable

Winans Way

Dead Run

Dickey Hill Rd.

Park Ave.

N. Forest

Franklintown

Franklintown Rd.

Dogwood Rd.

Dead Run

Security Blvd.

Park & Ride

I-70

Exit 94

Cooks La.

½

¼

mile

0

N

From downtown Baltimore, follow Route 40 west past Hilton Parkway and Edmondson Village Shopping Center. After passing intersections with Old Frederick Road, Winans Way, and Nottingham Road, turn right onto Cooks Lane. Follow Cooks Lane (which becomes Security Boulevard)1.0 mile to an intersection with North Forest Park Avenue. Turn right onto North Forest Park Avenue and follow it uphill 0.5 mile to an intersection with Windsor Mill Road. Turn right and follow Windsor Mill Road 0.3 mile to the park entrance on the right (opposite Tucker Lane). Enter the park between stone posts surmounted by cast-iron eagles. Follow the entrance road only 100 yards, then turn left into the large parking lot.

Another approach is from Interstate 695 (the Belt-way) west of Baltimore. From the Beltway, take Exit 16 for Interstate 70, then fork east toward Park & Ride. Follow Interstate 70 for 1.2 miles to Exit 94 for Security Boulevard. From the bottom of the exit ramp, follow Security Boulevard only a few hundred yards. At the first traffic light, turn right onto North Forest Park Avenue. Follow North Forest Park Avenue uphill 0.5 mile to an intersection with Windsor Mill Road. Turn right and follow Windsor Mill Road 0.3 mile to the park entrance on the right (opposite Tucker Lane). Enter the park between stone posts surmounted by cast-iron eagles. Follow the entrance road only 100 yards, then turn left into the large parking lot.

WALKING: (See Map 27 on page 273.) The route described here is marked with blue paint blazes, but the blazes are sometimes faint and infrequent.

Start at the back corner of the parking lot nearest the woods and tennis courts. Follow a path between the woods on your left and the courts on your right. Go straight past a trail that leads left toward the Carrie

Murray Outdoor Education Campus. Continue with woods on your left and a hedge and lawn on your right as the path becomes an arborway under the arched branches of Osage-orange trees. Follow the arborway path as it bends left, then continue straight where a side trail veers left into the woods (again toward the Carrie Murray Outdoor Education Campus). With a hedge and a lawn on your right, continue straight downhill and into the woods.

Follow the path downhill through the woods. Pass a trail intersecting from the right. Cross a small masonry bridge with iron hoops for railings. Continue along the side of the valley, with the slope falling off to your right. Follow the trail as it descends past immense beech and tulip trees. Part way down the bluff (and about a dozen yards before a manhole in the trail), bear half-left off the wide path in order to follow the blue blazes obliquely uphill on a narrow track. Follow the narrow, blue-blazed trail to and across the top of the slope. At a point where the trail abruptly drops about 3 feet, head straight downhill 25 yards, then turn right. Follow the trail through the woods, along the top of a ridge, then downhill to a trail junction overlooking Dead Run, where you should turn right.

With Dead Run on your left, follow the trail along the valley and then next to a stone wall by the stream, where the trail is in very poor condition. Pass a bridge and emerge onto a broad meadow. Follow the grassy swath uphill and around to the right. Continue along a rolling swath of lawn to the sadly decaying Crimea mansion.

From the driveway in front of the mansion—and with your back to the front door—turn left and follow the looping driveway clockwise past the Honeymoon House and a garage. Be alert for cars. Follow the edge of the road to the parking lot.

22

HERRING RUN PARK

Walking and bicycling—up to 5.5 miles (8.8 kilometers) round-trip. South of Harford Road in Baltimore, a paved path follows Herring Run for 2 miles to a point just downstream from Sinclair Lane, where the path ends. Most of this shallow valley is well-kempt park, and particularly attractive is the stretch between Harford Road and Belair Road, where paths on both sides of the stream form a circuit of 1.8 miles, as shown on Map 28 on page 285.

Very different is the area below Sinclair Lane, shown on Map 29 on page 286. Here you can explore a wasteland of weeds, brush, and woods dotted with rubbish and the charred remains of automobiles and campfires. This area is still awaiting park development. What would you do if you were assigned the task of designing an inexpensive yet viable park here? Intrepid mountain bikers may particularly enjoy this area, where a number of tracks have been worn by kids on all-terrain motorcycles.

Herring Run Park is open from sunrise to sunset. Dogs must be leashed. The area is managed by the Baltimore City Department of Recreation and Parks; telephone 396-6101.

UPSTREAM FROM SINCLAIR LANE, Herring Run has already been developed into Baltimore City's longest linear park, stretching from Baltimore County south past Mount

Pleasant Golf Course, Morgan State, Lake Montebello, Harford Road, and Belair Road. The focus of the following discussion, however, is the mile or so of riverside land downstream from Sinclair Lane. Although owned by the city and assigned to the Department of Recreation and Parks, the banks of Herring Run between Sinclair Lane and Pulaski Highway are as yet largely undeveloped for park purposes, nor are there any proposals for improvement of the area in the near future. Most of the west bank is weedy meadows and willow thickets crisscrossed by dirtbike paths. The mounded east bank is old landfill. Herring Run itself, which carries stormwater runoff from the northeast sector of the city and from parts of Baltimore County, is a sort of urban arroyo of gravel bars and gabions—that is, crushed rock encased in large wire cages that are stacked along the banks to retard erosion. Usually Herring Run is gentle and shallow, but the litter caught in bushes far up the banks shows how high the river gets during heavy rains. In some places floodwaters have washed out the earth behind the gabions, which are now collapsing into the stream. Nonetheless, as Lancelot Brown, the eighteenth-century English landscape architect, would have said, this unprepossessing wasteland "has capabilities"—a phrase Brown used so often to hook and reel in clients that he became known as Capability Brown.

Now it is your turn to exercise your capacity for park design. If you have taken some of the other walks described in this book, you have had a chance to form your own opinion about what makes a successful park. You probably have seen problems of gross misuse, under- and overuse, and conflicting use from which parks sometimes suffer. You may have had occasion, as at North Point State Park (Chapter 17), to consider questions of park design. The area discussed here—and shown on Map 29 on page 286—has been included despite its crudeness so that you can determine what you would recommend, if you were the city's planning consultant.

Perhaps you will like this trashy wasteland (as I do) and be attracted by its potential for park development. And if you don't, you can recover your spirits by going to the area farther north along Herring Run, shown on Map 28 on page 285.

In Baltimore, the impetus to create or refurbish a park usually comes from neighborhood improvement associations and from various local "friends of parks" groups. Herring Run enjoys the support of a somewhat more comprehensive organization called the Herring Run Watershed Association (address: 3507 Dudley Avenue, Baltimore 21213). If such a group were to express a persistent interest in the area south of Sinclair Lane, it is likely that the city would eventually arrange for the preparation of a park development plan to explore the issue.

Obviously, one of the first steps taken by park planners is an inspection of the area to determine the basic terrain with which they must work, as well as those less permanent features of the landscape that are worth preserving and enhancing. Standard land planning practice includes an initial site inventory and analysis of such factors as topography, slopes, geology, soils, stream patterns and quality, vegetation and forest types, animal life, historic sites, and existing structures and other facilities—although it is sometimes difficult to determine afterwards what practical use has been made of this mass of information. Planners must also note problems that need to be remedied, such as serious erosion or eyesores that should be screened with trees and shrubs. Access to the park must be provided from major roads and surrounding residential areas as well as between separate areas of the park. Finally, planners should be cognizant of zoning constraints and concurrent development plans for nearby sites that might enhance or conflict with the contemplated park. For example, part of the city's property along Bosley Lane east of Herring Run is used as a depot for the city's garbage trucks.

Soil (or more accurately rubbish) is a critical factor at Herring Run. Much of the land along the stream between

Sinclair Lane and Pulaski Highway is underlain by unburned refuse that will continue to settle for many years. The futility of building playing fields on this foundation of trash is demonstrated by just such an attempt near Armistead Gardens on the west bank by the Harbor Tunnel Thruway, where large hollows have developed in the fields since they were graded in 1978. Only several old, rusted baseball backstops now show that the undulating and often soggy expanse of weeds seen today was once ballfields.

After becoming familiar with the area, the planners then meet with the residents of nearby neighborhoods to determine their general concerns and recommendations as well as their specific requests for different kinds of facilities, from tennis courts to tot lots. Despite their own professional opinions about what might be suitable, the planners quickly learn that most residents want facilities that will improve the tone of the neighborhood and provide conveniences and amenities for their own use, but attract as few outsiders as possible. Residents near the park understandably expect that facilities that attract crowds be located at a distance from their homes or not built at all. For example, in 1984 the city contemplated building an ice rink in upper Herring Run Park, but local residents objected and the rink was put elsewhere. In most instances, however, a consensus is gradually reached through a series of public meetings, where objections and proposed solutions are reviewed.

In addition to site characteristics and neighborhood preferences, another conspicuous design constraint is development cost, especially during the present period of chronic city and state budget crisis. Roads, structures, and extensive regrading of the surface are particularly expensive. In 1978, the city spent $500,000 for improvements on the west bank of Herring Run just north of the Harbor Tunnel Thruway. The funds paid for a drainage system, several football and baseball fields, two tennis courts, picnic tables, toilets, a playground, a parking lot, and an access road. An inspection of the site shows that relative to the whole area between Sinclair Lane and Pulaski Highway, the money did not go very far. And as noted before, the project was also a complete waste because of subsequent settlement of the land. According to the Herring Run Watershed Management Plan released in 1993, this entire area of old ballfields will be allowed to grow up in brush and eventually into trees.

Upkeep is yet another consideration. Maintenance is funded largely by the city's ordinary tax revenues and accordingly is in very short supply. A park should require a minimum of maintenance while continuing to be attractive and to serve the use for which it was intended. Even the mowing of grass entails burdensome expense, and the city has welcomed the recommendation—set forth in the 1993 watershed management plan—that buffer zones 50 to 100 feet wide and consisting of tall grasses, wildflower meadows, shrubs, and trees be established on either side of Herring Run and its tributaries in order to stabilize the banks, filter and slow down rainwater runoff, and provide wildlife habitat. Already several Green Shores reforestation areas have been planted with trees, and in other areas the city plans to stop mowing near the river.

In addition to ordinary wear and tear, planners must anticipate the indefatigable zeal of vandals to deface, smash, raze, and utterly obliterate anything of less than Gibraltar-like permanence. For example, the park toilets built near Armistead Gardens in 1978—indeed, the very structures housing the toilets—were quickly destroyed by vandals who knocked man-sized holes through the concrete-block walls, rather as though the lavatories were bank vaults loaded with gold. What remained of the structures has since been torn down by the city. Even something as ordinary as a sign is immediately attacked by vandals. Upstream from Sinclair Lane, a series of signs and exercise stations for jogging and calisthenics was installed in 1978 along the bicycle path at a cost of $4,000 (donated by the Sun Life Insurance Company of America), but within three or four years vandals rendered most of the signs unreadable. The problem is not just an urban one; a nature trail for the blind built at the McKeldin Area of the Patapsco Valley State Park was similarly destroyed. And at the Hereford section of Gunpowder Falls State Park, a handsome old covered bridge was burned down.

Another form of abuse that plagues our parks is the dumping of trash. Some businesses appear to make regular use of the parks to dispose of their used tires, rubbish, demolition rubble, or whatever. Residents and even large public and private institutions bordering our parks often use parkland as a place to dump their lawn clippings and leaves. The only really effective deterrent against dumping is the presence of people. Incidentally, the first Saturday in April is Baltimore's annual Shape Up Parks Day, when volunteers turn out to pick up trash and litter.

Finally, from the often conflicting constraints dictated by the character of the site, the desires and fears of different groups, and budgetary and maintenance considerations, planners must establish and develop a design that makes the most of the opportunities presented. Any ideas for the area at Herring Run south of Sinclair Lane?

AUTOMOBILE: Herring Run is located in east Baltimore. If you are mainly interested in the section that has already been improved for park purposes, go to the **Harford Road** entrance described below. But if you are chiefly interested in the wild, derelict area that was discussed in the main body of this chapter, go to **Sinclair Lane**. In any case, the two areas are not so far apart that you cannot easily walk or ride from one to the other.

For each of these areas, two avenues of approach

are outlined: one from central Baltimore and the other from the Beltway.

Harford Road: From the intersection of Charles Street and 33rd Street near the Homewood Campus of Johns Hopkins University, follow 33rd Street east absolutely straight for 1.5 miles to the intersection with Hillen Road. Pass straight through the intersection with Hillen and follow the main trend of the road as it bends right and turns into 32nd Street. Continue past one traffic light to another at Harford Road, and there turn left. Follow Harford Road northeast 0.9 mile, in the process passing over Herring Run and going past the intersection with Walther Avenue. Just before the next intersection (where Argonne Drive leads left and Parkside Drive leads right), turn very sharply left into Herring Run Park. Follow the entrance road downhill to the parking area by the stream.

Another approach is from Interstate 695 (the Beltway) northeast of Baltimore. Take Exit 31A for Route 147 (Harford Road) south toward Parkville. Follow Harford Road south for 4.3 miles. Immediately after passing the intersection where Argonne Drive leads right and Parkside Drive leads left, turn right into Herring Run Park. Follow the entrance road downhill to the parking area by the stream.

Sinclair Lane: From downtown Baltimore, follow Route 40 east (Orleans Street, then Pulaski Highway). After passing under three railroad bridges and going under the Erdman Avenue bridge, turn right onto Mapleton Avenue at a traffic light, then turn right again onto Erdman Avenue (Route 151). Follow Erdman Avenue 1.4 miles, then turn right onto Sinclair Lane. Follow Sinclair Lane 0.7 mile to a crossroads with

Shannon Drive at a traffic light, and there turn left and park on the side of Shannon Drive.

Another approach is from Interstate 695 (the Beltway) east of Baltimore. Take Exit 35A for Route 40 west toward Baltimore. Follow Route 40 west about 4.0 miles, then exit onto Route 151 and Truck Route 40 (Erdman Avenue) west. Follow Erdman Avenue 1.2 miles, then turn right onto Sinclair Lane. Follow Sinclair Lane 0.7 mile to a crossroads with Shannon Drive at a traffic light, and there turn left and park on the side of Shannon Drive.

WALKING and BICYCLING: If you parked at **Harford Road**, cross Herring Run on the little footbridge under the big bridge. With Herring Run on your left, follow the paved footpath that leads downstream to Belair Road, as shown on Map 28 opposite. At Belair Road, you can turn left across the bridge and return upstream on the opposite bank, or you can continue downstream on the paved path, crossing Mannasota Avenue, Brehms Lane, and Sinclair Lane along the way.

If you parked at **Sinclair Lane**, you can head upstream or down on the paved path, but I am assuming that you came here because you are interested in the area downstream, which is shown on Map 29 on page 286.

Cross Sinclair Lane at the traffic light at the corner with Shannon Drive. With the stream valley on your left, follow the asphalt bicycle path downstream. Where the bicycle path ends, continue on a dirt track along the river. Ford a small stream (but only if the water is not more than ankle deep) and continue with Herring Run on your left. Be alert for places where the

MAP 28 — Herring Run: Harford Road to Sinclair Lane

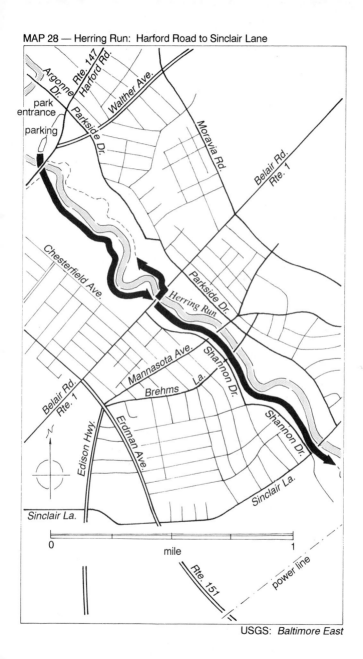

USGS: *Baltimore East*

MAP 29 — Herring Run: Sinclair Lane downstream

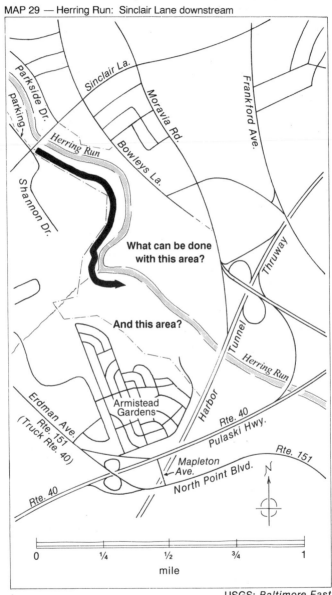

USGS: *Baltimore East*

earth is collapsing into the stream or into sink holes. Continue as far as the bridge at the Harbor Tunnel Thruway. Unfortunately , there is no provision for pedestrians or mountain bikers to cross to the other side of Herring Run, so you should return to Sinclair Lane by the way you came.

To explore the east bank of Herring Run, cross the bridge at Sinclair Lane, then head downstream as you did on the west bank. When you reach the old mounded landfill, watch out for wires, brick bats, and other refuse that might trip you up. One of the things that this area obviously needs—at least in many places—is another 4 or 5 feet of earth to cover the junk that still protrudes from the surface in some places—and also to provide the substance for intelligent regrading. (In Washington, D.C. earth dug from the Metro tunnels was used to compact and cover the old landfill at Anacostia River Park.)

IF YOU HAVE ENJOYED this book, you may also like some of the other guidebooks listed below, which are widely available at bookstores, nature stores, and outfitters. Or you can write to Rambler Books, 1430 Park Avenue, Baltimore, MD 21217 for current prices and ordering information.

DAY TRIPS IN DELMARVA

"The Delmarva Peninsula consists of southern Delaware and the eastern shores of Maryland and Virginia (hence the name Del-Mar-Va). . . . Few realize the wealth of sights this land mass holds, which is why *Day Trips in Delmarva* is such an infinitely enjoyable book."—*Baltimore Magazine* • "The best organized, best written, most comprehensive and practical guide to daytrips in the Delmarva Peninsula."—*The Easton Star-Democrat*

COUNTRY WALKS NEAR WASHINGTON
MORE COUNTRY WALKS NEAR WASHINGTON

"Cream of the local outdoors-guide crop. . . . You could probably fit both of these precise and passionately unstuffy works by Alan Fisher into one pocket, but you'll want to have them in your hand for most of the trips. . . . He starts each trip/chapter with history, perspective and a map, and ends it with meticulous step-by-step directions."—*Washington Post*

COUNTRY WALKS NEAR PHILADELPHIA

The author writes "books for thinking walkers, books for people who want to get out and stretch both their legs and minds."—*WalkWays*

COUNTRY WALKS NEAR BOSTON

"An invaluable paperback."—*Boston Sunday Globe*

COUNTRY WALKS NEAR CHICAGO

"A handy guide. . . . The general information sections—which, if combined, constitute three-fourths of the book—are excellent."—*Chicago Tribune*